Key management models

GERBEN VAN DEN BERG
PAUL PIETERSMA

Key management models

The 75+ models every manager needs to know

3rd edition

PEARSON

Harlow, England • London • New York • Boston • San Francisco • Toronto • Sydney
Auckland • Singapore • Hong Kong • Tokyo • Seoul • Taipei • New Delhi
Cape Town • São Paulo • Mexico City • Madrid • Amsterdam • Munich • Paris • Milan

Pearson Education Limited
Edinburgh Gate
Harlow CM20 2JE
United Kingdom
Tel: +44 (0)1279 623623
Web: www.pearson.com/uk

First published 2003
Second edition published 2009 (print and electronic)
Third edition published 2015 (print and electronic)

ISBN: 978–1-292–01627–6 (print)
       978–1-292–01629–0 (PDF)
       978–1-292–01630–6 (ePub)
       978–1-292–01628–3 (eText)

British Library Cataloguing-in-Publication Data
A catalogue record for the print edition is available from the British Library

Library of Congress Cataloging-in-Publication Data
A catalog record for the print edition is available from the Library of Congress

10 9 8 7 6
19

Print edition typeset in Helvetica Neue LT Pro 9.25 pt by 3
Print edition printed and bound by Ashford Colour Press Ltd, Gosport

NOTE THAT ANY PAGE CROSS REFERENCES REFER TO THE PRINT EDITION

Contents

About the authors viii
Publisher's acknowledgements ix
Preface xii
Using this book xv

PART 1 Corporate and business strategy 1

1   Ansoff's matrix and product market grid 3
2   BCG matrix 8
3   Strategic dialogue 11
4   BHAG 18
5   Blue ocean strategy 21
6   Business model canvas 24
7   Business scope (Abell) 28
8   Competitive analysis: Porter's five forces model 31
9   Core competencies 36
10   Internationalisation strategy framework 41
11   Road-mapping 46
12   Scenario planning 51
13   Strategy maps 55
14   SWOT analysis 58
15   Value disciplines 64

PART 2 Organisation and governance 69

16   7-S framework 71
17   Balanced scorecard 75
18   Benchmarking 79
19   Organisational growth model (Greiner) 84
20   Offshoring/outsourcing 89
21   Organisational configurations (Mintzberg) 92
22   Overhead value analysis 96
23   Risk management 100
24   The value chain 103

PART 3 Finance 107

25   Activity-based costing 109
26   Capital asset pricing model (CAPM) 112
27   Discounted cash flow (DCF) and net present value (NPV) 115
28   DuPont scheme 118
29   Economic value added (EVA) and weighted average cost of capital (WACC) 122
30   Financial ratio analysis: liquidity, solvency and profitability ratios 126
31   Investment stages 129
32   Real options theory 132
33   Risk–reward analysis 136
34   Value-based management 139

PART 4 Marketing and sales 143

35   4Ps of marketing (Kotler) 145
36   Branding pentagram 149
37   Client pyramid (Curry) 153
38   Crowdsourcing 156
39   Customer journey mapping 158
40   MABA analysis 162
41   Social network analysis 165
42   Stakeholder management 168

PART 5 Operations, supply chain management and procurement 173

43   Business process redesign 175
44   House of purchasing and supply 178
45   Kaizen/Gemba 181
46   Lean thinking/just-in-time 185
47   Purchasing model (Kraljic) 189
48   Root cause analysis/Pareto analysis 192
49   Six sigma 195
50   The EFQM model 199
51   Value stream mapping 203

PART 6 Innovation, technology management and e-business 207

52	Diffusion model 209
53	Disruptive innovation 212
54	Hype cycle 215
55	Innovation circle 218
56	Information Technology Infrastructure Library (ITIL®) 222
57	Stage-Gate model 226
58	Strategic IT-alignment model 229
59	The Open Group Architecture Framework (TOGAF®) 233

PART 7 Human resources (HR) and change management 237

60	Change quadrants 239
61	Compensation model 243
62	Eight phases of change (Kotter) 246
63	HR business roles 250
64	Motivational insights 254
65	Six thinking hats (De Bono) 261
66	Socially engineered change 264
67	Team roles (Belbin) 267
68	The Deming cycle: plan–do–check–act 271

PART 8 Leadership and (inter)cultural management 275

69	Bottom of the pyramid 277
70	CAGE distance framework 281
71	Competing values 284
72	Core quadrants 288
73	Cultural dimensions (Hofstede) 291
74	Culture dimensions (Trompenaars) 295
75	Focus–energy matrix 299
76	Seven habits of highly effective people (Covey) 303
77	Situational leadership 307

Appendix: Model matrix and categorisation 311
Index 319

About the authors

G.J.J.B. (Gerben) van den Berg (MSc) is a senior strategy consultant at Berenschot in the Netherlands. He has advised clients in a range of industries and across Europe. In his consulting practice, his core area of work is in strategy development, competitive positioning, corporate governance and (complex) organisational transformation. Gerben has a special interest in professional service firms. He is author of numerous books and articles on strategy and management, that have been translated into more than ten languages.

Paul Pietersma (MScBA MMC) is a strategy consultant and managing director of Strategy, Funding and Innovation at Berenschot in the Netherlands. He has over 15 years' experience in the consulting business in which he has advised many CEOs and boards of directors in a wide range of industries in the Netherlands, Belgium, Africa and the Caribbean. He has won the Dutch Professionals Award for Management Consultancy. He is the author of numerous books and articles on strategy and management, including the best-selling previous edition of *Key Management Models* (2nd edition), the internationally well received *The 8 Steps to Strategic Success* and several leading titles in Dutch.

Publisher's acknowledgements

We are grateful to the following for permission to reproduce copyright material:

Figures 1.1 and 1.2 after *Corporate Strategy*, revised edition, Penguin Books (Ansoff, H. I. 1987), with permission of the Ansoff Family Trust; Figure 2.1 from *Product Portfolio Matrix* (Henderson, B.) © 1970, The Boston Consulting Group; Figure 3.1 after *The 8 Steps to Strategic Success: Unleashing the Power of Engagement*, Kogan Page (Van den Berg, G. and Pietersma, P. 2014), with permission of Kogan Page; Figures 6.1 and 6.2 after The Business Model Canvas, www.businessmodelgeneration.com; Figure 7.1 after *Defining the Business: the Starting Point of Strategic Planning*, 1st ed., Prentice Hall (Abell, D.F. 1980) ©1980. Reprinted and electronically reproduced by permission of Pearson Education, Inc., Upper Saddle River, New Jersey; Figure 8.1 after *Competitive Strategy: Techniques for Analysing Industries and Competitors*, Free Press (Porter, M.E. 1980) Copyright © 1980 by Michael E. Porter, all rights reserved. Reproduced with the permission of Simon & Schuster Publishing Group, a Division of Simon and Schuster, Inc.; Figure 9.1 after 'The core competence of the corporation', *Harvard Business Review*, Vol. 68 (3), pp. 79-91 (Prahalad, C.K. and Hamel, G. 1990), Copyright © 1990 by the Harvard Business School Publishing Corporation, all rights reserved. Reproduced by permission of Harvard Business Review; Figures 12.1 and 12.2 after *The Sixth Sense: Accelerating Organisational Learning with Scenarios*, John Wiley & Sons, Inc. (Van der Heijden, K., Bradfield, R., Burt, G. and Cairns, G. 2002). Reproduced with permission of John Wiley & Sons, Inc. in the format republish in a book via Copyright Clearance Center; Figure 13.1 adapted from *Strategy Maps: Converting Intangible Assets into Tangible Outcomes*, Harvard Business School Press (Kaplan, R. and Norton, D 2004) Copyright © 2004 by the Harvard Business School Publishing Corporation, all rights reserved. Reproduced by permission of Harvard Business School Press; Figures 14.1 and14.2 after 'The TOWS matrix, a tool for situational analysis', *Long Range Planning*, Vol. 15(2), pp. 54–66 (Weihrich, H. 1982); Figure 15.1 after *The Discipline of Market Leaders: Choose Your Customers, Narrow Your Focus, Dominate Your Market* (Treacy, M. and Wiersema, F. 1997) Copyright © Jan 10, 1997 Michael Treacy and Fred Wiersema. Reprinted by permission of Basic Books, a member of the Perseus Books Group; Figure 16.1 The McKinsey 7-S framework from *In Search of Excellence: Lessons From America's Best Run Companies*, HarperBusiness (Peters, T. J. and Waterman, R.H. 1982) Copyright © 1982 by Thomas J. Peters and Robert H. Waterman, Jr. Reprinted by permission of HarperCollins Publishers; Figure 16.3 after *Managing on the Edge: How Successful Companies Use Conflict to Stay Ahead*, Simon and Schuster (Pascale, R.T. 1990); Figure 17.1 after 'The balanced scorecard: measures that drive performance', *Harvard Business Review*, Vol. 70(1), pp.71-80 (Kaplan, R.S. and Norton, D.P. 1992), Copyright © 1992 by the Harvard Business School Publishing Corporation, all rights reserved. Reproduced by permission of *Harvard Business*

Review; Figure 19.1 after 'Evolution and resolution as organisations grow', *Harvard Business Review*, Vol. 76(3), pp. 55-68 (Greiner, L.E. 1998), Copyright © 1998 by the Harvard Business School Publishing Corporation, all rights reserved. Reproduced by permission of *Harvard Business Review*; Figure 21.1 after Mintzberg, Henry, *Structure in Fives: Designing Effective Organizations*, 2nd ed., p.154 (1992), © 1992. Reprinted by permission of Pearson Education, Inc., Upper Saddle River, NJ, and the author; Figures 22.1 and 24.1 after *Competitive Advantage: Creating and Sustaining Superior Performance*, Free Press (Porter, M.E. 1985) Copyright © 1985, 1998 by Michael E. Porter, all rights reserved. Reproduced with the permission of Simon & Schuster Publishing Group, a Division of Simon and Schuster, Inc.; Figure 25.1 adapted from *Cost and Effect: Using Integrated Cost Systems to Drive Profitability and Performance*, Harvard Business School Press (Kaplan, R.S. and Cooper, R. 1998) Copyright © 1998 by the Harvard Business School Publishing Corporation, all rights reserved. Reproduced by permission of Harvard Business School Press; Figure 31.1 adapted from Robert Bosch Venture Capital GmbH, http://www.rbvc.com/en/investment_strategy/investment_strategy_page.html;

Figure 34.1 after 'Assessing empirical research in managerial accounting: a value-based management perspective' *Journal of Accounting and Economics*, Vol. 32, pp. 349-410 (Ittner, C.D. and Larcker, D.F. 2001), Copyright 2001, with permission from Elsevier; Figure 35.1 from Kotler, Philip; Keller, Kevin Lane, *Marketing Management: Analysis, Planning, Implementation and Control*, 12th Edition, p. 27 © 2006. Reprinted by kind permission of Pearson Education; Figure 37.1 from *Customer Marketing Method: How to Implement and Profit from Customer Relationship Management*, Free Press (Curry, J. and Curry, A. 2000) Copyright © 2000 by The Customer Marketing Institute BV, all rights reserved. Reproduced with the permission of Simon & Schuster Publishing Group, a Division of Simon and Schuster, Inc.; Figure 42.1 after 'Toward a theory of stakeholder identification and salience: defining the principle of who and what really counts', *Academy of Management Review*, Vol. 22(4), pp.853-886 (Mitchell, R.K., Agle, B.R. and Wood, D.J. 1997). Republished with permission of the Academy of Management, permission conveyed through Copyright Clearance Center, Inc.; Figure 44.1 from The House of Purchasing and Supply, Copyright A.T. Kearney, Inc., 2002, all rights reserved, reprinted with permission; Figure 47.1 after 'Purchasing must become supply management', *Harvard Business Review*, Vol. 61(5), pp. 109-117 (Kraljic, P. 1983), Copyright © 1983 by the Harvard Business School Publishing Corporation, all rights reserved. Reproduced by permission of *Harvard Business Review*; Figure 50.1 after *The EFQM Excellence Model* (EFQM 1992) EFQM: Brussels, Belgium; Figure 52.1 after 'A new product growth model for consumer durables', *Management Science*, Vol. 15(5), pp.215-227 (Bass, F.M. 1969), Copyright © 1969, INFORMS, reproduced with permission, http://www.informs.org; Figure 54.1 after *Mastering the Hype Cycle: How to Choose the Right Innovation at the Right Time*, Harvard Business School Publishing (Fenn, J. and Raskino, M. 2008) Copyright © 2008 by the Harvard Business School Publishing Corporation, all rights reserved. Reproduced by permission of Harvard Business School Press; Figure 57.1 after *Portfolio Management for New Products*, Perseus Books (Cooper, R.G., Edgett, S.J. and Kleinschmidt, E.J. 2002) p. 272, Exhibit 10.2, Copyright © Jan 4, 2002, Robert G.

Cooper, Scott J. Edgett and Elko J. Kleinschmidt. Reprinted by permission of Basic Books, a member of the Perseus Books Group; Figure 58.1 after 'Understanding strategic alignment', *Business Quarterly*, Vol. 55(3), p. 72 (Henderson, J.C. and Venkatraman, N. 1991); Figure 61.1 after *Compensation*, 9th ed., McGraw-Hill (Milkovich, G.T. and Newman, J.M. 2008) Copyright © McGraw-Hill Education 2008; Figure 62.1 after *A Force for Change: How Leadership Differs from Management*, The Free Press (Kotter, J.P. 1990) Copyright © 1990 by John P. Kotter, Inc., all rights reserved. Reproduced with the permission of Simon & Schuster Publishing Group, a Division of Simon and Schuster, Inc., and the author; Figure 63.1 after *Human Resource Champions*, Harvard Business School Press (Ulrich, D. 1996) Copyright © 1996 by the Harvard Business School Publishing Corporation, all rights reserved. Reproduced by permission of Harvard Business School Press; Figure 64.1 after 'Levels of existence: an open system theory of values', *Journal of Humanistic Psychology*, Vol. 10(2), pp.131-154 (Graves, C.W.), Copyright © 1970 by Sage Publications. Reprinted by permission of Sage Publications; Figure 65.1 after *6 Thinking Hats*, Little Brown (de Bono, E. 1985); Copyright © IP Development Corporation 1985, 1999, created by Dr Edward de Bono, used with permission of de Bono Global Pty Ltd. For further information on the Six Thinking Hats or the de Bono tools and programmes, please visit www.debono.com; Figure 69.1 after 'The fortune at the bottom of the pyramid', *Strategy+Business*, Vol. 26 (Prahalad, C.K. and Hart, S.L. 2002), PwC Strategy& Inc. © 2002, all rights reserved, reprinted with permission; Figure 70.1 after *Redefining Global Strategy: Crossing Borders in a World Where Differences Still Matter*, Harvard Business School Press (Ghemawat, P. 2007) Copyright © 2007 by the Harvard Business School Publishing Corporation, all rights reserved. Reproduced by permission of Harvard Business School Press; Figure 73.1 after Geert Hofstede and Gert Jan Hofstede, *Cultures and Organizations: Software of the Mind*, revised and expanded 2nd ed. New York: McGraw-Hill USA, 2005, ISBN 0-07-143959-5. Reproduced with permission from the authors and copyright holder; Figure 74.1 after *Riding The Waves of Culture: Understanding Diversity in Global Business*, 2nd ed., McGraw-Hill (Trompenaars, A. and Hampden-Turner, C. 1998) Copyright © McGraw-Hill Education 1998; Figure 75.1 adapted from 'Beware the busy manager', *Harvard Business Review*, February (Bruch, H. and Goshal, S. 2002), Copyright © 2002 by the Harvard Business School Publishing Corporation, all rights reserved. Reproduced by permission of *Harvard Business Review*; Figure 76.1 after *The Seven Habits of Highly Effective People*, Simon & Schuster (Covey, S.R. 1989)

In some instances we have been unable to trace the owners of copyright material, and we would appreciate any information that would enable us to do so.

Preface

We are proud to present the latest edition of *Key Management Models*. This third edition is once again a comprehensive book on management models, introducing them, explaining them, praising them and criticising them as necessary. Our selection includes the best-known models and you will also find some lesser-known ones that will perhaps surprise you.

Although this book is about management models, in our consulting practice we often hear phrases like 'We were well prepared for the rise of this competitor, as the analysis with the Porter model had shown us that…', or 'We have been very busy lowering our prices to keep up in this climate of stiff price competition, but according to the BCG analysis, we…', or even 'The Berenschot strategic dialogue model helped us to get strong support for this decision'. When events put the survival of the organisation at risk and management is stuck running the day-to-day operational business, many people turn to management models for some common sense and information on why things have turned out the way they have – as if management models provide the sole truth and the ultimate solution. To us, management models are nothing more and nothing less than useful tools – useful for problem-solving, for analysis, for supporting and facilitating decision-making and/ or for improving efficiency and effectiveness of organisations and teams. In short, management models are, in our opinion, tools for resolving common problems and challenges in business. Unfortunately, no management model, or group of models, can guarantee that a manager or consultant will deal with an organisational problem objectively and to the best of his or her ability. At best they will provide a new way of seeing a situation that will, as a result, enable positive change to take place.

Models can nonetheless provide valuable insights and a sound framework for making appropriate business choices. Management models and theories can help managers and consultants to gain clarity in business by reducing the complexities and uncertainties involved – nothing more, but definitely nothing less. The 2007–2014 crisis has made that very clear. Everybody knew that the crash in the financial system, the worldwide economic crisis, ongoing globalisation and the fact that the internet was here to stay would mean huge challenges: different businesses, different business models and different demands on authenticity (practise what you preach), transparency (proof that you practise what you preach) and flexibility (an ability to change your practice quickly). With the right type of management models, these events and their impact might have been seen up-front, and/or analysis and assessment of the underlying threats and possibilities of these events could help to identify the options and solutions available to your organisation to deal with them.

However, the vast array of management models on offer can be bewildering, for both managers and consultants alike. Being so commonly available, management models are used very frequently. But all too often only a handful of internationally known models are used, e.g. models from famous authors such as Michael Porter and from large firms like McKinsey & Co. or the Boston Consulting Group. What about all the other models? Are they unknown? Probably not, but their application is perhaps unknown. Or it might not be clear what their purpose is or in which context they can best (or cannot) be used.

The selection of models in this third edition builds on the comprehensive selection in our previous editions. There are some revisions and some updates, but the book is still, first and foremost, a comprehensive anthology of management models. The selection includes both well-known models and some lesser-known ones that could surprise you. In the first edition of *Key Management Models*, published in 2003, our colleagues (Steven ten Have and Wouter ten Have, alongside contributions from Frans Stevens) rose to the challenge and were among the first to present in an orderly fashion the most commonly used management models. In the second edition, published in 2008, we (together with our distinguished colleague Marcel van Assen) revised, updated and further grew the initial selection to 60 management models that were most frequently used in practice.

For the selection of management models in this third edition, we asked managers and consultants from various disciplines and working in our offices around the world to tell us which models they use in their work. We also conducted surveys among readers of the previous editions to find out what models they would like to see in a new edition (e.g. which ones were missing). As a result, our compilation reflects ideas and insights that are 'proven technology' and is largely the result of practical rather than literary research. The criterion for inclusion, therefore, was not whether the models selected are scientifically or technically profound, but whether they actually work. Some of the models selected in this book might still stand up to a high degree of scientific scrutiny, but are simply selected as they have proven to be great memory aids or great tools for use in day-to-day business.

To arrive at the final selection, we assessed all suggestions with regard to whether they met our definition of a management model: a tool that can be employed (either for process and/or analytical purposes) to enhance the daily functioning of a business, by improving both management methods and the performance of the organisation, or to solve related problems.

This book presents the 75+ models we selected. In order to give you an overview and to provide an easy point of entry to choose a model to apply to your situation, we have grouped the models into eight functional categories (see the next section, 'Using the book'). This classification has been changed from the previous edition. Where the previous edition grouped the models according to the area of management where their use is most appropriate, this edition presents the models by functional category. We chose to do this because of the greater number of management models included and to identify more clearly the variety and function of the models and the differences in their scope. It also allows us to emphasise some functional disciplines, which, in our modest opinion, have become more relevant in recent years. We want to give special attention to finance, e-business (internet) and cultural management (globalisation). Next to these, strategy, governance, marketing, HR, innovation, leadership and operations are still, of course, also important functional areas for any organisation.

Each of the models is introduced with a description, followed by an explanation of how and when to use it, in order to reduce the risk that managers will be tempted to view a currently fashionable model as the ultimate solution to their organisational malfunctions. To put it clearly, this book is intended neither as a 'top 75+' of popular management models nor as a prescription for 'good' management and organisation – it is intended as an anthology of a wide variety of useful management models that have proved their value in practice. For the 'diehards' among our readers, we have again included recommended further reading and have drawn attention to the potential limitations or shortcomings of each model.

It is with both pleasure and pride that we present this compilation once again. We are confident that the managers and consultants who use it will possess the necessary maturity, intelligence and discernment to place the models we have included into perspective, and will use them to act on sound, creative, consistent management and advice. It was never our intention to produce a comprehensive overview of all management models; our aim is rather to supplement the readers' existing knowledge by providing additional ideas and insights through sound, easily comprehensible descriptions of actual and frequently used models. Thus enriched, managers and consultants will be able to determine quickly which model is the most appropriate for a given situation, while also recognising its limitations. We view this book as a means not only of giving expression to this complexity, but also of making it more manageable, by providing models to reduce complexity and visualise reality, so that management issues can be discussed based on a 'common language' and dealt with properly and swiftly. Use the models wisely in your own specific context: structuring reality is completely different from managing reality!

It is impossible to thank all those people who have been involved in the publication of this book personally. We would like to thank all our colleagues involved for their valuable efforts and commitment. We would also like to thank our employer, Berenschot, for the time and support given to rewrite *Key Management Models*. The company has remained the front-runner amongst Dutch consultancy firms since its foundation in 1938. Special thanks goes to our publisher, who after two successful previous editions again knew how to encourage us and has facilitated the writing of this edition superbly.

To all of you who read this book, we wish you lots of wisdom and pleasure – and, above all, many constructive results from applying the models to your own organisation.

Gerben van den Berg and Paul Pietersma

Using this book

Key Management Models, third edition, describes 75+ contemporary management models and explains how each can be used and applied in business and management. There are many different ways in which management models can be categorised – we have simplified our classification by grouping the selected management models into eight functional categories, as follows:

1 **Corporate and business strategy.** Models used for formulating, implementing and realising strategy.

2 **Organisation and governance.** Models used for designing organisational structures and to design governance mechanisms.

3 **Finance.** Models used to design performance metrics, including financial instruments.

4 **Marketing and sales.** Models used to formulate marketing and sales policies, to structure marketing and sales departments, and to develop operational marketing and sales instruments.

5 **Operations, supply chain management and procurement.** Models used to formulate operations, supply chain and procurement policies, and methods to design, optimise and implement best practices for operations, supply chains and procurement.

6 **Innovation, technology management and e-business.** Models related to innovation management, to formulate R&D and technology policies, to align R&D and technology objectives with corporate strategy, to develop R&D instruments and to identify and install e-business activities.

7 **HR and change management.** Models used to formulate HR policies and to design and implement HRM practices and instruments. Models and methods related to change management are also included in this category.

8 Leadership and (inter)cultural management. Models used to identify necessary leadership, assess current and future culture aspects, and models related to working in different countries and cultures.

The models in each section are listed alphabetically and marked with one or more icons that represent the functional category.

For ease of use, each management model is described according to:

- The big picture – the essence and purpose of the management model.
- When to use it – the usefulness and applicability of the management model.
- How to use it – a description of how to apply the management model using a step-by-step approach.
- The final analysis – the limitations of the management model and the potential pitfalls with regard to its use.
- References – an overview of literature sources on the origination of the management model or with more information on (the use of) the management model.

Each entry includes one or more examples of how to apply the model and, where useful, includes a case study to describe how the models can be used in a specific situation. Where relevant, we also refer to alternative, but equally applicable, models that are included in this book. But it is certainly not our claim to be exhaustive or exclusive. There are many more models and methods available than those described in this book. You can find them on numerous websites or in other books on business management (including FT Publishing's *Key Management Ratios* and *Key Strategy Tools*, and books by Berenschot consultants). In the end it should be you who picks the management models that are most appropriate to your situation, as each model should help you to organise and interpret the information you regard as relevant and help you to understand the choices you have to make based on that information.

[PART ONE]

Corporate and business strategy

These models help to analyse and plan a company's strategic position and provide answers to strategic questions.

Ansoff's matrix and product market grid

1

The big picture

The Ansoff product/market grid offers a logical way of determining the scope and direction of a firm's strategic development in the marketplace. The firm's strategic development consists of two related types of strategy: portfolio strategy and competitive strategy.

The portfolio strategy specifies the objectives for each of the firm's product/ market combinations. It points to the dots on the horizon. The competitive strategy specifies the route to take to reach those objectives.

In the Ansoff product/market grid setting, the objectives (portfolio strategy) were introduced as choosing a growth vector, specifying the ultimate future scope of business. The growth vector is expressed in two dimensions: products and markets (Figure 1.1).

Later, Ansoff introduced the geographical growth vector, replacing the growth vector from his product/market grid (Figure 1.2). The geographical growth vector has three dimensions, which the firm can use to define its desired future business scope:

- the market need (e.g. need for personal transportation or need for amplification of electric signals);
- the product/service technology (e.g. integrated circuit technology);
- the market geography (e.g. regions or nation states).

New	2. Market development	Concentric diversification	Conglomerate diversification
		4. Diversification	
		Vertical integration	
		Horizontal integration	
	1. Market penetration	3. Product development	
Current	Current		New

Products

Figure 1.1 Ansoff's growth vector components: products and markets
Source: after Ansoff (1987)

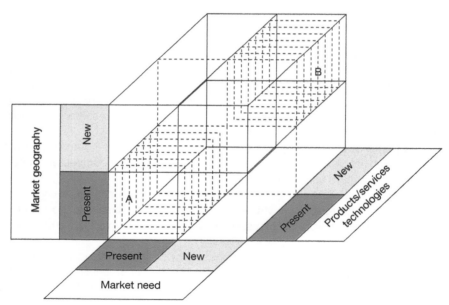

Figure 1.2 Ansoff's dimensions of the geographic growth vector: market need; products/services and technologies; and market geography
Source: after Ansoff (1987)

These three dimensions together form a cube. They offer a variety of combinations and strategic directions for a firm. Extreme choices are on the one hand to continue serving current regions with existing technologies to fulfil traditional needs or on the other hand to enter new regions with new technologies to fulfil new needs.

When to use it

Deciding a direction and a strategy for corporate growth depends upon a number of factors, including: the level of risk involved; the current set of products and markets; and whether the organisation wants to develop new or existing products or markets. In order to plan for the future in a systematic way, it is vital that managers understand the gap between the firm's current and desired positions. The Ansoff product/market grid and the Ansoff cube can be used as a framework to identify the direction of and opportunities for corporate growth.

Ansoff introduced four components that cover the portfolio strategy and help specify the desired future business scope:

1 Geographical growth vector

2 Competitive advantage

3 Synergies

4 Strategic flexibility.

The geographical growth vector can be determined with Ansoff's cube, by connecting the current scope of business with the desired future business scope.

A competitive advantage is needed both to enable the chosen scope and to be able to sustain a route towards it. The competitive advantage can be anything from a core competence or a patented technology to offering better after-sales service to clients than your competitors.

As a third strategy component, Ansoff suggests taking account of the synergy between the firm's competencies. This not only enables economies of scale but can also strengthen the firm's competitive position.

The fourth, and final, strategic component is the strategic flexibility. It is aimed at minimising the impact of unforeseen events and seeks to discard all unnecessary 'ballast'.

The four components are interlinked. Optimising one of the components is likely to depress the firm's performance in the others. In particular, maximising synergies is very likely to reduce flexibility. The process of selecting and balancing the strategic objectives is a complex matter.

How to use it

To use the product/market grid in practice, an organisation must first assess its existing product–market combinations and corresponding levels of competitive advantage. Then, its desired future business scope must be chosen as the geographical growth vector within the Ansoff cube.

Next, the feasibility of the chosen scope and direction should be assessed, with an analysis of the combination of the intended direction and extent of corporate growth and the firm's distinctive competitive advantages (core competencies). Not only should there be the means that enable the chosen scope, those means should also provide the firm with a sustainable competitive advantage.

Then, synergies have to be found and/or created either by making use of an existing outstanding competence (aggressive synergy strategy) or by developing or acquiring the necessary competence (defensive synergy strategy).

Finally, strategic flexibility has to be attained. This can be done externally to the firm through diversification of the firm's geographic scope, needs served and technologies so that a surprising change in any one of the strategic business areas does not produce a seriously damaging impact on the firm's performance. Alternatively, it can be attained by basing the firm's activities on resources and capabilities that are easily transferable.

A shortcut in determining the strategic objectives is to derive them from the strategic requirements of three archetype firms:

- An operating company will focus on synergies and a relatively narrowly focused geographical growth vector. Its investments are often irreversible, have long lead times and will often be in research and development (R&D) or physical assets. It must be able to anticipate change and minimise the changes of making bad decisions. Synergies will often be created around core competencies.

- A conglomerate firm will focus on flexibility. Its strategy would have no synergy or geographical growth vector. Instead it would include enough flexibility to be protected from strategic surprises or discontinuities in the environment of one or more of its subsidiaries.

- An investment fund can only focus on flexibility. It will have widely diversified holdings. Such firms seldom have the depth of knowledge of individual industries to enable them to seek a specific competitive advantage.

In fact, these 'pure form' firms do not exist. There are no stereotypes, as there are numerous shadings of characteristics. There are different degrees of integration in synergistic companies: some companies act as conglomerates in some parts and are synergistic in others, and some investment firms do have specialised knowledge of certain industries. Each firm will have to determine its own strategic objectives (portfolio strategy).

Next, a competitive strategy is adopted to determine the distinctive approach to succeed in reaching the chosen objectives in the strategic portfolio strategy (the path forward). Based on the original product/market grid, four generic competitive strategies were identified:

- Market penetration (current product/current market) – sell more of the same products and services in existing markets. This growth vector indicates growth through increase in market share for the present product/markets.

- Market development (current product/new market) – sell more of the same products and services in new markets.

- Product development (new product/current market) – sell new products and services into existing markets. This growth vector means growth by developing new products to replace or complement existing products.
- Diversification (new product/new market) – sell new products and services into new markets.

Also, depending on how 'different' the new product and the new market are, a variety of more specific growth vectors were identified within the diversification quadrant:

- Vertical integration – an organisation acquires or moves into suppliers' or customers' areas of expertise to ensure the supply or use of its own products and services.
- Horizontal diversification – new (technologically unrelated) products are introduced to current markets.
- Concentric diversification – new products, closely related to current products, are introduced into current and/or new markets.
- Conglomerate diversification – completely new, technologically unrelated products are introduced into new markets.

There are, of course, different roads that lead to Rome. The generic competitive strategies can only do little to answer the question of which competitive strategy would be the most beneficial. Each firm will have to determine its own strategic objectives (portfolio strategy) and its own strategic direction (competitive strategy).

The final analysis

Despite its age, Ansoff's work remains valid and is used a great deal in practice. Although the product/market grid is primarily used in its original form, it still offers a good framework for describing product/market opportunities and strategic options. It forms a good basis for further exploration and strategic dialogue.

What is groundbreaking, however, are the amendments Ansoff himself made to his own work. With the perspective of more than 20 years' experience, he concluded that his own, very well known product/market grid did not reflect reality enough and he introduced a different approach to corporate strategy. Revisiting all of Ansoff's work makes it clear that some of today's favourite management tools originate from his models.

References

Ansoff H.I. (1984) *Implanting Strategic Management*. Englewood Cliffs: Prentice Hall.

Ansoff, H.I. (1987) *Corporate Strategy* (revised edition). London: Penguin Books.

Ansoff, H.I. (1988) *New Corporate Strategy*. New York: John Wiley and Sons.

2

BCG matrix

The big picture

The Boston Consulting Group designed the 'BCG matrix' in the 1970s. It is one of the best-known methods for product portfolio planning, based on the concept of the product life cycle. It takes account of the inter-relation between market growth and market share. The underlying assumption is that a company should have a portfolio of products that contains both high-growth products in need of cash inputs and low-growth products that generate excess cash to ensure long-term success.

The use of the BCG matrix (see Figure 2.1) helps to identify and assess the priorities for growth in a product portfolio. The matrix comprises two dimensions: market share and market growth. Products are assessed based on these dimensions and each is then classified in one of four different categories: stars, cash cows, question marks and dogs. The basic premise of the model is to invest in (economic) growth opportunities from which the company can benefit.

When to use it

The BCG matrix can be used as a strategic tool to identify the profit and growth potential of each business unit of a company. By defining a strategy for each business unit (determining whether to 'hold', 'harvest', 'divest' or 'build'), the overall portfolio of an organisation can be maintained as a profitable mix.

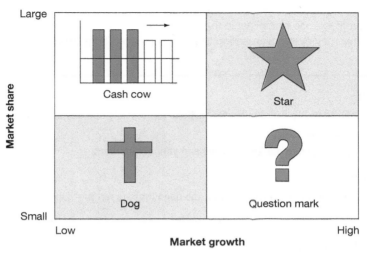

Figure 2.1 The BCG growth share matrix
Source: Boston Consulting Group (1970)

How to use it

First, determine a measure or rating of expected market growth for each product or service in the portfolio. Next, apply a growth share percentage of the rating to each product to define its relative market share. Finally, plot each of the products in the portfolio into the four quadrants that are defined by two dimensions: relative *market share* and relative rate of *market growth*. Although this is generally arbitrary due to small differences, it must be carried out consistently. This is the most difficult part, but using predetermined criteria may help. For example, a company's market share can be indicated as being small if it is less than one-third of that of its largest competitor. The growth rate of a market can be indicated as high when annual revenues grow by more than 10 per cent after correction for inflation. It is important to maintain the predetermined criteria and change them only during the product assessment phase. Otherwise, 'pet' projects and products will be shifted into a more favourable position, thereby defeating the object of the exercise.

- Stars are products that enjoy a relatively high market share in a strongly growing market. They are (potentially) profitable and may grow further. It is therefore advisable to invest in these products.

- Cash cows are products that are extremely profitable, and where no extra effort or investment is needed to maintain the status quo. A product becomes a cash cow when the growth of a product's market decreases but the company's market share remains high and stable.

- Question marks are products that have high market growth but small market share and so their growth rate is uncertain. Investments to generate further growth may or may not yield big results in the future. Additional investigation into how and where to invest is advised.

- **Dogs** should be dropped or divested when they are not profitable. If profitable, do not invest in them, but make the best of their current value. This may even mean selling the product's operations and/or brand.

Do's
- **Analyse your current business portfolio periodically and decide which products require investment.**
- **Pay attention to market changes and your competitors.**

Don'ts
- **Do not hesitate to drop or divest the dogs that are not profitable.**

The final analysis

Many people have questioned the basic assumptions of the BCG matrix, namely that markets are clearly defined; that market share is an appropriate indicator of cash generation; and that growth means that an infusion of cash is needed to extract a bigger payoff at a later stage. Many critics make the important point that throwing money at a product or product group does not make it grow or become more profitable automatically. We have therefore concluded that the BCG matrix can be very helpful in forcing decisions when managing a portfolio of products, but it cannot be employed as the sole means of determining market strategy.

When constructing a matrix, it often makes more sense to use relative market shares, as markets are not always clearly defined. A single market can comprise many different elements and many substitute products. Markets can be concentrated, or widely divided among many small players. Remember, too, that in immature markets, in particular, growth figures and market shares may not have reached a balance that justifies the rigorously positive or negative judgement of the BCG matrix.

References

Boston Consulting Group (1970) Product Portfolio Matrix, BCG.

Hambrick, D.C., MacMillan, I.C. and Day, D.L. (1982) 'Strategic attributes and performance in the BCG Matrix – A PIMS-based analysis of industrial product businesses'. *The Academy of Management Journal* 25(3), 510–531.

Henderson, B. (1968) 'The product portfolio'. *BCG Perspectives*, 66.

Henderson, B. (1973) 'The experience curve reviewed: IV the growth share matrix or product portfolio'. *BCG Perspectives*, 135.

Strategic dialogue

3

The big picture

The strategic dialogue is a generic eight-step model for formulating and implementing strategy (Figure 3.1). It treats strategy as an integral process of formulation and implementation. It focuses on content and process: doing the right things and doing things right. It is an iterative process with an approach that leads to choices while leaving room to keep options open. And it is an approach – the name 'strategic dialogue' says it all – that is based on engagement with key stakeholders: what the organisation can and will do are not formulated in an ivory tower, but rather in dialogue with key external partners and stakeholders, and these are explored and discussed with internal stakeholders. However, a dialogue doesn't imply a democracy: those responsible will still have the final say and have to make the strategic choices.

In a strategy process, there are three critical success factors:

- A good understanding of the context of the strategy definition: without shared understanding of cause, necessity and ambition, a company trying to formulate its strategy is drifting. And without knowing where you stand, there is no way to set a course.

- An adequate use of content in terms of quality, completeness and depth – a thorough analysis with appropriate models and instruments to obtain a complete understanding of the possibilities and impossibilities of the organisation and of the environment in which it is active. A thorough analysis is the basis for finding the right strategic options.

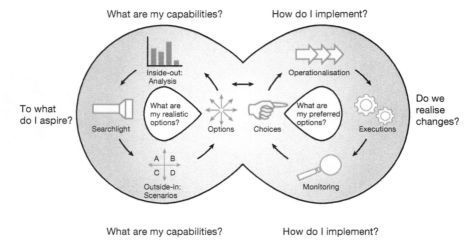

Figure 3.1 Strategic dialogue

Source: after Van den Berg and Pietersma (2014)

- An effective and inspiring process based on engagement: who are involved at what moment in time, what are the roles, and how is participation organised? In other words: applying the correct methods of engagement. These help to increase the intrinsic level of understanding, stimulate creativity and develop ideas.

For strategic success, organisations will have to understand the essence of context, the essence of content and the essence of the process. Organising both strategy formulation and strategy implementation processes as a dialogue will lead to strategic success. The strategic dialogue presumes that strategic success is the result of the formula:

Formulation × Mobilisation × Realisation

That is to say, strategic success comes from successful strategy formulation multiplied by mobilisation of the right people times successful strategy realisation (or implementation).

Formulation

Many companies devote most of their attention to the F of formulation. They formulate a strategy that, if correct, shows them the way amid the uncertainties of current and future markets. It could lead to the perfect plan. And then it is 'only' a matter of perfect execution. All too often, however, strategic plans are not flawless. It is difficult to make the right choices up front for unforeseen future developments. Often choices made – if they really are made in the first place – do not always reflect a combination of thorough analysis and sound entrepreneurship. And often the strategy states what the company will do, but not what the company will stop doing (which is often inherent in making choices). Emphasis on formulation is no guarantee for a consistent execution of the strategy, not for a consistent interpretation by all involved.

Realisation

Next to formulation, it is the R of realisation that typically receives the most attention in strategy processes. Sometimes there are elaborate and detailed implementation plans, which are as comprehensive as an encyclopaedia, and sometimes these are only fragmentary. Most of the time there is some kind of implementation plan, and attention will be given to communication and progress. Milestones and required breakthroughs in the implementation plan are monitored and periodically scheduled on the management agenda (however, they are often not properly addressed, as operational fires must be extinguished first). But even if there is a brilliant strategy with elaborate implementation plans and well-managed change projects, all too often everyone is still surprised that the strategy is not working and does not deliver what they had expected.

Mobilisation

The demands faced by companies in the twenty-first century are structurally different from before and this will be (or should be) reflected in the strategy process. Strategy processes have (or have to) become more agile and decisive. Strategy inherently is about the long term, but nowadays the pressure from banks and shareholders to achieve results in the short term is great. The tolerance for mistakes and risks remains low. Adjustments must be made instantly. You must therefore focus more than ever on the third variable: the M of mobilisation. This is about organising involvement and engagement in the process of both strategy formulation and strategy implementation. In short, it is about engaging key business partners and both external and internal stakeholders to get their understanding of and support for (or even buy-in on) your strategy.

When to use it

The strategic dialogue is a systematic approach to strategy formulation to be used in situations where both the formulation and implementation of a realistic and supported strategic plan are needed. It was originally developed as a methodology to overcome generic pitfalls that were frequently found during strategy formulation. These pitfalls are to be avoided in any strategy process and involve three aspects of the strategy formulation process: the scope of the process; the execution of the process; and the decision-making in the process. These aspects, and a description of some of the pitfalls, are shown in the following table.

Aspect	Pitfall	Description
Scope	'Me too'	Blindly following the most important (or annoying) competitor.
	'The grass is always greener'	Getting carried away with seemingly attractive new initiatives or possibilities and forgetting to make rational considerations.
	'Collective truth'	Too much reasoning from a collective vision, being too caught up with the organisation's own dynamics, and too little analysis.
	'We've always done it this way'	Holding on too rigidly to past experiences.
	'We know what they want'	Making assumptions about markets and customers instead of doing a thorough analysis.
Execution	'An elite activity'	Involving top management only and not the rest of the organisation.
	'No time to discuss'	Taking too little time for the process.
	'The controller as strategist'	Presenting budget adjustments ('last year's plan +5%') as strategy.
	'Paralysis by analysis'	Getting stuck in continuous analysis into the last digits behind the comma, often driven by a 'risk-averse mindset'.
	'Talk about them, not with them'	Engaging key external and internal stakeholders is experienced as difficult, inappropriate and/or inconvenient.
Choices	'It's all about the money'	Dominance of financial considerations (bottom line), making strategy more like an investment prospectus.
	'The hockey stick effect'	Placing ambitions over analysis, leading to overly optimistic long-term prognosis.
	'Let's make a compromise'	Trying to keep everybody happy and avoiding to make real choices
	'There is only one boss...'	Top management makes every decision (and wonders why nobody gets it or follows through on it).
	'Another good plan (for the file)'	Not putting the strategy into action.

We emphasise that the context or situation in which a new strategy is to be formulated affects both the content of the strategy and the process of formulating the strategy. This, of course, also holds for a strategy process with the strategic dialogue model. The scope and depth of the strategy process with the strategic dialogue model are also highly dependent on the specific contexts. This includes such contexts as restructuring, mergers or acquisitions and external disruptions (new technologies etc.). In each of these situations, compromises must be made between different aspects in the strategy process, as circumstances require specific demands. It may be that there is only a little time available, and the lead time will therefore be limited. It can also prevent the requirements of confidentiality limiting the group of people involved in expressing themselves. The nature of a specific situation determines the strategy process, sometimes creating more constraints than for a 'regular' strategy process.

How to use it

The strategic dialogue model is an integrated methodology of strategy formulation and implementation which has been developed on the basis of practical experience. It is not a one-size-fits-all standard prescription on how to do strategy, but it's a generic approach that you can customise to your organisation and circumstances. Every company and every environment are different and require a customised approach. The strategic dialogue model offers an iterative process which is applicable to a multitude of situations and strategic issues. In the strategic dialogue model, we identified eight distinct steps, each with distinctive purposes, scope and activities:

- Searchlight. The setting of the process of strategy formulation and implementation and finding a shared ambition and business scope.
- Outside-in: Scenarios. The mapping of potential strategic positions from plausible future business environments.
- Inside-out: Analysis. The exploration of strategic options based on the abilities and limitations in the company.
- Options. The translation of analytical information to insights and, from there, to generating strategic options.
- Choice. The estimation of the risks and feasibility of the various options, leading to the choice of strategy.
- Operationalisation. Making an implementation plan, setting the implementation process in detail and cashing in on 'quick wins'.
- Execution. The actual implementation of plans, policies and actions for change.
- Monitoring. The assessment of ongoing developments in the environment and organisational performance in relation to the strategy and strategic goals.

In each of the eight steps, other management models can be used for analysis, design or interaction. These are not equally important in every situation, nor is there a prescribed list of models to use in one or more of the steps. To get a clearer view of which ones to use, and when, see the references at the end of this chapter.

The schematic of the strategic dialogue model has the shape of two circles linked together: the process of formulation and of implementation (see Figure 3.1). These two circles together also form a lemniscate – the symbol for infinity – representing the integrated and iterative character of our approach to strategy. It depicts how everything is connected to everything else through logical links. Ideally, the strategy process will go through all eight steps of the model (an entire cycle) from left to right in the figure. The process of developing a mission statement, vision and strategy is described in the left-hand cycle. This process is fluid, interactive and creative. In the middle, the actual process of selection of strategic options takes place. This is where different options are weighed and choices are made. In the right-hand cycle, the emphasis is on the realisation and implementation of the choices made. This process is more rigid and action-oriented.

The final analysis

Formulating a successful strategy depends upon the quality of content and the method of implementation. However, of equal importance is the way in which the process is organised and the way the results are communicated to all parties. Efficient organisation and effective dialogue will greatly increase the success of the implementation phase. A number of factors are critical to get right when first setting up the process, in order to optimise the chances of delivering successful results:

- Determine who is to be involved, and which roles they are to assume during the strategy formulation process.
- Decide how to organise enthusiasm and buy-in for the strategy with the rest of the organisation – a plan without any commitment from those supposed to execute it is unlikely to succeed.
- Assess the quality of the team members' input with regard to both the analyses and the vision. Consider their willingness to think about the future in a systematic and fundamental way.
- Decide which other models and instruments would be of value as part of the process.
- Decide how to communicate with non-participants about and during the process. This becomes increasingly important once the results become visible.
- Include processes to ensure that agreed procedures are adhered to, by all those involved, especially during the implementation phase.

References

Van den Berg, G. and Pietersma, P. (2012) *The Grand Book on Strategy* Den Haag: SDU (In Dutch: *Het Groot Strategieboek*).

Van den Berg, G. and Pietersma, P. (2014) *The 8 Steps to Strategic Success: Unleashing the Power of Engagement.* London: KoganPage.

4

BHAG

The big picture

Every organisation benefits from a commonly understood, organisation-wide long-term goal. By formulating a BHAG (or 'big hairy audacious goal'), a statement can be given that helps an organisation to focus on a single common goal. The BHAG was first introduced by James Collins and Jerry Porras in their book *Built to Last*. To formulate a BHAG you need to answer three questions: what are you deeply passionate about; what can you be the best in the world at; and what drives your economic engine? Your answer to all three questions at once will be your BHAG: an inspiring direction for the organisation's future (Figure 4.1).

When to use it

Many organisations set out ambitious goals they hope to accomplish over the coming years. These goals are also intended to align the activities of the organisation, to guide decision-making and motivate employees to work together more effectively. A BHAG addresses just that: what will be the next great and inspiring leap forward for the company? The intended effect of this common long-term goal is to give purpose and a positive outlook on the future to the organisation.

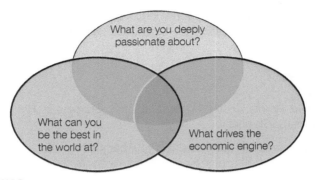

Figure 4.1 BHAG
Source: after Collins and Porras (1994)

How to use it

The BHAG model invites you to answer three questions:

- What are you deeply passionate about? According to Collins and Porras (1994), companies can only be really outstanding in areas where they are fully committed. The answer to this question should be formulated as 'a customer's problem that the company is going to resolve like no other'.
- What can you be the best in the world at? This question goes beyond one or two features or best-selling products. It is about identifying a core competence (see Chapter 9) that others cannot match.
- What drives the economic engine? This could be the number of customers, the number of billable hours worked or the price premium of the brand. It is about what essential variables lead to financial returns for the organisation.

By first answering each of the questions and then comparing and combining those answers, the BHAG is shaped. Ultimately there will be a shared understanding of what the BHAG is for the organisation. It is not necessary to formulate it as a catchy one-liner, although often this is the final outcome of such an exercise.

The final analysis

Not only does a BHAG help to state a common long-term focus for the organisation, but the process of formulating the BHAG also allows you to think explicitly about the *raison d'être* of the organisation. This can be useful to fundamentally reconsider the strategy and business model of your organisation. As the process of formulating a BHAG can be very inspiring, it can help to set a fertile ground for 'reinventing' your organisation.

The downside to the BHAG is that it requires both a lot of creativity and flexibility during the formulation stage and a lot of discipline from those involved. The process could easily turn into people trying to impress each other with soundbites, instead of discussing the fundamentals of the organisation among themselves.

References

Collins, J. and Porras, J. (1994) *Built to Last: Successful Habits of Visionary Companies*. HarperBusiness.

Collins, J. and Porras, J. (1996) 'Building your company's vision'. *Harvard Business Review* 74(5), 65–77.

Blue ocean strategy

5

The big picture

Blue ocean strategy focuses attention on the creation of new markets at the product development stage. The concept is designed to encourage managers to focus on the creation of uncontested markets.

Most strategic models focus on achieving competitive advantages, the central question being how to be better than the competition. The 'blue ocean strategy' model does not focus on winning from competitors, but on making the competition irrelevant by creating 'blue ocean' opportunities. Blue oceans are uncontested marketplaces in which new demands from customers are satisfied (Kim & Mauborgne, 2005). 'Red oceans', in contrast, are competitive arenas in which competitors fight and consequently weaken each other.

The blue ocean strategy model encourages innovation and influences the focus of strategy development. Instead of using competitors as a benchmark, managers look beyond the limits of existing market boundaries to seek new opportunities to create new value for customers. Rather than trying to beat the competition directly, managers should take action to develop a business offering that opens up and captures a new market space.

Red ocean strategy	Blue ocean strategy
• Compete in an existing marketplace • Beat the competition • Exploit existing demand • Make the value / cost trade-off • Align the whole system of a firm's activities with its strategic choice of differentiation *or* low cost	• Create an uncontested marketplace • Make the competition irrelevant • Create and capture new demand • Beat the value / cost trade-off • Align the whole system of a firm's activities in pursuit of differentiation *and* low cost

Figure 5.1 Blue ocean strategy
Source: based on Kim and Mauborgne (2005)

When to use it

Blue ocean strategy adds direction to the strategic management process. Development strategy often focuses solely on how to beat the competition. This will lead inevitably to a red ocean scenario in which competitors fight and consequently weaken each other. In order to direct the focus of strategy development towards the creation of blue oceans, the management team needs to answer four questions:

- Which of the factors that our industry takes for granted should be eliminated?
- Which factors should be reduced well below the industry's standard?
- Which factors should be raised well above the industry's standard?
- Which factors should be created that the industry has never offered?

In this process, it is essential to focus on what customers value, rather than merely focusing on competitors or the core competencies of the firm. Instead, one should start from scratch. By answering these questions, it is possible to create entirely new concepts for product(s). As a result, a new so-called 'value curve' can be created. This curve determines a new value proposition, which shows how the value of the new product differs from current products (Kim & Mauborgne, 1997).

Two types of blue ocean can be created by this process, either by launching a completely new industry or by creating new opportunities from within the existing industry by expanding the strategic boundaries of the industry. Most blue oceans are created this way.

How to use it

Blue ocean strategy is not a well-structured plan that is easy to implement. On the contrary, it is a concept that can be used to focus strategic development (by answering the questions in the previous section). Nevertheless, there are six core principles at the heart of blue ocean strategy that can be used as a guideline to tackle six key risks that are common to new product development strategy, namely search risk, planning risk, scope risk, business model risks, organisational risk and management risk. The six blue ocean principles can be interpreted as an 'implementation' guide for creating uncontested markets:

- The first principle – reconstruct market boundaries: identify commercially compelling blue oceans in which the *search risk* is minimised.
- The second principle – focus on the big picture, not the numbers: tackle the *planning risks* by focusing on the existing facts.
- The third principle – reach beyond existing demand: tackle the *scope risk* of aggregating the greatest demand for a new offering.
- The fourth principle – get the strategic sequence right: reduce the *business model risk* by focusing on how to build a robust model that ensures long-term profit.
- The fifth principle – overcome key organisational hurdles: reduce the *organisational risk* of executing a blue ocean strategy.
- The sixth principle – build execution into strategy: focus attention on the motivation and use of the competencies of employees to execute blue ocean strategy, thereby overcoming management risk.

The final analysis

The blue ocean strategy model is a theoretical model that may be a revelation for many managers. However, the model primarily describes what to do (on an abstract level) instead of demonstrating how to do it. The model and related ideas are descriptive rather than prescriptive. Moreover, the cases mentioned by Kim and Mauborgne as examples of successful blue ocean innovations are interpreted through a 'blue ocean lens', rather than being based on this model.

Although Kim and Mauborgne have made a valuable contribution to strategic management literature, not all firms should adopt this model. Blue ocean strategy may be a good strategy for many firms, but for others a fast-moving strategy, cost leadership, differentiation or focus strategy may be far more successful (Porter, 1979). Kim and Mauborgne provide the important insight that a firm can simultaneously pursue cost differentiation and low costs.

References

Kim, W.C. and Mauborgne, R. (1997) 'Value innovation: the strategic logic of high growth'. *Harvard Business Review* (January–February), 103–112.

Kim, W.C. and Mauborgne, R. (2005) *Blue Ocean Strategy: How to Create Uncontested Market Space and Make the Competition Irrelevant.* Cambridge MA: Harvard Business School Press.

Porter, M. (1979) 'How competitive forces shape strategy'. *Harvard Business Review* 57(2), 137–145.

6 Business model canvas

The big picture

The business model canvas as introduced by Alex Osterwalder (2010) describes the possible rationale of how an organisation creates, delivers and preserves value. It provides a canvas to describe, visualise, develop and explore business models. On the basis of nine basic building blocks, one can see at a glance how a company

Figure 6.1 Business model canvas
Source: after Osterwalder (2004)

does its business and earns money. The model is highly visual and shows how the building blocks interlock. It provides a common language to discuss current and (potential) future business models.

When to use it

The business model canvas has become popular thanks to its highly visual, integrated view, showing how a business actually functions. It is a perfect tool – as it was originally intended – for generating new business models and ideas for and new ways of doing business. But it is also a perfect tool to analyse the existing business of your organisation and find areas of improvement.

The model can also be used in strategic decision-making for your own organisation. It can provide inspiration and/or strategic insights by analysing your competitors' businesses. It can also be very helpful in making strategic options to choose from more tangible. With the business model canvas, alternative business models can be developed or completely new business models conceived that had previously not been considered.

How to use it

The business model canvas consists of nine generic building blocks:

1 Customer segments. For whom do we create value? Who are our most important customers? What characterises our clients? How can we segment our markets?

2 Value proposition. What value do we provide our customers? What customer problems do we solve? How does that vary between customer segments?

3 Servicing model or channels. How do we (want to) reach our customers? What are customer demands on delivery and service? What works best, what is cost-effective? How does my supply chain look?

4 Customer relationships. What relationship do customers in each segment expect? Which service level is required for which type of customer? Does the customer have a relationship with us too or are they just transaction-oriented?

5 Revenues. How do we earn from our customers? What do they pay for? How much do customers pay now or how much are they willing to pay? How do we generate income with each transaction?

6 Key resources. Which resources are necessary to create and deliver for the value proposition, the channels and the customer relationship? Do we have unique resources and/or exclusive access to resources?

7 Key activities. Which activities are needed to create and deliver for the value proposition, to use the channels, to foster relationships and to reach

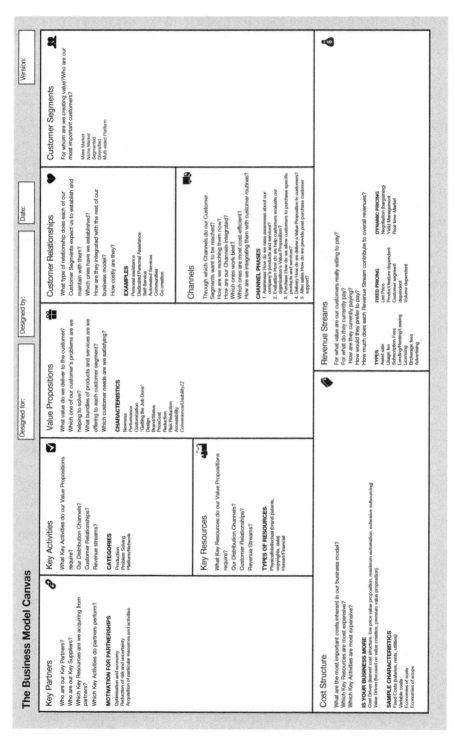

Figure 6.2 The business model canvas

Source: Businessmodelcanvas.com

the customers? Do we have unique activities? What do we do that is different from our competitors?

8 Key partners. Who are our main partners? What resources do they have and what activities do our partners do (better than us) that enable us to deliver value to our customers?

9 Cost structure. What are the costs of creating and delivering added value to our customers? Which of our (or our partner's) important resources are the most expensive? Which main activities cost the most? How do we incur costs with each transaction?

When using the business model canvas the first step is to print out an enlarged blank canvas (see Figure 6.2). This can then be used as a drawing board on which groups of people can together start sketching and writing, or sticking on Post-it notes. Each of the nine building blocks are to be considered and discussed. There are also many digital tools available for the business model canvas (an app for tablet computers, an online toolbox and a serious game).

The final analysis

A pitfall of the business model canvas is that the analysis of its nine building blocks is often based on assumptions rather than facts. Particularly poor knowledge about existing customers but also about new segments often leads to unsubstantiated assumptions. A second pitfall is that a substantiation of a strategic option is prematurely regarded as the best or only business model for that strategic option (too much concrete, insufficient exploration). The business model canvas is particularly suitable for creating multiple, alternative models. It is a hands-on tool that fosters understanding and creativity.

References

Business Model Generation website: http://www.businessmodelgeneration.com

Osterwalder, A. (2004) *The Business Model Ontology, A Proposition In A Design Science Approach*. University of Lausanne.

Osterwalder, A. and Pigneur, Y. (2010) *Business Model Generation: A Handbook for Visionaries, Game Changers and Challengers*. Hoboken, New Jersey: John Wiley & Sons.

7

Business scope (Abell)

The big picture

The business definition model introduced by Derek Abell (1980) defines and considers a company on the basis of three dimensions: the customers (who), their needs (what) and the technology and competencies the company dedicates to serve those needs (how). The model – by popular account – determines your business scope: stating what your company and business are about. The model is

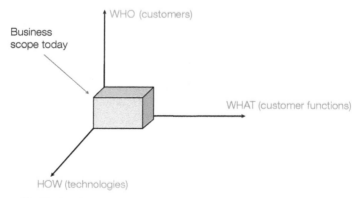

Figure 7.1 Abell's business scope

Source: after *Defining the Business: the Starting Point of Strategic Planning*, 1st ed., Prentice Hall (Abell, D.F. 1980) ©1980. Reprinted and electronically reproduced by permission of Pearson Education, Inc., Upper Saddle River, New Jersey.

often used to gain insight into the company and its proposition to the market. It also gives an insight into the company's possibilities for development in each of the three dimensions. Using this model, the current and the future potential of the company can be visualised and discussed (Figure 7.1).

When to use it

Abell's business scope model can be used to define the business scope of a company, offering an insight into the current position of the company in its market(s). It can also be used to identify the potential of the organisation, giving an insight into the positions the company could occupy in the market(s). It is often used in strategic discussions and decision-making, especially in identifying and setting goals in relation to the areas in which the organisation wants to pursue its (commercial) potential.

How to use it

To determine the business scope using Abell's model, there are three questions to be answered:

- Who – determine what customer groups the company can deliver value to. This question should be asked from the customer perspective.
- What – determine what needs customers have to identify what activities add value to these customer groups.
- How – determine what technologies, competencies and systems applied by the company will allow it to perform better (i.e. fulfil the needs of the customer better) than its competitors.

By first answering each question for the current situation of the organisation, a shared understanding and point of view is created. This could then serve as a common point of reference. By next answering each question for the future of the organisation (for instance taking a point in time 3–5 years from now), insight into the potential of the organisation is gained. In this way, the business scope model can be very useful for determining strategy and setting strategic goals: how ambitious should and can the organisation be? Should it look into new customer groups as well as new activities and new technologies? And how radically new should and can those be?

The final analysis

The model provides a clear framework for discussions about the current and potential business scope of the company. Besides extending the business scope, a discussion on limiting that scope can also lead to surprising insights.

Using the model is fairly straightforward; however, in practice, the 'how' question might prove more challenging. To fully answer this question much more detail is needed than in the other two questions. It is sometimes helpful to divide the 'how' question into two sub-questions: 'How: with what partners?' and 'How: with what technology?'

Very often the 'how' question leads to a fundamental discussion about the business model of the company and it is this limitation that might make the business scope model less suitable. Other models, e.g. the business model canvas (see Chapter 6), may be more appropriate to discuss the business model of the organisation.

References

Abell, D.F. (1980) *Defining the Business: the Starting Point of Strategic Planning.* Prentice Hall.

Van den Berg, G. and Pietersma, P. (2014) *The 8 Steps to Strategic Success: Unleashing the Power of Engagement*. London: Kogan Page.

Competitive analysis: Porter's five forces model

8

The big picture

Porter's (1980) competitive analysis identifies five fundamental competitive forces that determine the relative attractiveness of an industry: new entrants, bargaining power of buyers, bargaining power of suppliers, substitute products or services, and rivalry among existing competitors (Figure 8.1). The weaker these forces are, the more attractive an industry or company becomes. Competitive analysis provides an insight into the relationships and dynamics of an industry, and allows a company to make strategic decisions regarding the best defendable and most economically attractive position.

When to use it

The model can be used to gain a better understanding of the industry context in which the business is operating. For example, a company may use it to analyse the attractiveness of a new industry by identifying whether new products, services or businesses are potentially profitable. The model can also be used to evaluate a firm's strategic position in the marketplace, as it takes account of a broad range of competitors beyond the obvious or immediate. This creates an understanding of the strengths of both the company's current competitive position and the desired position.

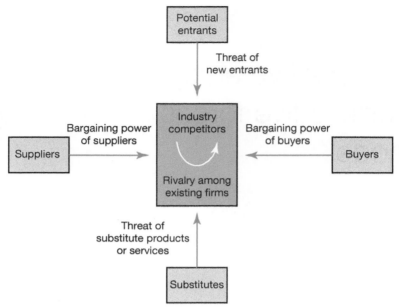

Figure 8.1 Porter's five forces
Source: after *Competitive Strategy: Techniques for Analysing Industries and Competitors*, Free Press (Porter, M.E. 1980) Copyright © 1980 by Michael E. Porter; all rights reserved. Reproduced with the permission of Simon & Schuster Publishing Group, a Division of Simon and Schuster, Inc.

How to use it

The five forces model is an aid to evaluating the competitive arena from all perspectives based on five fundamental forces. By identifying the strength and direction of each force, it is possible to assess quickly the strength of the organisation's position, together with its ability to make a profit or maintain profitability in a specific industry.

For each of the five forces, consider how well your company can compete.

1. New entrants

Are there entry barriers for new contenders?

- The greater the importance of economies of scale, the higher the entry barrier will be.
- Competing with established brands and loyalty is harder (e.g. Coca-Cola).
- High up-front (risky) capital requirements make entry difficult.
- High switching costs for products are a great advantage for existing players.
- Is access to distribution channels difficult or legally restricted?
- Do existing companies have cost advantages that are independent of market scale (e.g. patents, licences, proprietary know-how, favourable access to raw materials, capital assets, experienced workers, subsidies)?

- A government-regulated industry could limit entry by requiring operating licences (e.g. UMTS wireless communication).
- Expecting a low level of retaliation by existing players makes entry easier for newcomers.
- The concept of 'entry deterring price' – the bigger the margin, the more new entrants there will be.

2. Substitutes

How easily can your product or service be substituted with a different type of product or service?

For example, the bus is a substitute for the train. Porter argues that a substitute is particularly threatening if it represents a significant improvement in the price/performance trade-off.

3. Buyers' bargaining power

To what extent can buyers bargain?

- When buyers buy in large volumes, they are more likely to command better prices. For example, large grocery retailers pay lower wholesale prices than small stores.
- The larger the fraction of costs represented by the purchase price, the harder buyers will bargain.
- Undifferentiated products make it easier to play suppliers off against each other.
- Low switching costs increase buyer power.
- Low-profit buyers will be tough negotiators.
- The potential for 'DIY' production or backwards integration is a strong bargaining lever. Partial in-house production or 'tapered integration' not only is a strong bargaining tool, but it also provides a better understanding of a supplier's actual costs!
- The less the buyer's performance is affected by the product, the more price-sensitive the buyer will be.
- The more information buyers have, the better their bargaining position is.

4. Suppliers' command of industry

What level of influence do suppliers have?

Suppliers can have a significant impact on an industry's profitability and margin distribution, depending on several levers. Competitive forces from suppliers mirror those of buyers:

- A few suppliers selling to relatively more buyers will be able to have a bigger say.

- The absence of substitutes increases supplier power, as buyers have little choice.
- Suppliers with alternative customers, industries and channels have more power.
- The supplier's product is indispensable or of great value to your company.
- Switching suppliers will incur high expenses or rapidly depreciate your company's assets.
- Suppliers may integrate forwards by producing for and selling to your customers.

5. Existing competitors

What advantages do competitors have? Last, but not least, rivalry between existing competitors leads to tactics such as aggressive pricing and promotion, battles for customers or channels, and increased service levels. If there is an escalation of moves and counter-moves (e.g. price wars), all industry rivals may end up losing. However, advertising battles may also be of benefit as it makes clear the differentiation between companies and brands. Although rivalry and its intensity change as the industry expands its marketing and technologies, the following are indicators of a competitive threat from existing industry rivals:

- many and/or equally strong competitors;
- slow industry growth, leading to a focus on dividing, rather than expanding, the industry;
- high fixed costs and asset bases making rivals compete to turn stock and fill capacity;
- products are considered to be commodities and are made available at low cost, which encourage buyers to switch supplier at no risk and to buy by price;
- diversity of competitors and their strategies, making it difficult to anticipate competitive moves;
- high stakes, e.g. the challenge of building a customer base in cellular communication or sales on the internet;
- high exit barriers for economic, strategic, emotional or legal reasons. Major exit barriers are: specialised assets that are difficult to sell; fixed cost of exit (e.g. labour agreements, settlement costs); and the strategic importance of activities or brands for the corporation or its partners.

The final analysis

Although it is arguably the most widely used and recognised model for strategic analysis, this powerful model has one major disadvantage, namely that it tends to emphasise external forces and the ways in which a company can counter these forces. An organisation's intrinsic strengths and ability to develop its competencies independently of these forces are given much less consideration. The model can therefore be classified as reactive rather than proactive and is best used in combination with an inside-out approach.

Sometimes the model is extended with additional forces: government, partners (next to competitors) and compatible products (next to substitutes). These might help in getting an even more complete picture.

Reference

Porter, M.E. (1980,1998), *Competitive Strategy: Techniques for Analysing Industries and Competitors*. New York: Free Press.

9

Core competencies

The big picture

A core competence is something unique that a firm has, or can do, strategically well. Premiered by Prahalad and Hamel in their 1990 *Harvard Business Review* article (and their 1994 book), an assessment of an organisation's core competencies is an essential element in formulating strategy nowadays. Giving proper attention to what your organisation stands for and what strengths it has to stand out from the competition helps to answer the question as to what future possibilities your organisation possesses. The concept of core competencies is based on Barney's (1991) resource-based view of the firm: the idea that an organisation's inimitable and valuable tangible and intangible assets are key aspects of a firm's sustainable competitive advantage (Figure 9.1).

When to use it

The core competencies model is a strategic tool to determine the unique assets that can be used to create and offer value to customers. The process of defining core competencies encourages management to think about the strengths and capabilities that set the company apart from competitors. Whereas Porter's five forces model (Chapter 8) takes an outside-in approach and places the external environment at the starting point of the strategy process, the core competence model does the opposite. It builds on the assumption that competitiveness derives ultimately

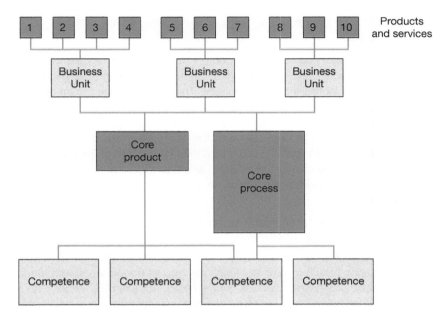

Figure 9.1 Core competencies

Source: after 'The core competence of the corporation', *Harvard Business Review*, Vol. 68 (3), pp. 79–91, (Prahalad, C.K. and Hamel, G. 1990), Copyright © 1990 by the Harvard Business School Publishing Corporation; all rights reserved. Reproduced by permission of *Harvard Business Review*

from a company's ability to build core competencies that spawn unanticipated products at lower cost and more speedily than competitors can. In this way, the core competence model can be used to create sustainable competitive advantage.

How to use it

The starting point for understanding core competencies is to realise that a business needs to have something that it can do well and that meets the following three conditions:

1 It provides consumer benefits.

2 It is not easy for competitors to imitate.

3 It can be leveraged widely to many products and markets.

A company that identifies, develops or acquires unique assets with which to build valuable products may create a long-lasting competitive advantage. The fundamental question relates to where this uniqueness comes from and how it can be sustained. Typically fundamental questions are asked such as:

● What value will we deliver to our customers in, say, 10 years' time?

● What new 'competencies' (a combination of skills and technologies) will we need to develop or obtain to provide that value?

- What are the implications with regard to how we interact with our customers?

Thinking about and trying to define a company's core competencies will stimulate management to rethink and – ideally – mobilise the organisation's intrinsic strengths. Foresight is a key ingredient in this process. The future will see the introduction of products and services that are not yet feasible. New industries and products will exist that are unimaginable today. Management needs to realise the impact of these uncertainties and to consider what the competitive arena might look like in the future. Hamel and Prahalad (1990) claim that the process of thinking about core competencies helps to identify the extent to which an organisation has the capability to seize a part of that unknown future. In order to develop foresight, managers need to do two things:

1 Do not consider the company as a number of business units, but as a collection of core competencies.

2 Determine what the company's unique competencies are (or should be) by considering how the company functions, and its performance with regard to specific processes, products and services. For example, rather than being considered solely as an automobile manufacturer, Volvo cars should be thought of as a company with unique competencies in product design, human safety and protection, and vehicle testing.

Some tips for determining core competencies
- **Throw away your existing notion of what your company is or could be.**
- **Explore and cross the frontiers of your business.**
- **Don't be afraid to talk about things you do not understand.**
- **Paradoxes are good – paradigms are bad.**
- **Pretend you are the customer.**
- **Think in terms of needs, not demands.**

Once management has an idea ('foresight') of what core competencies the company has or should have, it must build the *strategic architecture*. This is not a business plan, but a framework that prepares the company to capture a (potentially) large share of future revenues in emerging opportunities. The strategic architecture addresses issues and timing for what is called a broad opportunity approach:

- Which competencies have to be developed?
- Which new customer groups must be understood?
- Which new channels should be pursued?
- What are the new development priorities?

The final analysis

In theory, the process of defining core competencies stimulates management to think about the strengths and capabilities that set the company apart from competitors. In practice, however, defining core competencies clearly is so difficult that even Hamel and Prahalad seem unable to put their finger on it sometimes. In their zealous efforts to offer enough examples to bolster the universal application of core-competency thinking, they confuse core products and core competencies themselves.

Even with the benefit of hindsight, it is apparently difficult to identify core competencies, let alone come up with sharp definitions for the unknown future. Furthermore, it is frequently obvious that core competencies are not as unique and inimitable as management would like to think. Finally, if your core competencies are locked inside the heads of people that walk away from the organisation, you may want to reconsider what your core competencies really are.

Core competencies
- The collective learning within an organisation.
- The ability to integrate multiple skills and technologies.
- The capability to combine resources and knowledge to deliver superior products and services.
- What differentiates the organisation and what makes it competitive.
- The very fabric of the corporation.

Checklist for identifying a core competency
- Is it a significant source of competitive advantage?
- Does it uniquely identify the organisation?
- Is it widespread throughout the organisation?
- Is it difficult to copy?
- Is it difficult to put your finger on it, because it seems to be a combination of technologies, processes and 'the way things are done' in this organisation?

Examples of core competencies
- Sony – miniaturisation of electronic equipment.
- Honda – building high-performance engines and powered vehicles.
- Apple – making user-friendly computer interfaces and design.
- Canon – integrating precision mechanics, fine optics and microelectronics.
- 3M – persistently innovating adhesives and substrates.

References

Barney, J.B. (1991) 'Firm resources and sustainable competitive advantage'. *Journal of Management* 17, 99–120.

Hamel, G. and Prahalad, C.K. (1994) *Competing for the Future: Breakthrough Strategies for Seising Control of Your Industry and Creating the Markets of Tomorrow*. Boston, MA: Harvard Business School Press.

Prahalad, C.K. and Hamel, G. (1990) 'The core competence of corporation'. *Harvard Business Review* 68, 79–91.

Internationalisation strategy framework

10

The big picture

Doing business on an international level requires both thinking about the (new) markets the company is active in or about to enter, and the coordination and synergies of the new activities with current activities. The internationalisation strategy framework is a model that supports this balanced decision-making on how to internationalise the organisation's activities. The model is built around two types of questions commonly faced by organisations when they internationalise:

1 What is my rationale for internationalisation? Is the motivation for internationalisation driven by market opportunities in the selected country (extrinsic) or by expansion (intrinsic)? Does the company aspire to short-term gains (tactical) or to a long-term competitive position (strategic) in the country?

2 How do I coordinate and organise the new activities in this country? Should the company take on the whole range of activities (large spread) or should it be a single-operation business (focus)? Should the coordination (and related cost) of the new activities be organised as part of a globally integrated company or as a local business?

The answer to these questions and the related aspects can be interlinked, resulting in multiple tensions and trade-offs. From these, five generic business models for doing business internationally can be derived (see Figure 10.1).

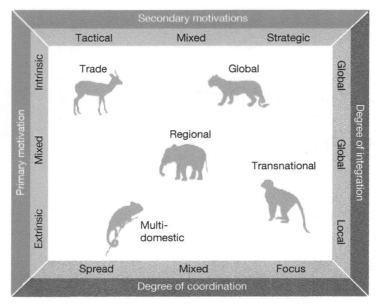

Figure 10.1 Internationalisation strategy framework
Source: after Lem, Van Tulder and Geleynse (2013)

When to use it

The internationalisation strategy framework is useful when considering expanding your business abroad (entering new markets and countries) and when discussing how to organise all your international activities. It presents five generic business models for doing business internationally:

- Trade model. The motivation of trade model companies is often intrinsically seeking easy combinations of available products or services with an opportunity in the local market. These companies are short-term opportunity-driven: always looking for (better) markets and responding quickly to competitors. They rarely ally with local stakeholders. This business model requires little coordination effort as risks associated are mostly operational and finance-related (payments, currencies). It is, however, difficult to build a sustainable competitive position from this business model. Typical entry modes for trade model companies include import/export and setting up local (trading) agencies.

- Multi-domestic model. The motivation of multi-domestic companies is extrinsically driven by market opportunities in the selected country of destination: products and services are to be adapted to local requirements and conditions, sometimes in local production facilities. These companies are short-term opportunity-driven, and in many cases they are the result of a successful local trade that grows into a permanent representation. This makes them well equipped for serving both small and large local markets. They are often embedded in the local business environment, and sometimes even regarded as 'national' companies by local stakeholders. This business model requires considerable decentralisation of business processes, making coordination within the company across countries more difficult. This also makes it difficult to achieve economies of scale and build a sustainable competitive position. Typical entry modes for multi-domestic model companies include setting up local (trading) agencies or allying (alliance or joint venture) with local sales agents and/or with local production facilities.

- Global model. The motivation of global model companies is intrinsic: they see opportunities in many local markets for their (one-size-fits-all) products and services, related both to sales and to resources and assets (e.g. cheap production facilities). These companies are long-term-driven: relying on their own internal competencies and the strength of their products, they enter selected countries to gain a lasting competitive position. They function primarily in the interests of global headquarters and engage little with local stakeholders. This business model allows for high efficiency, making coordination more easy. It does, however, allow very little for adaptability to local circumstances, which increases the risk of failure when local markets do not accept globally standardised products. Typical entry modes for global model companies include starting up wholly owned subsidiaries in sales and/or production (either through merger/acquisition or as greenfield investment).

- Regional model. The motivation of regional model companies is mixed, similar to the transnational model. By clustering activities on a regional level, i.e. in a geographically related group of multiple countries, companies can (re)arrange their spread of sales and/or production facilities into more regional centres. Their regional presence gives them freer access to countries in the region, making these companies more flexible with regard to entering local markets. Their lower 'sunk costs' in operations and lower-level engagement with local stakeholders also make them more flexible in leaving local markets and countries. This allows regional model companies to aspire to longer-term competitive positions in the region, but not necessarily in each country. The degree of coordination of this model is easier, as activities are clustered on a regional level. Coordination between regions in the company is less easy and depends both on the strength of the regions and on the level of cohesion between regions. Regional model companies make use of nearly all entry modes, at both regional and country levels.

- The transnational model. The motivation of transnational model companies is mixed, trying to strike a balance between multi-domestic model companies and global model companies: local market opportunities are primary motivators, but local conditions determine the attractiveness of local markets and countries. These companies will assess countries and markets extensively before entering. They do so, as they are willing to invest in a long-term presence and in the development of local markets. They therefore actively engage with local stakeholders. This business model is demanding in terms of coordination and investment strength, but allows for efficiencies of scale. Typical entry modes for multi-domestic model companies include allying (alliance or joint venture) with local sales agents and/or with local production facilities.

How to use it

First, you need to decide that you want to expand your business internationally. You then need to decide into which country or countries you want to expand your business. For this, an assessment of the country needs to be made. Naturally, this requires a thorough market analysis of the (availability of) target customer groups, competition, the (availability of) supply chain partners, etc. It also requires an analysis of the country, its legislation and regulators, culture, economic growth, political stability, etc. After choosing which country to expand into, you need to decide how you want to organise your activities in that country. This is where the internationalisation strategy framework comes in: by answering the questions the model is built around, you will find out how your motivation for internationalisation aligns with your coordination needs. An optimisation can then be found by trading off what local responsiveness is needed in the selected country and what levels of global integration (and economies of scale) can be organised in the company. From this, the most appropriate of the five generic business models can be chosen.

Very often an organisation's activities have spread into different countries, either grown historically or through mergers and acquisitions. The framework has proven to be even more appropriate for the discussion on rationalising or furthering an organisation's international presence.

The final analysis

The internationalisation strategy framework brings clarity to decision-making on the internationalisation of business. With the model, questions about motivation and coordination become apparent. They also become answerable. By honouring the many aspects that are to be considered when entering a new country, the internationalisation strategy framework model is very useful in discussing such entry. However, it does not provide any suggestions regarding what considerations to make when selecting a country to enter.

Another strong feature of this model is that it is very useful in discussing how to organise activities in multiple countries: many multinational companies have a historically grown collection of local presences. With this model they can assess and discuss how to optimise (or rationalise) the different local business models they have worldwide.

Although the internationalisation strategy framework was developed with doing business in Africa in mind, it can be used in relation to internationalisation in any part of the world.

Reference

Lem, M., Van Tulder, R., and Geleynse K. (2013) *Doing Business in Africa: A Strategic Guide for Entrepreneurs*. Utrecht: Berenschot International B.V. and RSM Erasmus University Rotterdam.

11 Road-mapping

The big picture

Road-mapping concerns the creation of a common vision. It is a process by which experts forecast future developments in technology and in the marketplace, and identify the consequences of those developments for (individual) firms. The road map model provides a description of how the process of development might be structured.

The road-mapping process clarifies future goals (based mainly on experts' views of technological development) and the road to achieving those goals. Based on this analysis, it is possible to identify how an individual firm could contribute towards making this development happen or how the firm can react to the development. This chapter uses a product–technology road map to explain the process.

A variety of road maps have been created in recent decades. When looking at technology-driven road maps, four different types and size can be identified:

- Industry road maps are those in which the expected development of an entire branch of industry is mapped out. The road-mapping process offers a way of minimising the risk to individual firms, because several different parties decide on the priorities for future development of the technology and what (research) should be contributed by each party. An industry road map can also be used to obtain finance (both private and public).

- The corporate road map is designed to help individual firms make strategic choices and may be based on the industry road map. This road map describes product–market combinations.

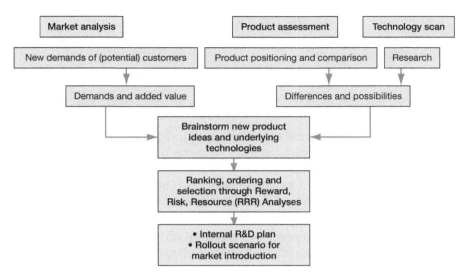

Figure 11.1 Road-mapping

- The product–technology road map is one in which a market analysis, product assessment and technology scan are combined to create an internal research and development (R&D) plan and rollout scenarios for introducing the product to market. The model described in this chapter is an example of a product–technology road map, which is created in combination with a technology road map.

- The competence–research road map focuses on the competence and research needed to create a particular (part of a) technology. This style of road map may either be compiled separately, or, as in the worked example, integrated as part of the whole.

When to use it

The product–technology road map can be used to focus more clearly on the future. It is useful for gaining professional insight into new market developments, particularly in technology-driven markets. New product development is essential for survival in these markets and is increasingly relevant due to the shortening of product life cycles. Road-mapping is therefore an essential strategy for firms that are continually searching for new products. Road-mapping aids the process of new product development by facilitating the structural identification of (new) markets, products and technologies.

Road maps generally consist of descriptions of:

- Delivery – the product descriptions and the research required.
- Purpose – market, product and technology analysis.

- Timing – the critical path and timing of delivery.
- Resources – the resources (money, people) and technology needed to create the products.

The advantages of road-mapping include the following:

- Road-mapping provides the participating organisation with valuable strategic information.
- Long-range strategic planning will be based on gathering well-structured information, which will enable better decisions to be made regarding future products and technologies.
- Internal and external data will be mapped, which will result in a well-structured vision of market factors, consumer needs, technological development, environmental factors and supplier changes.
- A better alignment between R&D spending and product development will result, because the opportunities for integrating new technologies into new products have been identified.
- Road maps may be the source of technology reuse options (same technology into new products).
- Results may reveal long-term strategic weaknesses and identify the gaps and uncertainties of products and technologies.
- Road maps are a powerful instrument for aligning the entire enterprise around a new development strategy and new product development. Project teams can quickly adapt to strategic changes.
- The potential for synergy is identified between suppliers and buyers, and between competitors.

How to use it

A technology–market road map is based on the results of:

1 Market analysis
2 A technology scan
3 Product assessment.

Market analysis looks from the outside-in and is carried out to identify new and long-term demands of customers. The results provide an overview of the new demands and the added value created by the firm(s). A technology scan looks from the inside-out and identifies the possible and likely new technologies. The product assessment also looks from the inside-out, and compares the product portfolio with other products available. The technology scan and the product assessment together provide an overview of the differences and possibilities for new products.

At the next stage, the results of the road map are discussed during a brainstorming session. During this session, new product ideas are evaluated by considering the rewards – USPs (unique selling points) and ROI (return on investment); the risks (technological and market readiness); and the resources (investment) required. Naturally, the products with the highest rewards and the lowest risk and resource requirements are the most valuable new products. Based on this analysis, an internal R&D plan can be created that is based on the research required to be able to produce the new product. In addition, it is possible to develop a rollout plan for market introduction.

Although the market analysis, product assessment and technology scan can be carried out by key people within the organisation (presumably with the help of an external consulting firm), the most successful road maps are created by key persons from a range of different organisations and universities. One of the main success factors of road maps is the involvement of 'champions'. Champions are respected and well-known experts in a particular (technological) area. When an industry champion lends their support to a road map, others will accept it more easily.

Other factors required for success are as follows:

- Road maps should be compiled by key individuals, who are known to be experts with specialist industry knowledge.
- Full management commitment is crucial if the road map is to have a positive impact on the organisation.
- Road maps should be updated on a regular basis to take account of ongoing product, market and technological changes.
- An impartial person (such as a consultant) can perform interviews and facilitate the road-mapping process.
- Taking a uniform approach is crucial for effective communication and can support linking between road maps.
- A road map should be used as a long-term approach to strategic development. If the strategic vision does not exceed a period of 2 years, it is not suitable for a road map.

The final analysis

Road-mapping is a method that facilitates the creation of a shared vision for the future; developing a shared view of the world is considered as important as the final road map. Therefore, road-mapping may not be successful for firms that have a vision of the world which differs from the dominant view (of the firms involved).

The main purpose of a road map is to inspire, by providing insights into ways to improve and renew. Although concrete activities and projects are described in a road map, the future is unknown and is not always predictable. A road map is therefore only a visualisation of the future. Although it is based on technological and market facts, it should not be used as a document of prediction. Frequent updating of the road map is essential in order to incorporate current developments into the 'planned' vision of the future.

References

European Industrial Research Management Association (EIRMA) (1997) *Technology Road Mapping*. No. 52. Paris: EIRMA.

Farrukh, C., Phaal, R. and Probert, D. (2003) 'Technology road-mapping: linking technology resources into business planning'. *International Journal of Technology Management* 26(1), 2–19.

Scenario planning

12

The big picture

Scenario planning asks questions about the future. It is a means of assessing strategy against a number of structurally quite different, but equally plausible, future models of the world. Scenarios provide a context in which managers can make decisions. By seeing a range of possible worlds, decision-makers will be better informed, and intentions based on this knowledge will be more likely to succeed.

Scenario exercises are based on the principles of transparency and diversity that try to make sense of the future development of key market forces.

- Transparency – refers to the process of making explicit assumptions about the relationships between key driving forces.
- Diversity – implies that there is no single 'best' scenario or 'high' or 'low' market projection. Diversity recognises that the future is uncertain and considers a number of different strategic routes (Ringland, 2002).

The contrasting objectives of scenario planning can be expressed as follows (Van der Heijden et al., 2002):

- a specific goal (one-off, problem-solving projects) versus a more general objective (longer-term projects that enable the survival of the organisation);
- projects undertaken to open up an organisation that is closed to new ways of thinking versus projects to achieve closure on decisions and action in an organisation that is drifting.

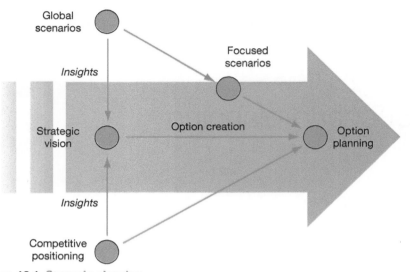

Figure 12.1 Scenario planning
Source: adapted from Van der Heijden et al. (2002)

These objectives lead to four types of scenario planning (see Figure 12.2):

1 Making sense – a one-time exploratory exercise of scenario planning to gain an in-depth understanding of complex situations.

2 Developing strategy – the use of scenarios to test the business proposition for the future in various, but relevant scenarios.

3 Anticipation – the organisational ability to see, perceive and understand what is happing in the business environment, which requires the organisation to mobilise as many resources as possible to observe, perceive, experience, make sense, rationalise and decide. The anticipation purpose of scenarios highlights the importance of being a skilful observer of the external world through strategic conversations.

4 Adaptive organisational learning – which goes one step further by introducing action in the process. This is comparable to the description of scenario learning of Fahey and Randell (1998), who showed that scenarios should be integrating into decision-making. This implies that the adaptive organisational learning framework moves from one-off strategy development to ongoing strategy planning and experience.

When to use it

Royal Dutch Shell uses scenarios for a wide range of purposes. In general, scenarios help the firm to understand the dynamics of the business environment, to recognise new opportunities, to assess strategic options and to take long-term decisions. Decision-makers can use scenarios to think about the uncertain aspects

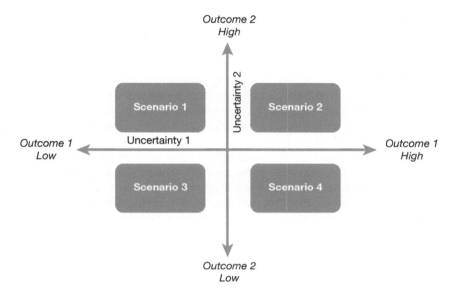

Figure 12.2 Categorisation of scenario objectives
Source: after Van der Heijden et al. (2002)

of the future that worry them the most, or to discover the aspects about which they should be concerned. Royal Dutch Shell provides four reasons why scenario planning is an important tool for strategy development:

- Confronting assumptions – this is related very closely to the discipline of mental models. By exploring the assumptions that people hold individually and collectively about the future, it helps the firm to act more effectively at that moment.

- Recognising degrees of uncertainty – scenario planning provides the organisation with a method for acknowledging and working with what they do not know.

- Widening perspectives – scenarios address blind spots by challenging assumptions, expanding vision and combining information from many different disciplines.

- Addressing dilemmas and conflicts – scenarios can help to clarify or resolve the conflicts and dilemmas confronting their users.

How to use it

Several methods of scenario planning have been put forward in management books (e.g. Schwartz, 1991; Ringland, 1998, 2002; Van der Heijden et al. 2002), but all scenario-planning processes start by identifying knowledge gaps and areas of uncertainty, and by setting up a scenario team comprised of employees and external facilitators. The process is structured during this phase. Next, key players are asked to explore the context (i.e. the business domain under study) through a series of interviews, with a view to challenging the team's current assumptions; this process is taken further during a series of workshops. Once the broad context of a scenario has been agreed, the driving forces are clustered and scenarios are developed. For each scenario, a coherent story is developed that highlights future implications. The relative impact of a scenario is explored in depth and its implications for the future are considered carefully. This new understanding is then tested via various business stakeholders.

Van der Heijden et al. (2002) adds *system thinking* as an additional step in the scenario planning process, in which the causal relationships in the stories are identified. By following these five steps, the scenario team develops a number of plausible futures for the organisation. The final step is to communicate the impact of the scenarios on the organisation: its strategic thinking, possible future strategies and corresponding actions. This implies that scenario planning is only valuable if various strategies or operational decisions are tested in different scenarios.

The final analysis

The effectiveness of using scenario planning lies in the ability of the scenario team to convince management to do what seems best. Changing the managerial world view is a much more demanding task than actually building the scenario (Wack, 1985). Furthermore, the one-off use of a single scenario is not a powerful tool for strategy building or action. Learning and action require us to consider scenario planning as an ongoing cyclical process of exploration and exploitation.

References

Fahey, L. and Randall, R. M., (1998), *Learning From the Future: Competitive Foresight Scenarios,* John Wiley & Sons.

Ringland, G. (1998) *Scenario Planning: Managing for the Future*. New York: John Wiley & Sons.

Ringland, G. (2002) *Scenarios in Business*, New York: John Wiley & Sons.

Schwartz, P. (1991) *The Art of the Long View: Planning for the Future in an Uncertain World*. New York: Doubleday/Currency.

Van der Heijden, K. Bradfield, R., Burt, G. and Cairns, G. (1996) *Scenarios: The Art of Strategic Conversation*. New York: John Wiley & Sons.

Van der Heijden, K., (2002) *The Sixth Sense: Accelerating Organisational Learning with Scenarios*. New York: John Wiley & Sons.

Wack, P. (1985) 'Scenarios: shooting the rapids'. *Harvard Business Review* 63(6), November – December, 139–150.

Strategy maps

13

The big picture

In 1992 Kaplan and Norton introduced the balanced scorecard (BSC, see Chapter 17). The premise for the BSC was to start with a clean sheet of paper. Based on the analysis of hundreds of scorecards, Kaplan and Norton found there are patterns that – in a chain of cause-and-effect logic – connect the strategy as intended with the drivers that will lead to the strategic outcomes. These patterns together form a framework, which is visualised as a map.

A strategy map (Kaplan & Norton, 2004) describes the process of transforming intangible assets into tangible customer and financial outcomes. Strategy maps help organisations see their strategy in a cohesive, integrated and systematic way (Figure 13.1).

When to use it

A strategy map is a generic architecture for describing the strategic goals and the contribution that is expected (and/or needed) in each of the four perspectives of the BSC. With a strategy map, and the corresponding BSC with performance indicators, management has a framework for managing the organisation towards the intended strategic outcomes. They help to clearly portray the value-creating processes within the organisation and the critical role of intangible assets. According to Kaplan and Norton, especially in today's knowledge-intensive economies, these intangible

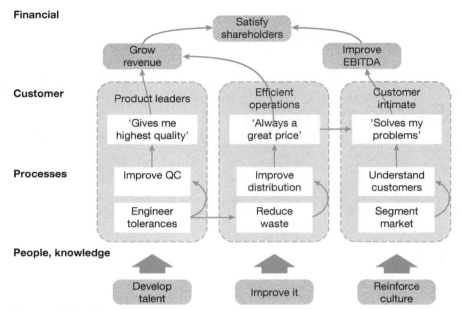

Financial

Customer

Processes

People, knowledge

Figure 13.1 Strategy map

assets are the ultimate drivers of strategic success. Captured in the perspective on the BSC of 'learning and growth' (see Chapter 17), the 'internal processes' of an organisation are strongly influenced – if not determined – by these intangible assets, which in turn determine how the organisation can deliver on the values required by customers (the 'customer' perspective). And how well the organisation is able to match those, of course, determines the financial outcome of the organisation. In this way, the framework with the four perspectives of the BSC provides management with a clear and easy-to-grasp overview of how they drive a strategy to success.

Another important aspect of strategy maps is that they also make the translation of strategy into performance targets more easy. As they can be combined with a corresponding BSC, the strategy map can even be cascaded all the way 'down' to the individual employee level. This can be extremely useful in convincing and motivating people that they can contribute to the strategy individually!

How to use it

To build a strategy map, the intended strategy of the organisation must first be clear. Often the strategy is stated as several strategic themes, such as growing in segment or region X, improving operating efficiency of product group Y. These themes can then be mapped out on the strategy map. Most of the time, the themes reflect what needs to be done within the organisation. They thus match the 'internal process' perspective of the BSC. From there, relations with the other perspectives can be derived, identifying the relevant aspects for the other perspectives. This starts with the 'learning and growth' perspective and 'builds up' towards the 'customer' and finally the 'financial' perspective. From this exercise, it becomes clear how the strategic themes drive the customer and financial outcomes.

From the strategy map it is then relatively easy to set up a corresponding BSC. On each of the four perspectives from the cause-and-effect exercise, the performance indicators can be derived. Next, the targets can be set, which are both feasible (as you know what affects the performance) and ambitious (as you still want to realise your strategy). And the initiatives can be formulated that are needed to realise the targets.

When the strategy is formulated as several themes, it is also relative easy to appoint responsibility for each of the themes, as monitoring progress can be done based on the corresponding BSC. In this way there is transparency and management can be held to account.

The final analysis

Strategy maps can help greatly in describing the intended strategy, as they depict the strategy on one page. By explicitly showing what drivers are important for the realisation of that strategy and what the cause-and-effect relations are between those drivers, it is a great tool to communicate the strategy and to manage the realisation of the strategy effectively. Another strong point is the possibility of operationalising the strategy with the BSC, also allowing for appointing responsibility for the actual execution and realisation of the strategy.

A common critique of strategy maps is that they involve nothing more than 'stacking' the four perspectives of the BSC. Visually, that is how it appears, but this overlooks the strength of using the cause-and-effect relations between aspects of the four different perspectives. In particular, these relations mean that the use of a strategy map leads to both a well balanced and solid operationalisation of the strategy.

On the other hand, strategy maps cannot help you decide on strategy. Although Kaplan and Norton think of strategy as a set of hypotheses that can be made explicit and tested, strategy maps will not provide suggestions or solutions to the challenges faced by the organisation. At best, at least theoretically, as that is not how they were intended, strategy maps can help to operationalise those suggestions or different strategies (or different competing strategic themes) to determine which one is the most feasible (internal perspectives) and the most profitable (external perspectives).

References

Kaplan, R. and Norton, D. (2001) *The Strategy-focused Organisation: How Balanced Scorecard Companies Thrive in the New Business Environment*. Boston: Harvard Business School Press.

Kaplan, R. and Norton, D. (2004) *Strategy Maps: Converting Intangible Assets into Tangible Outcomes*. Boston: Harvard Business School Press.

14

SWOT analysis

The big picture

Any company undertaking strategic planning must at some point assess its strengths and weaknesses. When combined with an inventory of opportunities and threats within or beyond the company's environment, the company is making a so-called *SWOT analysis* (or TOWS analysis), establishing its current position in the light of its *strengths, weaknesses, opportunities and threats* (Figure 14.1)

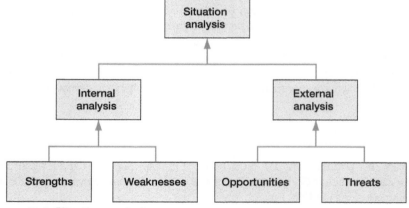

Figure 14.1 Situation analysis
Source: after Weihrich (1982)

When to use it

The SWOT analysis provides helpful information for matching resources and capabilities to the competitive environment in which the organisation operates. The model can be used as an instrument for devising and selecting strategy, and is equally applicable in any decision-making situation, provided the desired objective has been clearly defined.

How to use it

The first step in carrying out a SWOT analysis is to identify the company's strengths, weaknesses, opportunities and threats. A scan of the internal and external environments is therefore an important part of the process. Strengths and weaknesses are internal factors. They are the skills and assets (or lack of them) that are intrinsic to the company and which add to or detract from the value of the company, relative to competitive forces. Opportunities and threats, however, are external factors: they are not created by the company, but emerge due to the activity of competitors, and changes in the market dynamics.

- Strengths. What does the company do well? For example, does the company benefit from an experienced sales force or easy access to raw materials? Do people buy the company's products (partly) because of its brand(s) or reputation? Note: a growing market or new products are not classed as strengths – they are opportunities.

- Weaknesses. These are the things that a company lacks or does not do well. Although weaknesses are often seen as the logical 'inverse' of the company's threats, the company's lack of strength in a particular discipline or market is not necessarily a relative weakness, provided that (potential) competitors also lack this particular strength.

Strengths and weaknesses can be measured with the help of an internal or external audit, e.g. through benchmarking (see also Chapter 18). Opportunities and threats occur because of external macro-environmental forces such as demographic, economic, technological, political, legal, social and cultural dynamics, as well as external industry-specific environmental forces such as customers, competitors, distribution channels and suppliers.

- Opportunities. Could the company benefit from any technological developments or demographic changes taking place, or could the demand for its products or services increase as a result of successful partnerships? Could assets be used in other ways? For example, current products could be introduced to new markets, or R&D could be turned into cash by licensing concepts, technologies or selling patents. There are many perceived opportunities; whether they are real depends upon the extent and level of detail included in the market analysis.

- Threats. One company's opportunity may well be another company's threat. Changes in regulations, substitute technologies and other forces in the competitive field may pose serious threats, resulting, for example, in lower sales, higher cost of operations, higher cost of capital, inability to break even, shrinking margins or profitability, and rates of return dropping significantly below market expectations.

After the internal and external analysis, the results can be placed in a so-called *confrontation matrix* (Figure 14.2). In this matrix, the strengths, weaknesses, opportunities and threats can be listed and combined. Then points can be given to each of the combinations: the more important they are, the more points are awarded. This confrontation leads to an identification of the organisation's primary, and often urgent, strategic issues.

Company name
Date:

	O1	O2	O3	O4	O5	T1	T2	T3	T4	T5	TOTAL
TOTAL											100
S1											
S2											
S3											
S4											
S5											
W1											
W2											
W3											
W4											
W5											

Figure 14.2 The confrontation matrix
Source: adapted from Weihrich (1982)

The next step is to evaluate the actions the company has to take based on its SWOT analysis. Should the company focus on using its strengths to capitalise on opportunities, or acquire strengths in order to capture opportunities? Moreover, should the company try actively to minimise weaknesses and avoid threats? (See Figure 14.3.)

	Strengths (S)	Weaknesses (W)
Opportunities (O)	**SO strategies** *Use strengths to take advantage of opportunities*	**WO strategies** *Take advantage of opportunities by overcoming weaknesses or making them relevant*
Threats (T)	**ST strategies** *Use strengths to avoid threats*	**WT strategies** *Minimise weaknesses and avoid threats*

Figure 14.3 SWOT analysis

'SO' and 'WT' strategies are straightforward. A company should do what it is good at when the opportunity arises, and avoid businesses for which it does not have the competencies. Less obvious and much more risky are 'WO' strategies. When a company decides to take on an opportunity despite not having the required strengths, it must:

- develop the required strengths;
- buy or borrow the required strengths; or
- outmanoeuvre the competition.

In essence, companies that use 'ST' strategies will 'buy or bust' their way out of trouble. This happens when big players fend off smaller ones by means of expensive price wars, insurmountable marketing budgets or multiple channel promotions. Some companies use scenario planning (Chapter 12) to try to anticipate and thus be prepared for this type of future threat.

The steps in the commonly used three-phase SWOT analysis process.

Phase 1: Detect strategic issues

1 Identify external issues relevant to the firm's strategic position in the industry and the general environment at large, with the understanding that opportunities and threats are factors that management cannot influence directly.
2 Identify internal issues relevant to the firm's strategic position.
3 Analyse and rank the external issues according to probability and impact.
4 List the key strategic issues and factors inside or outside the organisation that significantly affect the long-term competitive position in the SWOT matrix.

Phase 2: Determine the strategy

5   Identify the firm's strategic fit, given its internal capabilities and external environment.

6   Formulate alternative strategies to address key issues.

7   Place the alternative strategies in one of the four quadrants in the SWOT matrix:

   (i)   SO – internal strengths combined with external opportunities is the ideal mix, but requires an understanding of how the internal strengths can support weaknesses in other areas;

   (ii)   WO – internal weaknesses combined with opportunities must be judged on investment effectiveness to determine whether the gain is worth the effort of buying or developing the internal capability;

   (iii) ST – internal strengths combined with external threats requires knowing the merit of adapting the organisation in order to change the threat into an opportunity;

   (iv)   WT – internal weaknesses combined with threats creates a worst-case scenario. Radical changes such as divestment are required.

8   Develop additional strategies for any remaining 'blind spots' in the SWOT matrix.

9   Select an appropriate strategy.

Phase 3: Implement and monitor strategy

10 Develop an action plan to implement the SWOT strategy.

11 Assign responsibilities and budgets.

12 Monitor progress.

13 Start the review process from the beginning.

The final analysis

A SWOT analysis is a valuable self-assessment tool for management. The elements – strengths, weaknesses, opportunities and threats – appear deceptively simple, but, in fact, deciding what the strengths and weaknesses of a company are, as well as assessing the impact and probability of the opportunities and threats in the external environment, is far more complex than it looks at first sight. Furthermore, beyond classification of the SWOT elements, the model offers no assistance with the tricky task of translating the findings into strategic alternatives. The inherent risk of making incorrect assumptions when assessing the SWOT elements often causes management to dither when it comes to choosing between various strategic alternatives, frequently resulting in unnecessary and/or undesirable delays.

References

Abell, D.F. and Hammond, J.S. (1979) *Strategic Marketing Planning: Problems and Analytical Approaches*. Prentice Hall.

Armstrong, J.S. (1982) 'The value of formal planning for strategic decisions'. *Strategic Management Journal* 3, 197–211.

Hill, T. and Westbrook, R. (1997) 'SWOT analysis: It's time for a product recall'. *Long Range Planning* 30(1), 46–52.

Menon, A., Bharadwaj S.G., Adidam, P.T. and Edison, S.W. (1999) 'Antecedents and consequences of marketing strategy making. A model and a test'. *Journal of Marketing* 63(2), 18–40.

Weihrich, H. (1982) 'The TOWS matrix, a tool for situational analysis'. *Long Range Planning* 15(2), 54–66.

15

Value disciplines

The big picture

The basic idea of this model is that no company can be all things to all people. The key issues upon which a company will fail or succeed in delivering unique value to its customers by fulfilling their needs can be identified and discussed with the value disciplines model. Every good business should have a value proposition, an operating model, and a value discipline.

Treacy and Wiersema (1995) claim that there are three generic value disciplines that enable an organisation to deliver value to its customers:

- operational excellence – in pursuit of optimal running costs;
- product leadership – to offer the best product (technically, and using the latest technology) and, above all, to be the first to do so;
- customer intimacy – to offer the best total solution, by being the most dependable and responsive to the customers' needs.

Treacy and Wiersema argue that market leaders are successful because they do not pursue all the value disciplines simultaneously. Although combinations of the three value disciplines are not impossible, they give rise to conflict, confusion and (other) inefficiencies. Treacy and Wiersema therefore claim that it is imperative to choose between the values. In addition, they claim that the value discipline, if chosen deliberately and acted upon vigorously, can produce significant value for the organisation (Figure 15.1).

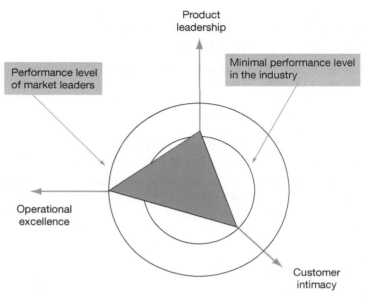

Figure 15.1 The value disciplines
Source: after Treacy & Wiersema (1997)

When to use it

Organisations constantly question the needs of their customers, and the true value of what they offer. The value disciplines model helps to answer these questions. The use of the value disciplines model often provides new insights, especially when an organisation reflects on its *raison d'être* and how it serves (or wants to serve) its (desired) customers.

How to use it

Opting for a specific value proposition depends upon matching the possibilities of the organisation with the requirements necessary to fulfil the customer's needs. Three rounds of discussion are usually necessary to gain a full understanding of the situation. In the first round, the focus is explicitly on customers and competitors within the sector; in the second round the focus is on the company itself; and in the third round the company chooses its primary value discipline.

In the first round, senior management agree answers to the following questions:

- Which type of value means the most to our current customers?
- How many customers focus on each type of value?
- What is the industry standard? Are there any competitors doing a better job in this regard?
- Why are we better or worse than our competitors?

The second round requires senior management to determine what the three value disciplines would mean for their business, including any major changes that might be called for. This results in several options for consideration:

- Leaders in operational excellence offer relatively high-quality products at relatively low prices. However, these organisations do not offer the newest products or services. Instead, they observe the market's direction and execute the activities recognised as the critical success factors exceedingly well. Their focus is on efficiency, streamlining processes, supply chain integration, low inventories, no frills and the dynamics of managing volume. Standardisation of (modular parts of) products and processes is the key.

- Product leaders are inventors and brand marketers. These organisations experiment constantly with new products, services or experiences. Their markets are either unknown or highly dynamic. Margins can be sky high, simply because of the high risks involved. The focus must therefore be on research and development, design and short time to market in order to score a few big hits to make up for their unquestionably countless failures. Technological innovation and product life cycle management are the keys.

- Leaders in 'customer intimacy' will do anything to satisfy their (small set of) customers, as long as they believe the customer is worth it. These organisations do not believe in one-off transactions. They invest time and money in long-term relationships with a few customers. They want to know everything about their customers and work closely with them. The focus is on exceeding expectations, customer retention, lifetime value, reliability and 'always being nice'. Knowing your customers and their wishes and considerations is the key.

In the third round, each of the options is fleshed out. Often, internal high performers are involved in this final round, not only to relieve the strain on executive agendas, but also to ensure their support, by giving them (a feeling of) influence over the company's future activities. Finally, every option has to be detailed with regard to how the organisation can be aligned with the chosen (new) value discipline. This means describing the organisation's operating models, business processes, structure, culture, management systems and information technology, as well as the corresponding value drivers that apply when choosing that value discipline. In addition, (rough) estimates of financial feasibility, potential revenues, key success factors and the potential pitfalls have to be determined. After the third round, senior management will make the decision regarding which option is right for the organisation.

The final analysis

The value disciplines model of Treacy and Wiersema is highly regarded and is accepted worldwide. Too often, however, the model is misused, for instance when consultants and managers force an organisation to choose and excel with only a single value proposition. In this way, the model leads to forced decision-making.

Such a one-dimensional choice will focus too short-sightedly on a single value proposition. True market leaders do not just excel in one (predetermined) value discipline, but also compete on all value disciplines, or even initiate new value disciplines, such as sustainability. In addition, market leaders also try to jack up the industry standards.

Furthermore, in many industries the industry standard on one of the value disciplines is relatively high. In these industries, one could raise the question of whether companies have a choice. For instance, any business-to-business service provider is likely to end up with operational excellence. So is any wholesaler. High-tech companies are likely to be product leaders; otherwise, they could not be in business. Also, changing a multi-billion, globally operating company away from focusing on efficiency when the stock market plunges seems an unlikely course of action. Hence, the model should not be used too rigorously or stand-alone.

The value disciplines model also focuses on value for the customer, and inherently emphasises the natural tendency of organisations to move along with changing customer needs and market developments in an attempt to do everything possible to avoid losing a customer. However, over-focusing on customer needs will ultimately result in the organisation paying less attention to its own competencies and capabilities.

Finally, the three value disciplines do not capture all possible strategic options. For instance, corporate strategic decisions, such as 'build or buy' and corporate vs product branding are not covered by the model. We therefore recommend using the model in combination with other strategic models.

Reference

Treacy, M. and Wiersema, F. (1997) *The Discipline of Market Leaders: Choose your Customers, Narrow your Focus, Dominate your Market.* London: HarperCollins.

[PART TWO]

Organisation and governance

These models help to organise a company's processes, resources and people. They address important 'how to' questions when designing excellent organisations.

7-S framework

16

The big picture

The 7-S framework is a diagnostic model used to organise a company effectively. The model views the organisation as a holistic entity with seven different aspects that are interconnected. The model was developed originally to encourage broader thinking about how to organise a company effectively. Translating strategic choices to the organisation requires comprehensive consideration of how the strategy could work, in conjunction with seven key elements: strategy, structure, systems, skills, staff, style and shared values. The premise of the model is that these seven elements have to be aligned, because they mutually reinforce each other.

When to use it

The 7-S framework is an appropriate model for defining and analysing the most important elements of an organisation. The framework enforces the user to work with a high level of discipline, and at the same time allows for both 'soft' and 'hard' perspectives on the organisation. The model can be used to analyse the present organisation or a future situation, and it may help to identify gaps and inconsistencies between them. It can also be used to assess the viability of a strategic plan from the perspective of an organisation's capability to succeed with the proposed strategy. In this case, the 7-S framework is like a compass, indicating whether all organisational elements are pointing in the same direction (Figure 16.1).

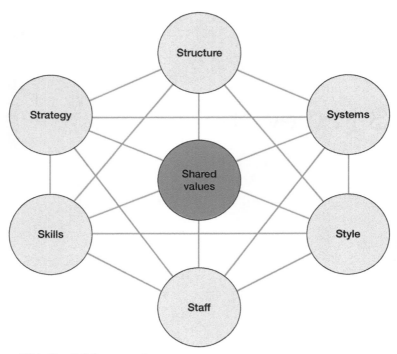

Figure 16.1 The 7-S framework

Source: after Peters and Waterman (1982)

The seven 'S's' that make up the 7-S framework are as follows:

- Strategy – refers to the organisation's objectives and the deliberate choices that are made in order to achieve them, such as prioritising certain products and markets, or the allocation of resources.
- Structure – refers to organisational structure, hierarchy and coordination, including the division of labour and the integration of tasks and activities.
- Systems – the primary and secondary processes that the organisation employs to get things done, such as manufacturing systems, supply planning and order-taking processes.
- Shared values – those values that underlie the company's very reason for existence. They are therefore placed at the centre of the framework. Shared values include the core beliefs and expectations that employees have of their company.
- Style – refers to the unwritten yet tangible evidence of how management really sets priorities and spends its time. Symbolic behaviour and the way management relates to the workers are the indicators of the organisation's style.
- Staff – comprises the people in the organisation, in particular their collective presence.

- Skills – the distinctive capabilities of the workforce and the organisation as a whole, which are independent of individuals.

The seven interdependent organisational elements may be classified as either 'hard' or 'soft'. Hard (rational, tangible) elements are strategy, structure and systems. Soft (emotional) elements are shared values, style, staff and skills.

How to use it

The 7-S framework can best be used as a matrix or table for assessing the impact of the proposed strategy of the organisation. Construct a matrix in which conflicts and possible solutions or combinations of the seven Ss are listed. Then decide either how to adjust the strategy or how to change the organisation to adapt the strategy. If this method is followed with a high level of discipline, the 7-S framework makes a strategy more 'wholesome' than most strategies have ever been (Figure 16.2).

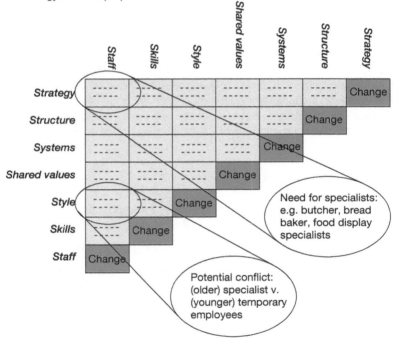

Sammy's supermarket chain: Sammy's is moving away from its traditional middle-of-the-road retail model towards an upscale, fresh, full-service, convenience-oriented grocery and fresh market. An initial decision to hire specialists may have consequences reaching far beyond the scope of the strategy at it was proposed.

Figure 16.2 The 7-S matrix

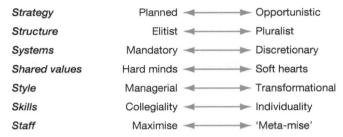

Strategy	Planned	←——→	Opportunistic
Structure	Elitist	←——→	Pluralist
Systems	Mandatory	←——→	Discretionary
Shared values	Hard minds	←——→	Soft hearts
Style	Managerial	←——→	Transformational
Skills	Collegiality	←——→	Individuality
Staff	Maximise	←——→	'Meta-mise'

Figure 16.3 The 7-S vectors of contention

Source: after Pascale (1990)

Note that the founders of the 7-S framework intended to use it in a much more sophisticated way: it was postulated that a firm's success depends on the successful management of vectors of contention (opposite poles) of the 7-S elements or dimensions. The smartest companies use conflict to their advantage (Figure 16.3).

The final analysis

The 7-S framework is a clear and robust diagnostic model. However, the 'soft' elements of the 7-S framework present a challenge to use because it is hard to define them in a measurable way. Consequently, the 7-S framework is often used in a stripped-down manner: listing issues against a checklist. The integral use of the framework, which consists of analysing the relationships between the seven Ss or analysing organisational conflicts within the seven Ss, is often omitted. Used in this way, it does not provide improvement suggestions. After all, the development of a new organisational capability requires more than an understanding of why current capabilities are insufficient. However, there are plenty of additional models that operate on the level of the individual Ss, which may unlock unforeseen potential.

References

Pascale, R.T. (1990) *Managing on the Edge: How Successful Companies use Conflict to Stay Ahead*. New York: Simon & Schuster.

Peters, Th.J., Waterman, R.H. (1982) *In Search of Excellence*. Harper Business.

Ragiel, E.M., Friga, P.N. (2001), *The McKinsey Mind: Understanding and Implementing the Problem Solving Tools and Management Techniques*. McGraw-Hill.

Balanced scorecard

17

The big picture

The balanced scorecard (BSC) was developed by Kaplan and Norton in 1992 as an alternative to traditional performance measurement approaches that focus solely on financial indicators, and are based purely on a company's past performance. The BSC is a top-down method for defining an organisation's goals and objectives (Figure 17.1). It comprises four different perspectives in which progress is monitored. For each perspective, relevant key performance indicators are identified, based on the organisation's mission and vision. These help to clarify the organisation's long-term vision. In this way, an organisation is able to monitor its goals, strategy and objectives, and make any necessary corrective measures promptly.

When to use it

The BSC can be used as an alternative to traditional financial accounting methods. It measures a company's performance across four perspectives: *financial*, *internal business processes*, *learning and growth* and *customers*. Financial measures are complemented by non-financial measures that drive long-term financial success, by asking questions such as:

- What is important for our shareholders?
- How do customers perceive us?

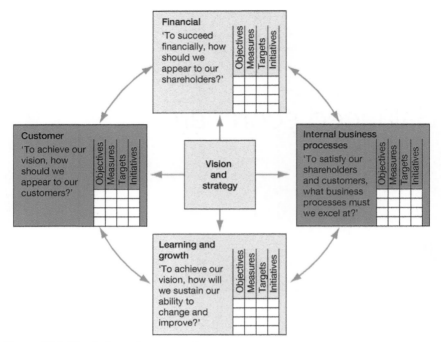

Figure 17.1 The balanced scorecard

- Which internal processes can add value?
- Are we innovative and ready for the future?

The BSC monitors not only past performance, but also present performance and tries to capture information about how well the organisation is positioned for the future. It is used to monitor organisational performance transparently and via multiple measures. It enables management to take appropriate corrective action when necessary, which will lead ultimately to substantial and lasting performance improvement.

How to use it

To create a BSC, a company first has to define its mission and vision, as these determine the desired performance and thus the success factors and key performance indicators for the four different perspectives:

- Financial perspective. Managers need timely and accurate financial data to manage their business. Important indicators are return on investment (ROI) and value added (economic value added, see Chapter 29). However, other measures can be added depending on the characteristics of the company and the industry in which it operates.

- **Customer perspective.** Customer service and satisfaction are viewed as important issues for all organisations, as poor customer performance ultimately leads to a company's decline: dissatisfied customers will find other suppliers to fulfil their needs! Measuring satisfaction, retention, market and account share provides an insight into how customers perceive the company. Possible indicators include customer profitability, return policy, handling service calls, market share in target segments, and claims and complaints handling.
- **Internal process.** Information on the performance of the company's operational activities helps to monitor and steer the effectiveness of the organisation's activities. Indicators on internal processes give management an insight into the effectiveness of their operations. Quality, response and cycle time, costs, new product development, time to market, but also break-even time realised, and new sales as a percentage of total sales are indicators for measuring the performance of a company's operation.
- **Learning and growth.** Indicators for the learning and growth perspective provide an insight into the successfulness of human resources management and knowledge, and innovation management. Important indicators in this perspective are employee satisfaction, staff retention rate, revenue/value added per employee, strategic redundancy in job skills, new ideas per employee and information availability relative to need.

Do's
- **Use the BSC to articulate your strategy, to communicate your strategy and to help align individual, organisational and cross-departmental initiatives to achieve a common goal.**
- **Refresh the BSC as often as needed, so that you can focus on and monitor the right goals.**

Don'ts
- **The BSC is not a tool for controlling behaviour or evaluating past performance.**

The final analysis

There is nothing new about the call for measuring non-financial indicators, but Kaplan and Norton (1992) have to receive the credit for advocating the impact of balanced measures from different perspectives. A CEO is still likely to be biased towards financial measures. The BSC forces a company to focus on a balanced set of key performance indicators which are recognisable throughout the organisation and which will lead ultimately to substantial and lasting performance improvement.

However, it is not easy to find a correctly balanced set of performance indicators. Note that an appropriate number of indicators in a BSC for top management is 12–16 if there is full consensus in a company's management team regarding these indicators. In addition, the main indicators have to be broken down into underlying indicators that can be acted upon by middle and lower management. Otherwise, there is a risk that employees will focus only on the few overall goals on the scorecard.

Finally, the BSC has to be updated regularly, depending on the type of business, to prevent the wrong measures being carried out.

References

Kaplan, R. and Norton, D. (1992) 'The Balanced Scorecard: Measures that drive performance'. *Harvard Business Review* Jan–Feb, 71–80.

Kaplan, R. and Norton, D. (1996) *The Balanced Scorecard: Translating Strategy into Action*. Cambridge MA: Harvard Business School Press.

Benchmarking

18

The big picture

Benchmarking is the systematic comparison of organisational processes and performances based on predefined indicators. The objective of benchmarking is to find the gap between the best practices and the present performance of the organisation in order to create new standards and/or improve processes.

There are five basic types of benchmarking:

1 The historical benchmark – a comparison of the indicators and performances of the organisation with its performance at a previous moment in time.
2 The internal benchmark – a comparison of performance and practices between parts of an organisation, e.g. between business units.
3 The competitive benchmark – a comparison of the indicators and performances of an organisation with those of its direct competitors.
4 The functional benchmark – a comparison of the indicators and performances of an organisation and those of a number of organisations within the broader range of the industry.
5 The generic benchmark – a comparison of the indicators and performances of an organisation with those of organisations from unrelated industries to find overall best practices.

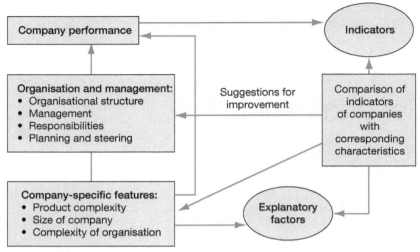

Figure 18.1 Benchmarking

All types of benchmark can be helpful: they give an organisation an insight into its strengths and weaknesses; they are objective; they uncover problems and indicate possible improvements; and they point out norms, new guidelines and fresh ideas to improve an organisation's performance.

Different methods for benchmarking vary to the extent that they include situational characteristics and/or explanatory factors to account for differences between organisations (Figure 18.1). Moreover, some benchmarking methods include prospective trends and developments of best practices, or other practical issues that may arise in an industry.

When to use it

The use of benchmarking depends on the goal. Bearing in mind the difference between intention and action, we can define the objective of benchmarking as the provision of an answer to any one of the following questions:

- How good are we at what we do?
- Are we as good as others at what we do?
- If the grass is really greener on the neighbours' lawn, how did they do that?

Usually, benchmarking is about comparing the organisation against the average of the benchmark population. This gives companies an insight into their own situation and into how the organisation performs compared with the average. Often, however, it is even more ambitious for the organisation to compare itself not against the average but against the best, or, for example, the top 25 per cent. By coupling this comparison to certain good or best practices, it often becomes very clear in which areas improvement actions are relevant.

The scope of a benchmarking project is determined by: the impact it may have on the organisation; the degree to which the results can be communicated freely, in order to increase the success rate of corresponding improvement projects; and the level of effort required to achieve results that are valuable in practice.

However, benchmarking does not lead to answers regarding how to improve, and it usually can't give declarations of differences in performance, but rather gives insights into what to improve. Benchmarks offer no judgment and only when there is no explanation for a deviation does it make sense to look for improvements (e.g. relatively high training costs can be the result of a certain strategic choice that has to do with investing in employee skills).

How to use it

Benchmarking juxtaposes existing information. Good benchmarking is often trickier than it appears at first sight. First, there should be very clear and unambiguous definitions. Then, measurement methods that objectively and properly measure what the organisation wants to compare are to be defined. When measuring at the organisation itself is already difficult, measuring at other organisations is likely to be even more so, if not impossible. Besides, organisations in general are often reluctant to disclose information to a competitor, even when the outcomes of the benchmark are made available to all participants. So many organisations make use of (independent) benchmark databases.

Next, the organisations (or peers) that are being used in benchmarking should be selected. Ideally they would perform better than, or at least equally as well as, the target organisation (or peers), as this brings most lessons to improve the organisation. In general, peers are identified via industry experts and publications. However, differences in products, processes, structure or the type of leadership and management style make it difficult to make direct comparisons between organisations. It is possible to overcome this difficulty in a practical way. Assumptions about the performance of the target firm can be made more accurate by benchmarking the indicator (e.g. 'delivery reliability') according to a number of explanatory factors. It is possible to compare organisations in cross-section for some indicators, based on explanatory factors. Reliable delivery of a product, for instance, depends on the complexity of the product. Therefore, a group of firms that have a similar level of product complexity will have similar indicators and will be a suitable peer group for benchmarking reliable delivery performance (see Figure 18.2).

After carrying out the benchmark, reporting on comparative performance per participant is done and improvement directions for deviations are defined per participant.

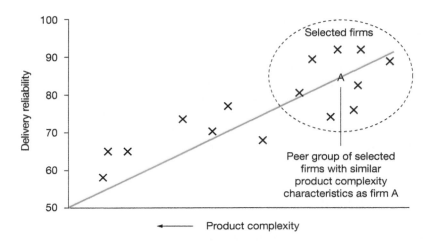

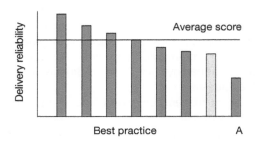

Figure 18.2 Example of benchmarking: (a) selecting a peer group; (b) finding best practice

Benchmarking entails the following (sometimes overlapping) steps:

1 Determine the scope of the project.
2 Choose the benchmark partner(s).
3 Determine measure(s), units, indicators and the data collection method.
4 Collect the data.
5 Analyse discrepancies – get to the facts behind the numbers.
6 Present the analysis and discuss implications in terms of (new) goals.
7 Generate an action plan and/or procedures.
8 Monitor progress by continuously performing a benchmark.

The final analysis

Benchmarking is not straightforward. Too often, semi-committed managers or consultants perform benchmarking without the use of predetermined measurements or the proper tools for detailed analysis and presentation. Undoubtedly, many benchmarking projects end in dismay; an exercise often justifiably portrayed as being as futile as comparing apples and pears. Even when performed in a structured way, the 'we are different to them' syndrome prevents benchmarking from leading to changes for the better. Furthermore, competitive sensitivity can stifle the free flow of information, even inside an organisation.

By applying explanatory factors, benchmarking can not only provide comparative data that may prompt management to improve performance (indeed, it highlights improvement opportunities), but it also indicates original, but proven, solutions to apparently difficult problems. We therefore argue that it is precisely the differences between the firms in the peer group that should be encouraged, rather than trying to exclude organisations because of so-called 'non-comparable' products or processes.

A word of warning however: becoming as good as the benchmark (i.e. the average of the benchmark-population) should never be a goal in itself: no organisation will beat competition by being only equally as good!

Reference

Watson, G.H. (1993) *Strategic Benchmarking: How to Rate your Company's Performance against the World's Best*. New York: John Wiley & Sons.

19 Organisational growth model (Greiner)

The big picture

Greiner's growth model helps to identify the root cause of problems that a fast-growing organisation is likely to encounter, and makes it possible to anticipate them before they occur. It describes the phases that organisations pass through as they grow, regardless of the type of organisation. Each phase is characterised by a period of evolution in the beginning with steady growth and stability, and ends with a revolutionary period of organisational turmoil and change. The resolution of each revolutionary period determines whether an organisation will move forward to the next phase of evolutionary growth.

The Greiner growth model was based originally on five phases of growth, represented by five dimensions: (1) an organisation's size; (2) an organisation's age; (3) an organisation's stage of revolution; (4) an organisation's evolution; and (5) the growth rate of its industry. In 1998, however, Greiner added a sixth phase, namely 'growth through alliances' (see Figure 19.1).

When to use it

Greiner's growth model should be used as a starting point for thinking about the growth of your organisation. It will help you to understand the specific problems that belong to the particular growth phase your organisation is in, and therefore provides you with the possibility to anticipate these problems in time. Finally, this

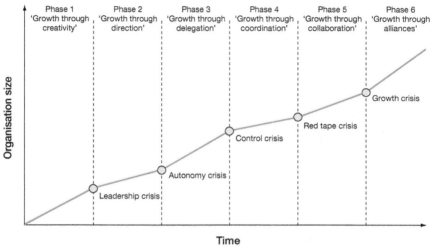

Figure 19.1 Greiner's growth phases

model demonstrates that changes in management style, organisational structures and coordination mechanisms are appropriate and necessary at different phases in the development of a company.

How to use it

Based on the five dimensions described earlier, Greiner identified six phases of growth:

Phase 1: Creativity

In this phase, the emphasis is on creating both a product and a market. Characteristics of the period of creative evolution are as follows:

- The founders are in charge, they are technically orientated and/or entrepreneurial, and are focused on making the product and selling it.
- Communication is frequent and informal.
- Hard work is rewarded by modest salaries and promise of ownership benefits.

As the company grows, the organisation becomes more complex, and soon the founders are struggling with the burden of managing the company, instead of running it. Conflicts become more frequent and partners argue over new products and markets. Through lack of decisive direction, the company enters a *leadership crisis*. The first critical choice is to locate and install a strong business manager who can pull the organisation together. This will lead to phase 2.

Phase 2: Direction

Companies that enter the second phase have succeeded in installing a capable business manager. The characteristics of this phase are:

- functional organisation structure;
- accounting and capital management;
- incentives, budgets and work standards;
- more formal communication and hierarchy;
- directive top-down management.

The directive management style funnels energy efficiently into growth. However, as the organisation grows even more complex, top management is no longer able to oversee all operations, and lower-level management feel tied down, despite their greater knowledge of markets and products. The *autonomy crisis* is born. The solution adopted by most companies is to move towards more delegation.

Phase 3: Delegation

Delegation evolves from the successful application of a decentralised organisational structure. It exhibits the following characteristics:

- operational and market-level responsibility;
- profit centres and financial incentives;
- decision-making based on periodic reviews;
- top management acts by exception;
- rare and formal corporate communication, supplemented by 'field visits'.

Once again, the organisation embarks on a period of relative prosperity, until top executives feel a loss of control. Managers abroad and in the field are acting ever more independently, running their own campaigns. As Greiner effectively puts it, freedom breeds a parochial attitude. Soon, the organisation falls into a *crisis of control*. Top management's attempt to regain control usually drowns in the vast scope of operations and markets. The solution is in finding ways to coordinate rather than control.

Phase 4: Coordination

Those companies that survive the control crisis as a single entity will have found and implemented the techniques of phase 4:

- merging of local units into product groups;
- thorough review of formal planning;
- supervision of coordination by corporate staff;
- centralisation of support functions;
- corporate scrutiny of capital expenditure;

- accountability for return-on-investment at product group level;
- motivation through lower-level profit-sharing.

As limited resources are used more efficiently and local management looks beyond its own needs, the organisation can grow once more. Product group managers have learned to justify and account for their decisions and are rewarded accordingly. Over time, however, the watchdog mentality begins to take its toll on middle and lower management. Eventually the rules and procedures become a goal rather than a means. The corporation is getting stuck in a *red tape crisis*. The organisation needs to increase its market agility, and people need more flexibility.

Phase 5: Collaboration

A new evolutionary path is characterised by:

- team action for problem-solving;
- cross-functional task teams;
- decentralisation of support staff to consult specific task teams;
- matrix-type organisational structure;
- simplification of control mechanisms;
- team behaviour education programmes;
- real-time information systems;
- team incentives.

This phase ends with an *internal growth crisis*, which means that the only way the organisation is able to grow further is by collaborating with complementary organisations.

Phase 6: Alliances

In this phase, organisations try to grow through extra-organisational solutions, such as mergers, creating holdings and managing the network of companies around the corporation.

Greiner's growth model can be applied as follows:

1 Know where your organisation currently stands, based on the descriptions above.
2 Think about whether your organisation is at the beginning of a period of stable growth or whether it is close to a *crisis*.
3 Realise the consequences of the coming transition not only for yourself, but also for your team. This helps to be prepared for the inevitable changes.
4 Plan and take preparatory actions to make the transition as smooth as possible.
5 Repeat these steps on regular basis, e.g. every 6–12 months.

The final analysis

Although the basic model was published in 1972, Larry Greiner's growth model is still very helpful in understanding growth-related problems and the impact of possible solutions on an organisation. However, it is risky to classify the stages of organisational growth to the point where solutions are taken for granted. One must understand that this model should be used only to understand the state of the company, rather than to decide which solutions are best.

This model provides a simple outline of the broad challenges faced by a management team that is experiencing growth. The rate of growth, the effective resolution of revolutions and the performance of the company in each phase will still depend on the essentials of good management, such as leadership, a winning strategy, motivation of employees and a good understanding of your customers.

Reference

Greiner, L.E. (1998) 'Evolution and revolution as organisations grow'. *Harvard Business Review* 76(3), 55–68.

Offshoring/outsourcing

20

The big picture

This model can be used to decide whether organisational activities could and should be outsourced or offshored. Outsourcing is the delegation of non-core operations to an external source that is specialised in the management of that operation. Offshoring is comparable to outsourcing, but in this case the business process – such as production, manufacturing or services – is moved to another country. This decision-making model helps to determine whether it is wise to off-shore or not (Figure 20.1).

When to use it

Companies usually choose to outsource or offshore parts of their business for one or more of the following reasons: to reduce fixed costs; to increase focus on core competencies; or in order to use their labour, capital, technology and resources more effectively. The decision to move to another country is taken because there is a cost or skills advantage in doing so, or because there is a need for international focus.

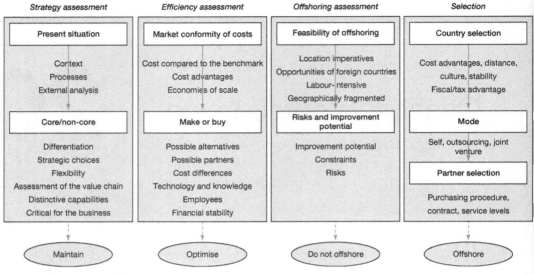

Strategy assessment	Efficiency assessment	Offshoring assessment	Selection
Present situation	**Market conformity of costs**	**Feasibility of offshoring**	**Country selection**
Context Processes External analysis	Cost compared to the benchmark Cost advantages Economies of scale	Location imperatives Opportunities of foreign countries Labour-intensive Geographically fragmented	Cost advantages, distance, culture, stability Fiscal/tax advantage
Core/non-core	**Make or buy**	**Risks and improvement potential**	**Mode**
Differentiation Strategic choices Flexibility Assessment of the value chain Distinctive capabilities Critical for the business	Possible alternatives Possible partners Cost differences Technology and knowledge Employees Financial stability	Improvement potential Constraints Risks	Self, outsourcing, joint venture **Partner selection** Purchasing procedure, contract, service levels
(Maintain)	(Optimise)	(Do not offshore)	(Offshore)

Figure 20.1 Offshoring

How to use it

The following steps are necessary in deciding which processes to off-shore, and to which country:

1 Why choose off-shoring? Examples of reasons to offshore may include knowledge that competitors are moving offshore to gain a cost advantage, or that profit margins are under pressure because of higher price competition.

2 To which countries and with which partners? In selecting an offshore partner, it is important to consider the types of experience, skills and culture that you need from your supplier in order to work together successfully. For example, the factors to consider in each potential country include labour potential, expected quality of production, and the cost advantage. Develop several alternatives for further assessment before making a decision.

3 What are the costs, profits and risks, and which processes are eligible for offshoring? Step 3 involves a thorough cost–benefit analysis for each of the different alternatives. Important components to consider include wage levels, extra costs and charges, price levels and the effect on the internal *value chain* of the company. Analyse which parts of the organisation might be offshored, and what the effects on the overall value chain are likely to be.

4 What happens next? Finally, carry out a detailed feasibility analysis for each country, partner, process, and contract.

At this point, there are still a number of uncertainties. Plans need to be elaborated upon further before any go/no-go decisions are taken. The same four-stage model can be applied to decisions concerning outsourcing, but excluding the international component.

The final analysis

The risk of using this model is in the temptation to skip certain steps in order to move quickly to the implementation stage, e.g. by sourcing potential offshore partners before thinking carefully about the strategic effects and consequences for existing personnel.

Offshoring has been a controversial issue amongst economists. On the one hand, it is considered of benefit to both the country of origin and the destination, by providing jobs and lowering the costs of goods and services. On the other hand, job losses and wage erosion in developed countries will also result. Economists who are against offshoring argue that highly educated workers with higher value jobs, such as accountants and software engineers, have been displaced by highly educated and cheaper workers from countries such as China and India. Furthermore, falling employment in the manufacturing industries has caused fear amongst workers. The controversy emanates mostly from the fear of uncertainty, as the effects of offshoring have not (yet) been conclusively proven. This model rationalises the choices regarding offshoring and outsourcing by helping decision-makers to reduce uncertainty.

Reference

Aron, R. and Singh, J. (2005) 'Getting offshoring right'. *Harvard Business Review* 5 (Dec.), 135–143.

21 Organisational configurations (Mintzberg)

The big picture

The organisational configurations framework of Mintzberg (1983) describes six organisational configurations. These help with understanding what drives decisions and activities in an organisation. The essence is that a limited number of configurations can help to explain much of what is observed in many organisations. The basic configurations help with discerning organisations and their (typical) core problems. The use of the basic configurations can help to prevent choosing and designing 'wrong' organisational structures as well as the ineffective coordination of activities (Figure 21.1).

When to use it

Mintzberg's configurations approach can be used to explore the organisational structures and processes associated with each strategy of an organisation. Management is able to determine not only the category into which their organisation falls, but also the changes that are required to make the organisation internally consistent, and to solve current coordination problems.

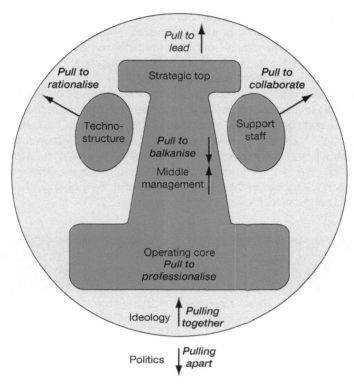

Figure 21.1 Six elementary building blocks of organisations

Source: after Mintzberg, Henry, *Structure in Fives: Designing Effective Organizations*, 2nd ed., p.154 (1992), © 1992. Reprinted by permission of Pearson Education, Inc., Upper Saddle River, NJ, and the author.

How to use it

When using Mintzberg's configurations model to analyse and redesign (parts of) an organisation, one must start by identifying the organisation's basic building blocks. According to Mintzberg, all organisations consist of six elementary building blocks:

1 the operating core
2 the strategic top management
3 the middle management
4 the techno-structure
5 the support staff
6 the ideology part.

Typically, the first three building blocks are connected by a single chain of formal authority. In the figure, these parts are therefore illustrated as a single piece. The techno-structure and support staff on both sides influence the core indirectly, whilst the ideology represents the norms and values (the 'strong culture') that surround, yet penetrate the very fabric of the organisation. These six organisational building blocks are internal determinants of how an organisation evolves. In addition, there are many external forces, such as shareholders, suppliers and customers, all of which have an impact on the organisation.

After the identification and configuration of the organisational building blocks, a company has to analyse and design appropriate coordination mechanisms. Labour, governance and control can be distributed differently between the building blocks of the organisation. Hence, the use of different coordination mechanisms determines the final structure of an organisation. Moreover, when organisations lack appropriate coordination, they are likely to become politicised, because various parts of the organisation will fight to fill the power vacuum. Mintzberg distinguishes six coordinating mechanisms, as shown in the following table:

Configuration	Prime coordinating mechanism	Key part of organisation	Type of decentralisation
Entrepreneurial organisation	Direct supervision	Strategic top	Vertical and horizontal centralisation
Machine organisation	Standardisation of work	Techno-structure	Limited horizontal decentralisation
Professional organisation	Standardisation of skills	Operating core	Horizontal decentralisation
Diversified organisation	Standardisation of output	Middle management	Limited vertical decentralisation
Innovative organisation	Mutual adjustment	Support staff	Selected decentralisation
Missionary organisation	Standardisation of norms and values	Ideology	Decentralisation
Political organisation	None	None	Any

Next, Mintzberg claims that the essence of organisational design is the manipulation of design parameters such as job specialisation; behaviour specialisation; training; indoctrination; unit grouping; unit size; planning and control systems; and liaison devices (e.g. positions, task force committees, integration managers and matrix structure). The most important parameter in Mintzberg's organisation configurations model, however, is the way in which power is distributed throughout the organisation. The distribution of power refers to the types of decentralisation, and varies for each organisational configuration as shown in the table.

Finally, the choice of the design parameters is also determined by contextual factors that are mostly beyond management's control (e.g. age, size, technical system and elements in the environment, such as various stakeholders).

The final analysis

Due to the robust nature of Mintzberg's basic configurations, there is a risk of using the configurations as blueprints. It is extremely difficult, however, for organisations to match or even compare these configurations because of the relatively limited number of criteria for defining the organisational configurations, but also because there are many hybrids or combinations of multiple configurations in practice. In our opinion, it is irrelevant whether an organisation can be classified exactly as innovative or entrepreneurial. The essence of Mintzberg's model is that it helps one to understand the relationship between the nature of an organisation and its coordination mechanisms. As Mintzberg says, there is no single right way to manage an organisation: what is good for General Motors is often completely wrong for Joe's Body Shop.

References

Mintzberg, H. (1989) *Mintzberg on Management*. New York: Free Press.

Mintzberg, H. (1992) *Structure in Fives*. New York: Prentice Hall.

22 Overhead value analysis

The big picture

Overhead value analysis (OVA) is a technique used to find opportunities to reduce overhead costs. The model focuses on the reduction and optimisation of indirect activities and services in organisations. An OVA makes improvement opportunities

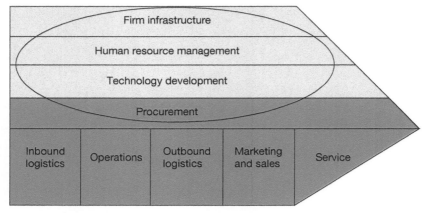

Figure 22.1 Overhead depicted in the value chain

explicit, and compares the costs of indirect activities with the output of the primary processes, for which it uses Porter's value chain model (see Figure 22.1; see also Chapter 24).

When to use it

An OVA can be used to reorganise and eliminate excess overhead activities. In practice, however, management uses it as both a preventive measure and a last resort. The intended result is not necessarily limited to lowering costs; many organisations simply want to increase awareness of the service demands of the (internal) customer. It is clear that an OVA has a significant impact on the indirect activities of the people involved.

An example OVA project

Deteriorating financial results and a lack of organisational versatility were the early signs that the client, a manufacturer of military and advanced remote control technology, needed to reassess its indirect organisational functions. An OVA team set out to identify overhead activities and made an initial, but orderly, list of all activities and costs. Next, it was decided to engage in a full OVA project to restructure the organisation and drastically reduce the number of indirect functions. The result was a transformation from a functional organisation to a market-driven business unit structure: departments delivered value to their internal customers, and many tasks that had formerly been divided into primary and secondary functions were decentralised. The change process enjoyed wide support in the organisation, as all parties involved felt that they were participating in their own 'reinvention'.

How to use it

There are six basic steps for an OVA:

1 The first step is to *create a foundation* including a definition of the required output, the required activities and an assessment of the end product.
2 The second step is to make an *orderly listing of activities and costs*. This step includes estimating the costs of input/resources, the costs of activities and the allocation of the cost to products, generally with the help of *activity-based costing* (ABC).
3 In step three, a *customer evaluation* of the service and output is required. Relevant aspects are necessity (i.e. critical, desired or nice-to-have), quality, quantity and cost. Customers are asked for both an assessment of the current output and an indication of the improvements that need to be made. Both interviews and questionnaires are used in the customer evaluation.

4   In step 4, the OVA team must *identify cost-saving opportunities* based on the possible improvements identified. This forces the organisation to make a statement with regard to priorities for output and required activities.

5   Step 5 is to *prioritise opportunities* with the aid of the four elements used earlier in the customer evaluation:

- Necessity: is value added?
- Is quality of output sufficient?
- Is quantity of output sufficient?
- Can it be done at reasonable cost?

The identification and prioritisation of opportunities overlap with the question of whether or not to eliminate, change, automate, integrate and/or outsource certain activities. This is very much a pragmatic process executed by management in conjunction with experts and managers of the overhead departments.

6   Finally, as a project in itself, the last step is to *implement* the set of changes discussed and decided upon in the previous five steps.

The success factors of an OVA project are:

- **The organisational objectives are known.**
- **The organisational structure is in place.**
- **The scope of OVA is determined.**
- **No other projects are interfered with, or otherwise disrupt the OVA.**
- **There is sufficient support throughout the organisation.**

The final analysis

The results of an OVA are often represented as statistics, whereas most of the data-gathering is, in fact, qualitative. As the required data are obtained from employees whose jobs may be put up for debate, it may be helpful to use a benchmark to verify the data provided. Other potential pitfalls of OVA are:

- insufficient data and information;
- insufficient support for results and arguments;
- insufficient support for implementation.

Both management and analysts should make the process as easy as possible for the *people (employees) involved*. Getting everybody involved to the point where plans are regarded as being self-made is a major contribution to the potential success of OVA. OVA is often used in combination with *activity-based costing* (see Chapter 25).

References

Davis, M.E. and Falcon, W. D. (1964) *Value Analysis, Value Engineering: The Implications for Managers.* New York: American Management Association

Mowen, M.M. and Hanson, D.R. (2006). *Management Accounting: The Cornerstone for Management Decisions.* Mason, Ohio: Thomson South-Western.

Porter, M.E. (1985) *Competitive Advantage: Creating and Sustaining Superior Performance.* New York: Free Press.

23 Risk management

The big picture

Risks are an ubiquitous and characteristic side-effect of taking action by organisations (see also Chapter 33). Although there are many different types of risk (financial, economic, project, market, technical, social, operational, safety, etc.), the structured

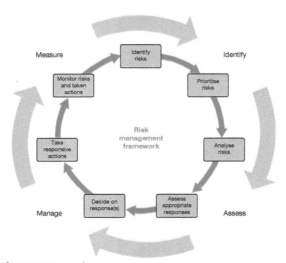

Figure 23.1 Risk management

approach of risk management helps to identify risks and take appropriate action to minimise the likelihood of the occurrence or reduce the (negative) impact of that risk (Figure 23.1).

When to use it

Every activity brings some risk as zero risk does not exist, so it is about minimising the negative impact of risk. That is what risk management offers. Many organisations operate in (market) environments where taking high levels of risk is necessary to compete. In some industries, the risks taken are thus high and/or the negative impact of the risks severe, so that designated risk management becomes a primary function of the organisation (e.g. in banking, insurance, and the pharmaceutical and petrochemical industries). Sometimes risk management is even regulated through legislation (e.g. Solvency2 for insurers and BASEL III rules for banks) and standards (e.g. ISO 31000 and OHSAS 18001).

How to use it

Risk management is a systematic set of methods and techniques that help to analyse, prevent, mitigate, reduce and even eliminate risks. It consists of four inter-related phases: risk identification, risk assessment, risk management (or handling) and risk measurement (or monitoring). When starting with risk management and setting up your framework, you start by identifying risks. Using a multi-perspective approach covering as many possible types of risks – from operational, to financial, to environmental, to safety, etc. – a long list of risks will be drafted. Next the risks are to be prioritised according to the potential (negative) impact they can have on the organisation: to what extent are which assets vulnerable to this risk?

Then, the prioritised risks are analysed: what is the probability that the risk will occur? What will trigger its occurrence? What relationships are there between risks and their triggers? What is the worst-case scenario for the organisation (what likely combination of risks could occur simultaneously)?

When the risks are better known and understood, an assessment is to be made of what appropriate responses the organisation can take to these risks. Different gravity of the impact on the organisation, different exposure of assets, different probability and different triggers will require different actions. The appropriate actions can be categorised into mitigating actions to, eliminating actions, preventive actions, actions regarding reduction of consequences and actions regarding handling of consequences. As your risk management framework is being set up for the first time, you will have to decide on which action to take when the identified risk occurs. When it is possible to prevent or mitigate a risk, that action will be preferred. When only the impact of the risk can be mitigated or reduced, decision criteria to choose what action to take will include minimisation of cost of action and potential collateral damage. When the risk management framework is set up, the decision on what action to take will most likely be documented (in a script or scenario) and then periodically checked for new insights into and revision of the appropriate action decided on earlier.

Risk management's most common activity is monitoring risks. This predominantly involves the risks that are identified, but monitoring will also lead to identification of other or new risks. Monitoring also includes the monitoring of the actions taken to mitigate, prevent or handle risks and their impact.

The final analysis

Risk management is a model that can be used to understand how to cope with risks. It provides a framework in which, per phase or per activity, several tools and methods can be used both to find the risks and to take appropriate actions. In many businesses and markets, taking risks is part of the game, and risk management is thus a primary function of the organisation.

There is, however, a tendency to place a lot of emphasis on risk management. Especially when things go sour, organisations (and regulators) tend to take overly strong actions and impose a very strict risk management framework on the organisation (or the whole industry). Excess risk management can be counterproductive: risk management is about managing the effects of doing business, but too much will inhibit doing business.

Risk management is not an all-encompassing solution: although almost all risks will be identified by organisations, keeping an eye on them is more difficult. In particular, when risks are assessed to have a very low probability, they tend to drift off the radar, and when they actually do happen, the organisation is unprepared to take the appropriate action.

References

Crouhy, M., Galai, D. and Mark, R. (2013) *The Essentials of Risk Management*, 2nd edn. McGraw-Hill.

Hopkin, P. (2012) *Fundamentals of Risk Management: Understanding, Evaluating and Implementing Effective Risk Management*, 2nd edn. London: Kogan Page.

Lam, J. (2014) *Enterprise Risk Management: From Incentives to Controls*, 2nd edn. John Wiley & Sons.

The Institute of Risk Management: www.theirm.org

The value chain

The big picture

According to Porter (1985), competitive advantage can only be understood by looking at the firm as a whole. Cost advantages and successful differentiation are found by considering the chain of activities a firm performs to deliver value to its

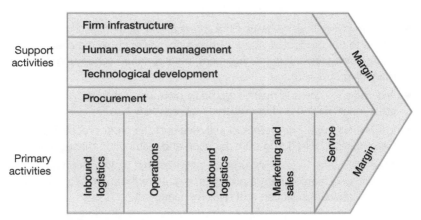

Figure 24.1 Value chain analysis

customers. The value chain model divides the generic value-adding activities of an organisation into primary and secondary activities. An advantage or disadvantage can occur within any of the five primary or four secondary activities. Together, these activities constitute the value chain of any firm (Figure 24.1).

When to use it

The model can be used to examine the development of competitive advantage. By identifying the potential value to the company of separate activities, a firm can gain insight into how to maximise value creation whilst minimising costs, and hence create a competitive advantage.

The value chain is also useful for outsourcing and offshoring decisions. A better understanding of the links between activities can lead to better make-or-buy decisions which can result in either a cost or a differentiation advantage.

How to use it

In order to analyse the competitive advantage (or lack of one), Porter suggests using the value chain to separate the company's activities therein into detailed discrete activities. The relative performance of the company can be determined once the firm's activities have been broken down to a sufficient level of detail.

Porter has identified a set of generic activities. The primary activities include inbound logistics, operations, outbound logistics, marketing and sales, and services. The support activities include procurement, technology development, human resource management and the firm's infrastructure. Each activity should be analysed for its added value. Also the total combined value of all these activities when considered in relation to the costs of providing the product or service has to be analysed, as this will dictate the level (or lack of) profit margin:

- Inbound logistics – activities include receiving, storing, listing and grouping inputs to the product. It also includes functions such as materials handling, warehousing, inventory management, transportation scheduling and managing suppliers.
- Operations – include machining, packaging, assembly, maintenance of equipment, testing and operational management.
- Outbound logistics – refers to activities such as order processing, warehousing, scheduling transportation and distribution management.
- Marketing and sales – includes all activities that make or convince buyers to purchase the company's products, e.g. advertising, promotion, selling, pricing, channel selection and retail management.
- Service – is concerned with maintaining the product after sale, thus guaranteeing quality and/or adding value in other ways, such as installation, training, servicing, providing spare parts and upgrading. Service enhances

There are various ways in which we have seen consultants use the value chain.

A visualisation of the company or a competitor

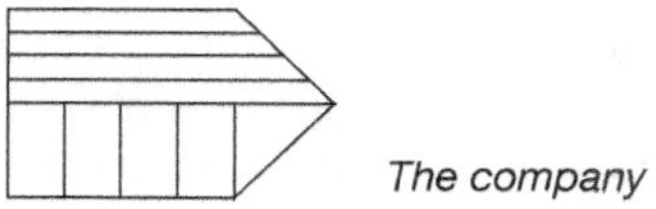

The company

A quick and dirty identification of (lack of) strengths

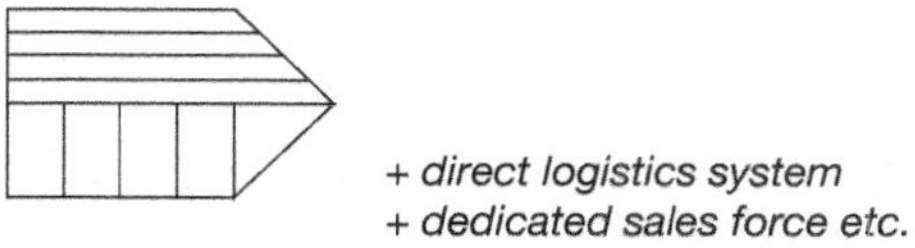

+ direct logistics system
+ dedicated sales force etc.

Comparison of competitive strengths

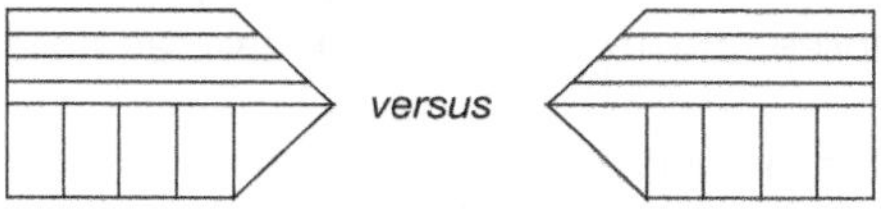

versus

Analysis to establish potential match for M&A or strategic alliances

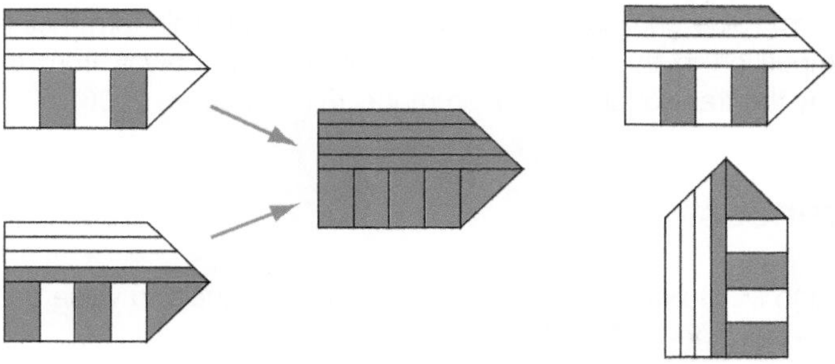

Figure 24.2 The value chain: a versatile tool for consultants

Source: based on Porter (1985)

the product value and allows for after-sale (commercial) interaction with the buyer.

● Procurement – is referred to by Porter as a secondary activity, although many purchasing gurus would argue that it is (at least partly) a primary activity. Included are activities such as purchasing raw materials, servicing, supplies, negotiating contracts with suppliers and securing building leases.

- Technology development – Porter refers to activities such as R&D, product and/or process improvements, (re)design and developing new services.
- Human resource management – includes recruitment and education, as well as compensation, employee retention and other means of capitalising on human resources.
- Infrastructure – such as general management, planning procedures, finance, accounting, public affairs and quality management – can make the difference between success and (despite the best intentions in the world) failure.

The final analysis

Since Porter introduced the value chain model in the mid-1980s, strategic planners and consultants have used it extensively to map out a company's strengths and shortcomings (see Figure 24.2). When strategic alliances and merger and acquisition (M&A) deals are analysed, the value chain is used frequently to gain a quick overview of a possible match. For example, if one company is strong in logistics, and the other in sales and service, together they would make an agile, highly commercial competitor.

There is one downside: it is difficult to measure or rate competitive strengths objectively. Especially when trying to map the entire value chain and apply quantitative measurements or ratings, many companies find themselves employing large numbers of strategic analysts, planners and consultants.

The term *value grid* has recently been introduced. This term highlights the fact that competition in the value chain has been shifting away from the strict view defined by the traditional value chain model (Pil & Holweg, 2006).

References

Pil, F.K. and M. Holweg (2006) 'Evolving from value chain to value grid'. *MIT Sloan Management Review* 47(4), 72–79.

Porter, M.E. (1985) *Competitive Advantage: Creating and Sustaining Superior Performance*. New York: Free Press.

[PART THREE]

Finance

These models provide a financial perspective to the organisation and its activities.

Activity-based costing 25

The big picture

Activity-based costing is a cost accounting model. It is used to allocate all costs, based on time spent on activities relating to products and services provided for customers. Traditional cost accounting models allocate indirect costs (overhead) based on volume. As a result, the costs of high-volume products tend to be over-rated, whereas the costs of low-volume products are under-rated. Contrary to traditional cost accounting methods, activity-based costing (ABC) calculates the 'true' costs of products, customers or services by attributing indirect costs based, not on volume, but on required or performed activities.

Instead of using broad arbitrary percentages to allocate costs, ABC seeks to identify cause-and-effect relationships to assign costs objectively. Once the costs of the activities have been identified, the cost of each activity is attributed to each product, to the extent that the product uses the activity. In this way, ABC often identifies areas of high overhead costs per unit and is able to direct attention towards finding ways to reduce the costs or to charging more for costly products.

There is an underlying assumption when using the ABC model that costs are generated not by the products or customers themselves, but by the activities required to make or serve them. As different products require different activities, each of which uses a different level of resources, the allocation of costs should be weighted accordingly.

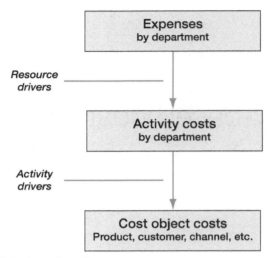

Figure 25.1 Activity-based costing

When making business decisions, knowledge of true costs can help to (Figure 25.1):

- establish economic break-even points;
- identify 'profit makers' and 'losers' (i.e. assess 'customer value');
- highlight opportunities for improvement;
- compare investment alternatives.

When to use it

Activity-based costing can be useful if the overhead is high and the products/customers are highly varied regarding complexity and handling costs. Activity-based costing turns indirect costs into direct costs. A more accurate cost management system than traditional cost accounting, ABC identifies opportunities for improving the effectiveness and efficiency of business processes by determining the 'true' cost of a product or service.

Other models that are similar to ABC are total cost of ownership (TCO) and life cycle costs. TCO is a calculation that reflects the total cost of the investment, including one-time purchases, recurring costs and operating costs. The TCO concept is widely used in information technology (IT) implementations where the benefits are hard to quantify and the focus is on minimising the project costs. A life cycle cost analysis calculates the cost of a system or product during its entire life span.

How to use it

There are five steps involved in performing a simple ABC analysis:

1 Define the cost objects, indirect activities and resources used for the indirect activities.
2 Determine the costs per indirect activity.
3 Identify the cost drivers for each resource.
4 Calculate the total indirect product costs for the cost object type.
5 Divide the total costs by quantity for indirect cost per individual cost object.

Cost objects are products, customers, services or anything else that is the object of the cost-accounting endeavour. Activities could be anything a company does to operate its business: receiving, loading, packing, handling, calling, explaining, selling, buying, promoting, calculating/computing, writing orders, reading orders, etc. Indirect activities are not directly attributable to cost objects. Resources are machines, computers, people or any other capacity or asset that can be (partly) allocated to an activity.

The final analysis

Activity-based costing enables segmentation based on true profitability and helps to determine customer value more accurately. As such, it is the first step towards activity-based management (ABM). ABC does not assess efficiency or the productivity of activities, even though this may be extremely important for improvement. In addition, ABC assumes that it is possible to identify unique cost objects, activities and resources. At the end of the day, the outcome of an ABC analysis is only as accurate as its input.

Reference

Kaplan, R.S. and Cooper, R. (1998) *Cost & Effect: Using Integrated Cost Systems to Drive Profitability and Performance*. Cambridge MA: Harvard Business School Press.

26

Capital asset pricing model (CAPM)

The big picture

The capital asset pricing model (CAPM) is a method of expressing the relation between risk and return for all types of equity. It brings together the risk of a security (often shares) – or a portfolio of securities – and the required return of a security given its risk. The risk of any type of equity is considered to consist of systematic risk, sometimes referred to as market risk or undiversifiable risk, and unsystematic risk, sometimes referred to as company or investment specific risk. According CAPM any provider of equity (either the company owner or an investor) will expect returns that are larger than the risk-free rate (the interest rate) plus the systematic risk of the investment. This premium is expressed with the so-called beta (β). Beta is the measure of risk involved with investing in a particular security relative to the market risk and the risk-free rate.

When to use it

In any provision of equity (= an investment) there are risks involved, as the actual return on the investment could be different from the expected return. Upon taking an investment decision, the risk element is to be taken into account in relation to the return on investment that is expected. The CAPM is often used in deciding whether or not to invest in a company and in calculating what return should be expected on that investment. It can be used by both company owners and external investors (e.g. venture capitalists). However, the model is better known for its use with regard to investments in a portfolio of companies: a portfolio of shares. It is used by banks, pension funds and other institutional investors.

How to use it

According to the CAPM, the relationship between the expected return of an individual security (share) and its market risk can be expressed as (Figure 26.1):

$$r = r_f + \beta \left(r_m - r_f \right)$$

where

r = expected return from an individual security (share)

r_f = risk-free rate

β = beta coefficient (measure of the market risk of an individual security)

r_m = expected return from an investment in all securities (shares) available on the market (market return).

The CAPM states what the security-appropriate required return should be. In other words, what the appropriate discount rates should be for that security, i.e. the rate at which future cash flows produced by the investment should be discounted given that security's relative riskiness. The riskiness is expressed using the security's beta (β). The market as a whole has – by definition – a beta of 1, as β reflects the specific sensitivity of a security to the non-diversifiable market risk. $\beta > 1$ signifies more than average 'riskiness'; $\beta < 1$ indicates lower than average 'riskiness'. Although the

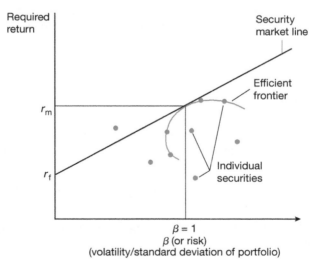

Figure 26.1 Expected return vs market risk

risk-free rate is presented as a steady factor in the formula, this rate is not fixed and will change with changing economic conditions.

The CAPM can also be – and is mostly – used to calculate the optimal set of securities in a portfolio. The CAPM assumes that the risk–return profile of a set of securities can be optimised, with an optimal portfolio being the set of securities with the lowest possible level of risk for its level of return on all securities in the portfolio. Additionally, as each additional asset introduced into a portfolio further diversifies the portfolio, the optimal portfolio must comprise every asset, with each asset value-weighted to achieve the above. The CAPM assumes that investors will want to hold fully diversified portfolios, as they tend to be risk-averse. This means that investors are assumed by CAPM to want a return on an investment based on its systematic risk alone, on its β. And as the unsystematic risk is diversifiable, the total risk of a portfolio with enough diversification through its securities can be viewed as equal to β.

A combination of assets, i.e. a portfolio, is referred to as 'efficient' if it has the best possible expected level of return for its level of risk. When the portfolio does not include any holdings of risk-free assets, a so-called 'efficient frontier' can be found. This efficient frontier represents portfolios for which there is the lowest risk for a given level of expected return. Equivalently, a portfolio lying on the efficient frontier represents the combination offering the best possible expected return for given risk level.

The final analysis

Today, the CAPM is still a popular model with investors, due to its simplicity and utility in a variety of situations and even though there are more modern approaches to asset pricing and portfolio selection. Although its construction requires many assumptions, most of these can be relaxed without changing the basic results of the model. In spite of doubts some have with the model, the use of β coefficients is widely spread (as they are frequently published) in the world of financial professionals and professional investors.

References

Arnold, G. (2010), *The Financial Times Guide to Investing: the Definitive Companion to Investment and the Financial Markets*, 2nd edn. London: Financial Times/Prentice Hall.

French, C.W. (2003) 'The Treynor capital asset pricing model'. *Journal of Investment Management* 1(2), 60–72.

Schlosser, M. (1989), *Corporate Finance: a Model Building Approach*. London: Prentice Hall.

Discounted cash flow (DCF) and net present value (NPV)

27

The big picture

Discounted cash flow (DCF) is a method to assess and compare the current and future values of an asset. DCFs are calculated to assess the future cash flows that could come from an investment opportunity. A DCF analysis is a valuation method used to estimate the attractiveness of an investment opportunity. The total incremental stream of future cash flows from a capital project is tested to assess the return it delivers to the investor. If this return exceeds the required, or hurdle, rate, the project is recommended on financial terms, and vice versa. The DCF analysis discounts the future cash flows to their present-day value. Using future free cash flow projections and discounting them to a present value, the potential for investment can be evaluated. If the value arrived at is higher than the current cost of the investment, the opportunity may be a good one. DCF also converts future earnings into today's money. Often these analyses are called net present value (NPV) calculations: determining today's (present) value of tomorrow's earnings (Figure 27.1).

When to use it

Discounted cash flow (and NPV) is used for capital budgeting or investment decisions to determine:

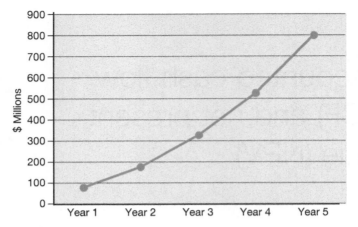

Figure 27.1 Net present value

- which investment projects a firm should accept;
- the total amount of capital expenditure;
- how a portfolio of projects should be financed.

A relevant cost is an expected future cost that will differ from alternatives. The DCF method is an approach to valuation, whereby projected future cash flows are discounted at an interest rate that reflects the perceived risk of the cash flows. The interest rate reflects the time value of money (investors could have invested in other opportunities) and a risk premium.

How to use it

The discounted cash flow can be calculated by projecting all future cash flows and making a calculated assumption on what the current value of that future cash flow is according to the following formula:

$$\sum_{1}^{n} \frac{\text{Future cash flows}}{(1 + \text{discount rate})^n}$$

The discount rate can be determined based on the risk-free rate plus a risk premium. Based on the economic principle that money loses value over time (time value of money), meaning that every investor would prefer to receive their money today rather than tomorrow, a small premium is incorporated in the discount rate to give investors a small compensation for receiving their money not now, but in the future. This premium is the so-called risk-free rate.

Next, a small compensation is incorporated against the risk that future cash flows may not eventually materialise, and that the investors will therefore not receive their money at all. This second compensation is the so-called risk premium and it should reflect the opportunity costs of the investors.

These two compensating factors, the risk-free rate and the risk premium, together determine the discount rate. With this discount rate, the future cash flow can be discounted to the present value. Based on the future cash flows and their present-day value, the DCF analysis can be used as basis for an NPV analysis. This NPV of a project or investment proposal can then be compared with other projects and proposals, allowing an investment decision to be made. A calculation example is presented in the following box:

Time	t	t + 1	t + 2	t + 3	t + 4 . . . n
Investment	−15.000	−5.000	−5.000		
Cash flows		2.000	4.000	4.000	5.000
Total cash flow	−15.000	−3.000	−1.000	4.000	5.000
Discount rate = 10%					
Discount rate $(1 / (1 + 10\%)^n)$	0	0.91	0.83	0.75	0.68
Net Present Value (NPV)	15.000−	2.727−	826−	3.005	34.151
NPV total	18.602				

The final analysis

First published in 1938 by John Burr Williams in a paper based on his PhD, 'Discounted cash flow statements', DCF analysis and NPV methods have become common all over the world.

DCF models are powerful, but they have their faults. DCF is merely a mechanical valuation tool, which makes it subject to the axiom 'garbage in, garbage out'. Small changes in inputs can result in large changes in the value of a company. The discount rate is especially difficult to calculate. Future cash flows are also hard to forecast, especially if the largest part of the future cash inflows is received after 5 or 10 years. Also the discount rate and, more particularly, the risk premium are sometimes difficult to calculate objectively. Alternative calculation methods, such as weighted average cost of capital (WACC, see Chapter 29), have more sophisticated approaches to assess the expected return for investors.

References

Brealey, R.A. and Myers, S.C. (2003) *Principles of Corporate Finance*, 7th edition. London: McGraw-Hill.

Walsh, C. (2008) *Key Management Ratios: the 100+ Ratios every Manager Needs to Know*. Harlow: Pearson.

Willams, J.B. (1938) *Theory of Investment Value*, Cambridge: Harvard University Press.

28 DuPont scheme

The big picture

The DuPont scheme can be used to illustrate the impact that different factors have on important financial performance indicators, such as the return on capital employed (ROCE), the return on assets (ROA) or the return on equity (ROE). While these ratios can be calculated using a simple formula, the model provides more insight into the underlying elements that make up the ratios. It is similar to sensitivity analysis, in the sense that the model makes it possible to predict the effect of variability in one or more input variables. The tool is well known in purchasing management, as it shows the tremendous impact that effective purchasing can have on profitability (Figure 28.1).

When to use it

The model can be used in several ways. First, it can be used as the basis for benchmarking, i.e. comparing different companies in an industry to answer the question why certain companies realise superior returns than their peers. Secondly, it can be used to predict the effect of possible management actions.

The DuPont scheme will show big differences between industries. If one looks at the ROE, a high score can be caused either by 'operational efficiency' or by 'capital efficiency'. High turnover industries (e.g. retailers) tend to face low profit margins, high asset turnover and a moderate equity multiplier. Other industries,

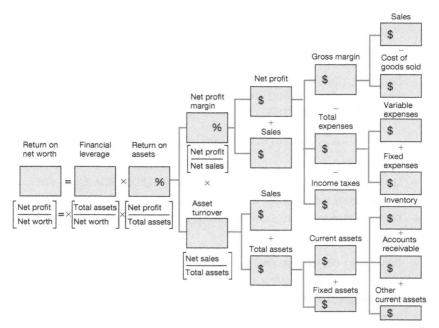

Figure 28.1 DuPont analysis

such as fashion, depend on high profit margins. In the financial sector, the ROE is determined mainly by high leverage, gaining large profits with relatively low assets. It is essential to choose peers carefully when analysing how to improve the profitability of a specific company (Figure 28.2).

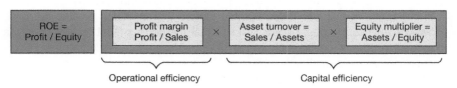

Operational efficiency   Capital efficiency

Figure 28.2 Return on equity = operational and capital efficiency

How to use it

The following steps have to be performed in a DuPont scheme:

1 Insert basic information into the model. In particular, identify the information on sales, interest-free liabilities, total costs, equity, current assets and non-current assets.

2 Calculate the other parameters using the formulas in the figure. This provides you with a basic view of current profitability.

3 Determine which possible improvements can be made, and how

much impact they will have on costs, sales and assets. The effect of a measurement (potential improvements) can be calculated and used as input in the model, whereas the model shows the effect on the ROCE, ROA and ROE.

4 Compare different potential performance-improving actions with respect to their required investments (time, money and organisational pressure), and their impact on profitability.

Do's

- Analyse peers to identify how they realise a certain ROCE, ROA and/or ROE. This indicates the areas that need to be improved.
- Analyse which parameters are essential to improve profitability.

Don'ts

- This is not a decision-making tool. The comparison of the impact of an improvement action is a first step. Often a detailed analysis to evaluate the possible outcome of potential improvement actions is also required.
- Do not overlook non-financial issues that are not addressed by this approach.

The final analysis

The DuPont scheme originates from the work of F. Donaldson Brown, who developed the scheme at DuPont in 1919. The scheme has thus proved its value, as it is still useful. It helps to determine the factors that influence profitability most. However, it lacks the possibility to validate that the correct numbers are used. As opposed to other models, such as the balanced scorecard (including key performance indicators; see Chapter 17), the DuPont scheme lacks parameters other than financial parameters, excluding other important factors such as employee motivation.

Besides these shortcomings, the main disadvantage is that identifying the factors that influence profitability most is only part of the story. The next step is to find appropriate actions that will improve profitability, but the DuPont scheme is not equipped for identifying and deciding on those actions. Other models, such as root cause analysis (Pareto analysis; see Chapter 48) are better suited to determining which actions are appropriate.

References

Bodie, Z., Kane A. and Marcus, A.J. (2004) *Essentials of Investments*, 5th edn, pp. 458–459. New York: Irwin/McGraw-Hill.

Groppelli, A.A. and Nikbakht, E. (2000) *Finance*, 4th edn, p. 444. New York: Barron's Educational Series.

Ross, S.A., Westerfield R. and Jaffe, J. (1999) *Corporate Finance,* 5th edn. Maidenhead: McGraw Hill.

Economic value added (EVA) and weighted average cost of capital (WACC)

The big picture

The economic value added (EVA) is a method to express the financial performance of an organisation. It expresses the performance of an organisation as its profits minus the cost of financing the organisation's activities. The idea is that value is created (added) when the profit exceeds the costs (see Figure 29.1). The concept of EVA was introduced by consulting firm Stern Stewart & Co (Stewart, 1990).

When to use it

The original purpose of EVA was to include two principles in management's decision-making: (1) the objective of a company is to maximise shareholder value; and (2) the value of a company depends on the extent to which future profits differ (positively) from the cost of capital needed to generate those profits. It was introduced to make better decisions regarding the organisation's strategy and the future activities it should pursue and invest in. Nowadays EVA is used not only for making investment decisions within organisations, e.g. investments in capital projects, but also for investments in companies (as a shareholder).

Economic value added helps to assess which alternative provides the best return, expressed as the highest value added. Analysing the economic value added gives an insight into how the proposed investment will perform relative to the risk (expressed as the cost of capital) to which it is exposed. The best performing

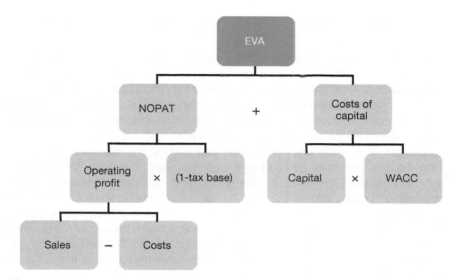

Figure 29.1 Economic value added

projects (or companies) will exceed the cost incurred to finance them (or, in other words, they will exceed the required minimal return on the capital employed).

Often EVA is seen as an elaboration on value-based management (VBM, see Chapter 34). Used especially for capital budgeting and investment analysis, EVA allows investments to be tested against the required capital charge. Properly executed, this approach aligns all activities and decision-making on the key drivers of value.

In particular, the inclusion of the cost of capital employed to realise the performance, the calculation of the WACC, is often used as alternative to NPV (see DCF and NPV, Chapter 27). In NPV a required rate of return is used as discount rate. This rate is often based on a risk-free rate plus a risk premium. An alternative discount factor can be the WACC. This already includes the costs the organisation has to incur to attract the funding for the project or investment decision. The WACC takes into account both the cost of using own means (backed by the organisation's equity) and the cost of using loans or externally attracted capital. These costs typically include the risk premium, as these are discounted in the interest rates of external funding parties and they are discounted in the expected return on equity (dividends) by shareholders.

How to use it

The EVA model consist of two elements:

- the profit or income from activities, expressed as the net operation profit after taxes (NOPAT);

- the cost of capital employed to perform those activities, expressed as WACC.

The NOPAT is calculated starting with the earnings before interest and taxes (EBIT), thus after depreciations and amortisations, and correcting this for all other items that influence operational performance and thus the profit statement. Then taxes are deducted, resulting in the NOPAT. This calculation is fairly straightforward, although the corrections to operational performance, such as amortisation of goodwill or depreciation of inventories, can sometimes be a bit more complex.

The WACC is more complex to calculate. Calculating this starts with identifying the cost of capital for each type of funds used. The costs for loans from external parties are the most obvious (the interest rate), but funds based on the organisation's equity also have a cost. And as some costs –in some countries – are tax-deductible (such as interest on some types of loans), it is important to express the costs as after-tax costs. Next, for each source of funds, the weight is calculated, i.e. the percentage of the total funding of the organisation. The WACC is then calculated as the sum of the costs of each source times the weight of that source in the overall funding, using the formula in Figure 29.2.

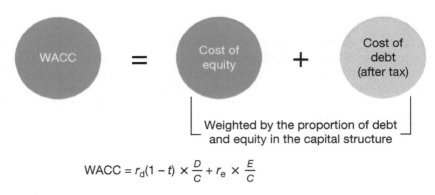

$$\text{WACC} = r_d(1 - t) \times \frac{D}{C} + r_e \times \frac{E}{C}$$

where:

- r_d is the cost of foreign capital (interest)
- t is the tax rate on corporate income
- D (Debt) is a foreign capital
- C is the total long-term capital invested
- r_e is the cost of own (share) capital (equity) – expected return on equity
- E is the Equity

Figure 29.2 Weighted average cost of capital.

Ultimately, the EVA can be calculated by subtracting the total cost of capital from the total profit from activities.

The final analysis

By taking into account the cost of all capital employed for performing the organisation's activities, the EVA shows the financial amount of wealth a business creates (or destroys). For that reason, it is popular with shareholders and investors for comparing companies and equity investments. For comparison based on similar intentions, an alternative measure is used also that employs elements of EVA: the calculation of return on net assets (RONA). RONA is a ratio that is calculated by dividing a firm's NOPAT by the amount of capital it employs (RONA = NOPAT/capital employed). This ratio does not, however, include the cost of capital employed and is therefore less suited to investment decisions for which the type of capital employed is of importance, such as decision-making within organisations regarding what business or what capital projects to invest in.

Although EVA is at first sight a very clear and easy-to-understand concept, the mathematics are less easy. Both the calculation of NOPAT and the calculation of WACC require some advanced understanding of accounting and of the EVA method. Next to its complexity there are also many modifications to EVA, varying from alternative methods for calculating the cost of equity, such as the capital asset pricing model (CAPM, see Chapter 26), to alternative methods for expressing the value of the organisation as a whole, such as the market value added model.

References

Stewart, G.B. (1990) *The Quest for Value*. New York: HarperCollins.

Walsh, C. (2008) *Key Management Ratios: the 100+ Ratios Every Manager Needs to Know*. Harlow: Pearson.

Young, S.D. and O'Byrne, S.F. (2000) *EVA and Value-based Management: A Practical Guide to Implementation*. McGraw-Hill.

30 Financial ratio analysis: liquidity, solvency and profitability ratios

The big picture

Financial ratios help to analyse the financial performance of all the activities of an organisation and all its products and services in all markets. Financial ratios are based on the balance sheet and profit and loss account of the organisation. Using financial ratios gives two types of insight: where the organisation performs best; and the financial constraints and possibilities the company has when considering new activities, project or strategies.

When to use it

It is wise periodically to analyse the financial position and financial performance of every organisation. In practice, these analyses occur very regularly as they are not only carried out with each investment opportunity or new strategic initiative, but they are also often integrated into the periodic reporting of the organisation.

Financial ratios standardise financial data, so that they are transparent and can be compared with those of competitors and/or with the organisation's historical performance (measuring progress). Most of the ratios can also be calculated per product, per market, per business unit or any other company cross-section.

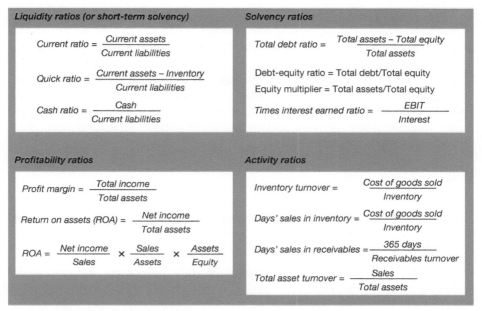

Figure 30.1 Financial ratio analysis

The financial ratio analysis provides a view of:

- the financial situation of the company;
- the extent to which the company will be able to pay its debts or attract investors.
- the possibilities of making more investments.

How to use it

There are four different types of financial ratios (see Figure 30.1), reflecting the performance of the organisation:

- Liquidity ratios indicate the extent to which the company is able to meet its financial obligations in the short term.
- Solvency ratios indicate the extent to which the company structurally meets all its financial obligations.
- Profitability ratios measure earnings capacity with the current capital.
- Activity ratios show the turnover periods.

To perform a financial ratio analysis, you simply collect the data from the financial administrative systems that are mentioned in each of the formulas and then calculate the ratios. The required data are generally rapidly available, as most ratios are part of regular management reports.

The final analysis

A financial ratio analysis provides insights into the current financial state of affairs of an organisation. It can also give an impression of the future financial situation if policies were to remain unchanged. The financial ratio analysis should not, however, be used in absolute terms. There is great risk involved in giving too much attention to the financial component of setting a new strategy: the results of the ratio analysis are never directional for a new strategy, but will only show the financial possibilities and limitations of the organisation.

References

Keown, A.J., Scott, D.F., Martin, J.D. and Petty, J.W. (1994). *Foundations of Finance: The Logic and Practice of Financial Management*. Upper Saddle River, NJ: Prentice-Hall.

Walsh, C. (2008) *Key Management Ratios: the 100+ Ratios every Manager Needs to Know*. Harlow: Pearson.

Investment stages

31

Investment stages is a model that can be used to determine the availability of different sources for financing business activities at different phases (stages) in the life of a company. To bring an idea to market, you will go through several stages (see also innovation circle, Chapter 55). In each stage different sources of financing are available. The most commonly used ones are depicted in Figure 31.1. The model can also be used in the opposite way: to see what type of financing is most commonly offered to a business that is seeking investment.

When to use it

When finding a new business, sources of financing are not always readily available. Start-up firms are often perceived to have high risks, and most generic sources of financing (banks, stock market, etc.) are often not keen to finance the business activities. When a business grows (and returns increase and risks decrease), more sources of financing become available (i.e. they will express their interest in investing in your business or lending you money).

Alternatively, the model can be used to find appropriate types of financing to offer to start-up firms, given the stage they are in. Each stage will have its required investments and typical levels of profitability. By knowing when to 'get in', the typical 'length of the ride' (before investments provide returns and loans are paid back) is known too.

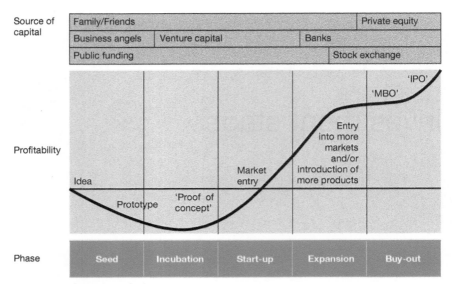

Source of capital

Family/Friends				Private equity
Business angels	Venture capital		Banks	
Public funding			Stock exchange	

Profitability

Idea

Prototype

'Proof of concept'

Market entry

Entry into more markets and/or introduction of more products

'MBO'

'IPO'

| Phase | Seed | Incubation | Start-up | Expansion | Buy-out |

Figure 31.1 Investment stages

Source: adapted from Robert Bosch Venture Capital GmbH, http://www.rbvc.com/en/investment_strategy/investment_strategy_page.html

How to use it

First an assessment is to be made of the stage your business is at. Is it still in its infancy, a promising idea that needs to be further developed, or is it already well established and looking to grow into new markets? Next, from the model, the most commonly used sources of financing can be derived that typically match the business's phase. For each source of financing, a search for available parties can be started. These parties are then contacted and asked to express their interest. Be aware that you can make them an offer too: what do they invest in? How will they get a return on their investment? Investors will seek securities for their investment. Often, in very early stages, these can include exclusive rights such as patents or shares in the start-up firm. After having closed a deal on financing business activities, closely monitor the fulfilment of the terms and conditions of the investor. And when business progresses, start looking out for additional and/or new sources of financing to grow the business further.

The model can also be used to assess the stage the business is at before investing in it. Depending on this stage, the amount and level of securities the business can offer for the investment can be determined. Make sure you are clear about intentions: investments will probably require to be returned (or withdrawn) at some point in the future, and will not be available for the whole time the business is in existence.

The final analysis

This is a clear and relatively simple model that merely matches sources of financing to the (typical) profitability of a business at a certain stage in its lifetime. Its usefulness lies in its double-edged approach: it can be insightful for both investors and investment seekers.

One shortcoming of this model is that it only matches on an abstract level. It requires a certain level of knowledge (or knowing where to access that knowledge) regarding financing and investing. The model does not allow any specific assessment to be made, e.g. of the advantages and disadvantages of a source of financing, nor does it allow assessments to be made of a specific business.

Another shortcoming is the implicit statement that the *nec plus ultra* in financing business is via a public offering on a stock market. In reality, all large firms have a multitude of sources of financing. And worldwide there are more family-owned companies than there are companies listed on a stock market.

References

Marks, K.H., Robbins, L.E., Fernandez, G., Funkhouser, J.P. and Williams, D.L. (2009) *The Handbook of Financing Growth: Strategies, Capital Structure, and M&A Transactions*, 2nd edn. Wiley.

Preston, S.L. (2007) *Angel Financing for Entrepreneurs: Early-Stage Funding for Long-Term Success.* San Francisco, CA: Jossey-Bass.

32

Real options theory

The big picture

Real options theory is related to decision-making as choosing from a set of possible decisions now, taking into account all decisions that are available to the decision-maker in the future. These future possible decisions are considered as options to the decision-maker: you don't need to decide yet, you still have the possibility to do so later. It leaves decision-makers with 'a right, not the obligation,' to take a (subsequent) decision at a future time. When facing a decision to be taken now, all related decisions at future times must be taken into account.

Real options theory stems from financial markets in which (put and call) options are traded to buy or sell shares in a company at a future time. The managerial flexibility to adapt decisions in response to (unexpected) future developments can be seen analogously as options. And just as the value of an option in a financial market can be calculated, likewise the future possible decisions (the options) can be given a present-day value. The word 'real' refers to the fact that it relates to the real world rather than to financial market decisions. By applying financial option valuation techniques, the value of having future decision-making opportunities can be quantified. The value of the option depends on the potential benefits offered by a future decision. The number of options depends on the number of possible future decisions there are (Figure 32.1).

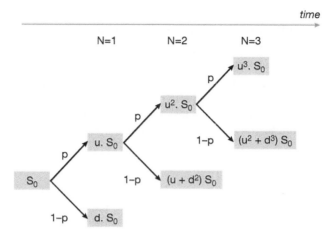

S_0 = cost of executing the option
N = future decision
d = downside effect of future decision
u = upside effect of future decision
p = change of effect occuring

Figure 32.1 Real options theory

When to use it

When facing a decision for which the expected outcomes of the alternatives are uncertain and where it is known that at a future time another decision can be made that will affect the outcome, real options theory can be useful to consider the different alternatives with their subsequent and related future decisions. It is often contrasted with more traditional valuation methods (e.g. discounted cash flow and net present value; see Chapter 27), which fail to accurately capture the economic value of flexibility in an environment of widespread uncertainty and rapid change.

A number of types of real options can be distinguished:

- **Defer options.** Also known as 'waiting to invest' options, these are often used in industries like natural resources extraction, farming, real estate and industries where price fluctuations are high.

- **Phasing options.** Also known as 'growth' options, these are often used in industries in sectors such as the high-tech industry, the pharmaceutical industry and those industries where multiple products are generated simultaneously. They are also often used in R&D-intensive industries for phasing investments, sometimes in combination with the Stage-Gate model (see Chapter 57).

- **Switching options.** These are also known as 'flexibility' options and are used when it is required to alter operating scale (up or down), switch product mix or change operating processes. Switching options are often used in industries like fashion, retail and industries with high volatility.

- Exit options. Also known as 'abandon' options, these are often used in capital-intensive industries.
- Learning options. This type of option is used in many industries, often to test uncertain markets or to test the suitability of new products or a specific project. Then, based on the result – the learning – a subsequent phase in entry or development or even full market introduction can follow.

How to use it

While financial options are precisely defined and parameterised, the definition and valuation of real options are more elusive. Nevertheless, the same valuation techniques are used. The following are the best known ones:

- The Black–Scholes model, named after Nobel Prize laureates Fischer Black and Myron Scholes, is a formula to calculate the value of options that can be exercised at a specified future date.
- The binomial (or trinomial) pricing model is a formula to calculate the value of options that can be exercised sequentially, with each future decision being an upside or downside (or stable) effect of that decision.
- Monte Carlo simulation is a method for estimating the expected value of the option by simulating a multitude of possible scenarios for uncertain developments (multiple possible effects of future decisions that are not necessarily to be taken sequentially).
- The fuzzy pay-off method is a formula for calculating the value of options that can be expressed as a set of decisions, the effects of which are not precisely known up-front.

All methods for valuation of real options base their calculations on (at least) four variables: the cost of executing the option (the net present value of the expected effects of the option when exercised), the time, the uncertainty of the expected effects (volatility of the option) and the risk-free interest rate.

The final analysis

Real options theory has helped management to make tremendously complex multi-faceted decisions in uncertain and changing environments. It distinguishes itself in that it takes into account uncertainty about the effects of alternatives of consecutive decisions that determine the future success of the company, coupled with management's ability to respond to this uncertainty via successive decisions. Real options theory is also very helpful in communicating about decisions, showing what future related choices are still available.

But real options theory also has its limitations. When the effects of the alternatives to a decision are not known, it does not work: the valuation formulas require a future cash flow (an effect expressed in a currency). Also, the valuation of a real option is based on the (cumulative) value of the future effects, but unlike financial options for which the underlying asset (shares) can be traded, the future effects of real options can rarely be traded separately. Another shortcoming is that interdependencies among alternatives are very difficult to incorporate into the valuation of the real option. Further the complexity of real options theory is a disadvantage in itself.

References

Collan, M., Fullér, R. and Mezei, J. (2009) 'A fuzzy pay-off method for real option valuation'. *Journal of Applied Mathematics and Decision Sciences*, March 2009.

Copeland, T. and Tufano, P. (2004) 'A real-world way to manage real options'. *Harvard Business Review*, March 2004.

Courney, H., Lovallo, D., and Clarke, C. (2013) 'Deciding how to decide: a toolkit for executives making high-risk strategic bets'. *Harvard Business Review*, November 2013.

Luehrman, T. (1998) 'Strategy as a portfolio of real options'. *Harvard Business Review*, October 1998.

Trigeorgis, L. (1996) *Real Options: Managerial Flexibility and Strategy in Resource Allocation*. Cambridge, MA: The MIT Press.

33 Risk–reward analysis

The big picture

The risk–reward analysis charts potential rewards of strategic options against the associated risk. The result is an assessment of the attractiveness of strategic options, serving as a basis for decisions to allocate resources. The risk–reward analysis works in the same way as a risk–return analysis for valuing financial products such as bonds and options (Figure 33.1).

Figure 33.1 Risk–reward analysis

When to use it

The risk–reward analysis can be performed at any level of detail. The CEO could do it on the back of an envelope, or he or she might ask a team of analysts to perform a fully fledged analysis, including extensive market research, return on investment (ROI) calculations, scenario development and sensitivity analysis. The fundamental steps remain the same.

By using this tool, one can compare completely different types of projects and combinations of projects. Combining projects may add up to a balanced resource allocation that fits the acceptable risk profile of the company. However, the model is not able to show variance in risk and reward if certain strategic options are combined in different models. The interconnectedness of strategic options is not taken into account.

How to use it

A risk–reward analysis starts with drawing up a list of feasible strategic options and their potential rewards. For example, options might include international market development; new product introduction; professionalising the purchase department; and outsourcing production. Together, investments, additional savings and/or reduced costs represent a potential reward that can be quantified. Often information on qualitative factors such as a better image, completeness of product range and strategic expansion of capacities like technology are also included to assess the potential return of a strategic option.

Subsequently, a thorough analysis must be carried out for each strategic option to assess the associated risk. Factors to consider in this respect include the level of investment, industry threats, cut-off from other options, effects on supply chain relations and exit barriers, but also factors such as exclusion of other options and vulnerability from overstretching financial reserves.

The options can then be plotted in a risk–reward analysis chart, with risk on one axis and reward on the other. Once all the options are plotted in the risk–reward analysis chart, a brainstorming session is useful to find ways to reduce the risk associated with options that have high reward potential. In a similar vein, methods must be found to increase the reward of relatively safe options. These discussions result in a prioritisation of the different options.

The risk–reward analysis can be extended with a third dimension to become a risk–reward *resource* analysis. The amount of resources required is then represented in the diagram (by bubble size). Options that require large amounts of resources are plotted with larger bubbles than options that require fewer resources. This enables one to trade off risks, rewards and resources or to find the best options.

Ultimately, the objective is to balance risks, rewards and resources according the company's desired risk profile. Organisations with an aversion to risk will focus on decisions for the long-term continuation of the organisation, and will therefore accept fewer possible rewards. A more entrepreneurial, risk-seeking company might accept higher risks as it chases higher rewards. Nevertheless, there should be a positive balance between the two.

The final analysis

One of the prevailing pitfalls in management is that decisions are made with limited information and a lack of multiple perspectives. Inaccurate, optimistic or unrealistic predictions about the potential rewards of strategic options push risk analysis into the background. The estimated risk, on the other hand, tends to be underestimated. The result is an overvaluation of the options the organisation has.

The drawback of the model is that the evaluation of the dimensions, risk, reward and possible resources, is the result of a complex interaction of factors. The weight of each factor and the interrelation among factors are generally affected by emotions.

To maximise the effect of the use of the risk–reward analysis, it is advisable to compare the possibilities extensively to minimise the number of options. Furthermore, it is recommended that the details of all potential risks and rewards are analysed sufficiently. The greatest pitfall is to oversimplify the situation and not pay enough attention to the interrelatedness and complexity of factors.

Reference

Sperandeo, V. (1994) *Trader VIC II: Principles of Professional Speculation.* Hoboken, NJ: John Wiley & Sons.

Value-based management

34

The big picture

Value-based management (VBM) is a tool for maximising the value of a corporation. VBM uses valuation techniques for performance management, business control and decision-making. The value of a company is determined according to its discounted future cash flows. Value is created when a company invests capital against returns that exceed the capital cost. All strategies and decisions are tested against potential value creation. There are several ways of using VBM. The simplest is the use of VBM for financial reporting. VBM can also be used for capital budgeting and investment analysis. All investments are tested against the required capital charge. Properly executed, this approach aligns all activities and decision-making on the key drivers of value.

A well-known model used in VBM is economic value added, or EVA (see Chapter 29). This model is preferred over more traditional, accounting-related models to measure a firm's performance, such as earnings per share or return on investment (ROI), as these do not include the costs of the capital invested to achieve the performance.

When to use it

Value-based management is used to set goals, evaluate performance, determine bonuses, communicate with investors and carry out capital budgeting and

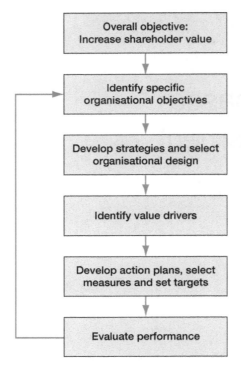

Figure 34.1 Value-based management accounting framework

Source: after Ittner and Larcker (2001)

valuations. Traditional accounting systems determine the value of organisations based on performance measurements such as earnings per share and return on equity. However, they take no account of the effectiveness with which resources are deployed and managed, i.e. the cost of the opportunity to invest capital. As a result, many companies that appear profitable on paper are, in fact, considerably less so. Attention must be paid to four areas for successful application:

1 Measurement
2 Management
3 Motivation
4 Mindset.

Three steps have to be taken regarding measurement. First, establish rules to convert accounting profit to economic profit (i.e. adjust conventional earnings to eliminate accounting anomalies affecting economic results). Secondly, identify VBM centres within the organisation: these may be large or small, but must all be accountable for their own results. Finally, link these centres to harmonise decisions across the organisation. This allows VBM to be tracked, unit by unit, on a monthly basis.

Measuring value is one thing; acting on the results is another. Management and value must therefore become inextricably linked. Budgeting and planning techniques must be adjusted to incorporate the concept, and a link must be established between the operating and strategic levers.

By basing incentive compensation on an increase in value, managers can be motivated to think and act as if they were owners because they are paid like owners – by increasing shareholder wealth, they simultaneously increase their own. Therefore, bonuses and other incentives must be linked to performance as opposed to budgets, allowing managers to focus on maximising wealth rather than merely meeting corporate expectations. Of course, a certain degree of risk must be involved, including penalties for underperformance. An additional advantage is that shifting from the constant negotiation of financial targets to a one-time setting of bonus parameters greatly simplifies the planning process.

How to use it

When using value-based management, the following issues have to be taken into account:

- Focus on better operational decisions instead of calculating the exact value. The true value of VBM is the interaction between the business issues and the value drivers.
- Avoid accounting complexity to the smallest detail.
- The absolute value is not important, but value creation is.
- Do not use VBM as a stand-alone tool, but integrate it into strategic planning and the planning and control cycle.
- Commitment and the active support of higher management are essential.

The final analysis

Despite being described as a measure of financial performance and, moreover, one which can be calculated theoretically, it is important to remember that VBM is not so much about generating a specific figure as about capital growth in general. Implementing VBM can be complex. In particular, information about future cash flows is needed. Within VBM there could be great emphasis on shareholder value and a focus on short-term cash generation. In general, it is not advisable to go into detail too deeply or to use complex methods.

References

Ittner, C.D. and Larcker, D.F. (2001) 'Assessing empirical research in managerial accounting: A value-based management perspective'. *Journal of Accounting and Economics* 32, 349–410.

Rappaport, A. (1986) *Creating Shareholder Value: A Guide for Managers and Investors*. New York: Simon & Schuster.

Stewart, G.B. (1990) *The Quest for Value*. New York: HarperCollins.

[PART FOUR]

Marketing and sales

These models provide a commercial perspective for the organisation and help to analyse and engage the markets in which the organisation is active.

4Ps of marketing (Kotler)

35

The big picture

Philip Kotler introduced what is commonly known as the *4Ps of marketing*: product, price, place and promotion. The '4Ps', or the marketing mix, is a description of the strategic position of a product in the marketplace. The premise of the model is that marketing decisions generally fall into the following four controllable categories:

- Product (characteristics)
- Price
- Place (distribution)
- Promotion.

When grouped into these four categories, marketing decisions can be justified and chosen deliberately, taking into account the intended effects (Figure 35.1).

When to use it

Marketing (and sales) is the functional field in any organisation that bridges the customers' perspective with the organisational perspective. An analysis of the elements that form the marketing mix of an organisation, the 4Ps introduced by Philip Kotler, gives insights into the company's current and potential interactions with current and potential customers and the position the company has in the perception of its

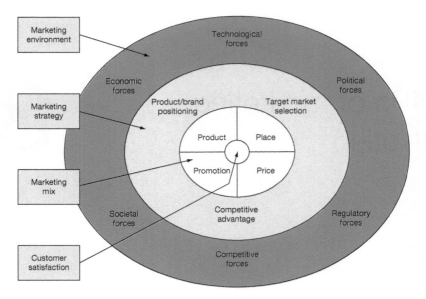

Figure 35.1 The marketing mix: Kotler's 4Ps

Source: after Kotler and Keller (2006)

customers. The marketing mix is a tactical toolkit that an organisation can use as an integral part of its marketing strategy to realise its corporate strategy. As an organisation can adjust the 4Ps categories on a regular basis, it is able to keep pace with the changing needs of customers in a specific market segment.

How to use it

There are three basic steps:

1   Step 1: Research. In order to develop a marketing mix that precisely matches the needs of the customers in the target market, an organisation first has to gather information on each of the 4Ps.

2   Step 2: Analyse the variables and determine the optimum mix. Next an assessment is to be made as to whether the 4Ps are well enough aligned to each other. An optimal marketing mix has to be determined, which will allow the organisation to strike a balance between satisfying its customers and maximising the organisation's profitability. This means making decisions regarding the issues in each of the categories illustrated in the following table.

Product decisions	Price decisions	Distribution (place) decisions	Promotion decisions
Brand name	Pricing strategy (skim, and penetration)	Distribution channels	Promotional strategy (push or pull)
Functionality styling		Market coverage (inclusive, selective or exclusive distribution)	
Quality	Suggested retail price		Advertising
Safety	Volume discounts and wholesale pricing		Personal selling and sales force
Packaging			
Repairs and support		Specific channel members	Sales promotions
Warranty	Cash and early payment discounts	Inventory management	Public relations and publicity
Accessories and services	Seasonal pricing	Warehousing	Marketing Communications budget
	Bundling	Distribution centres	
	Price flexibility		
	Price discrimination	Order processing	
		Transportation	
		Reverse logistics	

- Product – Do you actually produce what your customers want? Possible decisions and activities regarding the product include: new product development; modification of existing products; and elimination of products that are no longer attractive, or that are unprofitable. There is also a variety of activities closely linked to the product that can be considered, such as branding, packaging, guarantees and the handling of complaints.

- Place (distribution) – Are your products available in the right quantities, in the right place, at the right time? Can you achieve this whilst keeping inventory, transport and storage costs as low as possible? Analyse and compare the various distribution possibilities, after which the most appropriate option can be selected. Again, there are a number of activities related to this category, such as selecting and motivating intermediaries; controlling inventory and managing transport; and storing as efficiently as possible.

- Promotion – How can you best inform/educate groups of customers about your organisation and its products? Different types of promotional activities may be necessary, depending on whether the organisation wishes to launch a new product, to increase awareness with regard to special features of an existing one, or to retain interest in a product that has been available in the same form for a long time. Therefore, decisions must be taken as to the most effective way of delivering the desired message to the target group.

- Price – How much are your customers willing to pay? The value obtained in an exchange is critical to consumers, in addition to which price is often used as a competitive tool, not only in price wars, but also for image enhancement. Pricing decisions are thus highly sensitive.

3 Step 3: Check. Monitoring and control on an ongoing basis are essential to ascertain the effectiveness of the chosen mix and how well it is being executed.

The final analysis

Over the years, the 4Ps have become an institution. But one of the main problems with the 4Ps is that they have a tendency to keep increasing in number, prompting the question 'Where does marketing stop?' Of all the candidates, the 'people' factor is undoubtedly the most widely accepted 'fifth P'. After all, people manipulate the marketing mix as marketers; they make products/services available to marketplace as intermediaries; they create the need for marketing as consumers/buyers; they play an important role when it comes to service levels, recruitment, training, retention, and so on.

It is tempting to view the marketing mix variables as controllable, but remember that there are limits: price changes may be restricted by economic conditions or government regulations; changes in design and promotion are expensive and cannot be effected overnight; and people are expensive to hire and train. Do not forget to keep an eye on what is happening in the outside world, as some events may have a greater impact than you think.

Ultimately, successful marketing is a matter of gut feeling and acting on hunches. Whilst the marketing mix is a useful instrument when it comes to analysing and ordering, the multitude of marketing decisions has to be considered.

References

Kotler, P. and Armstrong, G. (2011) *Marketing management*, 14th edn. Upper Saddle River, NJ: Prentice-Hall.

Kotler, P. and Keller, K.L. (2000) *A Framework for Marketing Management*, 3rd edition. Upper Saddle River, NJ: Prentice-Hall.

Kotler, P. and Keller, K.L. (2006) *Marketing Management: Analysis, Planning, Implementation and Control*, 12th edn. Upper Saddle River, NJ: Pearson Education.

Branding pentagram

36

The big picture

The branding pentagram is a model that helps to translate corporate strategy into branding policy by stating the branding principles, 'loading' the brand, choosing the desired positioning, and translating branding into everyday actions.

When to use it

The branding pentagram is useful for organisations that are willing to develop or improve their branding. It serves as a framework to define the brand and its strategy:

- Who is the product or service for?
- What does the product or service do?
- How is it useful to me as a client?

A brand is the complete set of signals that surround a product, service or company. Branding is the process of managing these signals in a structured and consistent way. The branding pentagram is a framework for evaluating and elaborating five integral factors that influence branding strategy.

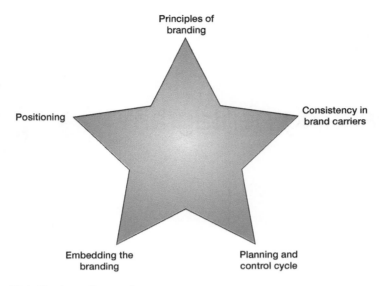

Principles of
branding

Positioning

Consistency in
brand carriers

Embedding the
branding

Planning and
control cycle

Figure 36.1 The branding pentagram

The pentagram consists of five interrelated points:

1 Principles of branding
2 Positioning
3 Consistency in brand carriers
4 Embedding the branding
5 Planning and control cycle.

By covering these five points (see Figure 36.1), an organisation not only states its brand(s) and branding policy, but also incorporates relevant branding activities into the organisation's daily practice.

How to use it

The five points of the pentagram can be addressed by elaborating on the following aspects, in the following order:

1. Principles of branding

The principles of branding consist of:

- *Brand mission* – which goals do I eventually want to achieve with the brand?
- *Desired brand perception* – what are the core values of the brand?
- *Brand architecture* – what are my choices regarding the brand portfolio?

2. Positioning

The positioning of the brand can be chosen based on:

- *Segmentation* – which segmentation criteria are used?
- *Target group* – which target group(s) is the brand aimed at (client/end user)?
- *Position* – how does the brand distinguish itself compared with (the critical success factors of) the competitors? This should be measured in terms of both the product offered (the proposal to the clients) and the performance of the organisation (the clients' perception).

3. Consistency in brand carriers

To maximise the effect of the brand, there must be consistency in the way the brand is carried. Consistency in brand carriers can be created by creating consistency in the way the brand is carried by the different products and services of the organisation, and by how the brand is 'carried out' and spoken of by the employees of the organisation, or the employees of an intermediary. Further consistency can be guarded via the different means the organisation uses to communicate.

4. Embedding the branding

This starts by ensuring consistency. The brand policy needs to align consistently with underlying functions and responsibilities. Responsibilities and authority for branding should be assigned to one of the management team or board members. A person should be appointed who will have direct responsibility for branding. Branding should be embedded by anchoring it in the organisation's culture and the behaviour of its employees.

5. Planning and control cycle

This starts with the formulation of SMART (specific, measurable, achievable, relevant, time-specific) targets of brand policy for both the short and the long term. Next, the planning and control cycle can be developed by determining the measuring method. The method must enable measurement of the degree of realisation and the evaluation of the measured degree(s) of realisation. Furthermore, this method must give input and initiation to adjustment based on the evaluation.

'Branding' is optimal when the *real* brand experience is equal to the *desired* brand experience. In such a case, the branding confers a sustainable, competitive advantage. Conversely, unsuccessful branding has a negative effect on a firm's competitive advantage.

The final analysis

Where brands are concerned, bear the following in mind:

- Brands, and therefore branding, are subjective by nature.
- Many of the worlds' best brands are companies, rather than specific products. A brand can just as easily be a service, an organisation or even an aspiration.
- Brands can take many forms and are not just names – nor are they restricted to physical products.

The model does not fill in the branding strategy of an organisation. It merely serves as a framework on which a company can build. The use of the model is therefore limited to *which aspects* should be borne in mind when elaborating a brand strategy, not *what the content* of the aspects should be.

Reference

Baker, M. and Hart, S. (1999) *Product Strategy and Management.* Harlow: Pearson Education.

Client pyramid (Curry)

37

The big picture

If you can successfully identify your most valuable customers, acquire them, keep them and increase their purchases, you will generate significantly more value than with a one-size-fits-all approach. The customer pyramid paradigm, revitalised by Jay and Adam Curry, provides a company with a mechanism for segmenting its customer base. The pyramid depicts the customer classification: the most valuable group of customers at the top and the vast majority of less valuable customers at the bottom (Figure 37.1).

When to use it

A customer analysis helps to classify customers into groups. Curry's customer pyramid forces an organisation to segment customers in terms of revenue generation, which indicates how important a customer is. The pyramid maps out what each customer contributes to the company results. Customers can then be treated differently in each segment of the pyramid. Marketing and sales resources are allocated differently in the various customer segments, related to the value of the customer to the company. In addition, Curry's customer pyramid provides an insight into cross-selling and up-selling opportunities (imagine customers 'moving up in the pyramid'; see Figure 37.1).

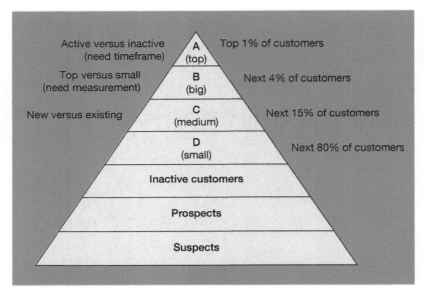

Figure 37.1 Curry's pyramid

How to use it

Customers can be segmented in the customer pyramid based on company-specific factors. These factors usually include, but are not limited to, turnover and profitability per customer. The segmentation reflects how an organisation considers and treats a (future) customer, segments of customers or the entire potential customer base. The *80/20 rule* is often used. This popular rule says that 20 per cent of the customers account for 80 per cent of the profit, and that the other 80 per cent only contribute the remaining 20 per cent. In practice, the percentages can be very different; the key idea behind the rule is that not all customers are profitable – some even cost you money!

Once a company knows who its most valuable (potential) customers are, it has to undertake the following steps:

1 Gather as much relevant information about (potential) customers as possible, in particular the big and top customers.

2 Analyse this information and, if necessary, redesign the information requirements.

3 Set goals for how you want your customers to perceive you, as provider of their products, services and/or experiences.

4 Choose media, systems and content for communicating and interacting with customers.

5 Develop rules of engagement and 'packages' for each customer segment.

6 Embed a customer-driven culture in the company.

7 Develop your customer management systems as you learn.

The final analysis

There is a plethora of models and tools available to support managers and business analysts in customer marketing and relationship management. One of the inherent dangers is the tendency to focus on data of existing customers as opposed to taking the time to consider the scope of potential customers.

An advantage of the pyramid model is that the categorisation of customers allows for account management and targeted marketing policies. However, the success of an organisation in targeting, acquiring and retaining customers is obviously influenced by many more factors than customer relationship management alone. For instance, pricing, the intrinsic value proposition of the product or service, a coherent marketing strategy or cultural endorsement of a customer-centred approach can also be very decisive.

References

Curry, J. (1992) *Know your Customers: How Customer Marketing can Increase Profits.* London: Kogan Page.

Curry, J., and Curry, A. (2000) *The Customer Marketing Method: How to Implement and Profit from Customer Relationship Management.* New York: Free Press.

38

Crowdsourcing

The big picture

Crowdsourcing is a method that captures the knowledge, ideas and creativity of a large group of people or even a group as large as society as a whole. Through interaction with the group by purposefully posing questions, the organisation can get useful, collective feedback.

This method can be used both externally (with key stakeholders) and internally (with key employees). A good medium for crowdsourcing is the internet or – especially in larger organisations – the organisation's intranet environment.

When to use it

Submitting a question to a relevant, interested audience or just to people in another field can generate new insights that help solve a problem or situation. Typically, crowdsourcing should be used in stages where (still) no decisions have to be taken, furthering the use of input from relevant stakeholders who are not involved in the decision-making stage itself.

In business-to-customer (B2C) environments, crowdsourcing methods are increasingly used for collecting information for strategic decisions, e.g. in marketing strategies. In one example a large crisp manufacturer launched a competition, inviting consumers (the general public) to make suggestions for new flavours, and then inviting the general public to vote for the best suggestion before putting the winner into production.

Figure 38.1 Crowdsourcing

Source: after crowdsourcing.org

How to use it

For crowdsourcing you will need access to a large, relevant network or community of the target group, i.e. the stakeholders whom you are looking to interact with. A good approach is to ask a question via social media and thus launch the discussion or to let people vote on ideas or products. On a smaller scale, crowdsourcing can also be done using industry-related discussion platforms or intranet.

The final analysis

Crowdsourcing is a contemporary and often refreshing alternative to finding answers to the challenges your organisation is facing. To make use of the 'the wisdom of the crowd', however, the input received needs to be filtered. The number of suggestions can be overwhelming and additional analysis is then needed to find the best or best applicable suggestions, either quantitatively with, for instance, Delphi methods or qualitatively with, for instance, expert panels. Similarly, the number of responses can also be relatively low, which brings with it the risk of placing too much emphasis on the opinions of a small group.

Reference

Surowiecki, J. (2004) *The Wisdom of Crowds: Why the Many are Smarter than the Few and How Collective Wisdom Shapes Business, Economies, Societies and Nations*. New York: Doubleday Publishing.

39

Customer journey mapping

The big picture

Customer journey mapping is a model for mapping all interactions between customers and the organisation from the perspective of the customer, with the intention of improving these interactions and, by doing so, increasing sales and customer satisfaction. Although the model has been around since the late 1980s, with the rise of the online customer interactions (social media, e-commerce, etc.) customer journey mapping is used by many companies to optimise activities and interactions both offline and online, and to align between both channels.

Customer journey mapping is a way of seeing things from the customers' point of view. It is not about just describing their experience, but also how they feel about what happens to them and then analysing what the company can do better to improve this experience.

When to use it

Customer journey mapping is a model for gaining greater customer insight. It can be used as part of a business improvement process – with potential for both improving the customer experience and reducing the costs of providing a service. It can also be used as part of a design or restructuring process, drawing up the perfect customer journey – or at least the best achievable one. Moreover, it can be used as part of training and insight material to help customer-facing teams improve their

	1. Recognise need	2. Become aware of products	3. Orientate	4. Decide	5. Purchase	6. Use	7. Repeat purchase
Key steps							
Key activities of organisation							
Key customer actions							
Emotional experience 🙂 🙁							
Perceived barriers							
Suggestions and improvments							
Optimisation potential							

Figure 39.1 Customer journey mapping

empathy with customers or to identify where attention and investment are required to improve customer experience – or where savings can be made while not harming customer satisfaction.

Another application of customer journey mapping is as a tool for providing input for the company's strategy: based on the mapped-out customer experiences and customer feedback, additional future business opportunities might be found.

How to use it

Customer journey mapping is all about the customer and his/her experiences with the company (see Figure 39.1). This requires essential knowledge of customers, so it is imperative that those involved in mapping the customer journey should have first-hand experience with customer interaction. In addition, customer satisfaction surveys are valuable input.

Customer journey mapping starts with analysing the interaction of customers with the organisation. Often this interaction is split into key steps. For each step, the activities of the organisation and the activities the customer has to perform are identified. And for each step – and each activity – the emotional experience for the customer should be assessed. This emotional experience is key to customer journey mapping and the starting point for identifying improvement potential in the company's interaction with customers. When there is a negative emotion from the customer, one should look into the activities performed by the organisation. Are they up to standard? Do they meet the customer expectations? And one should also look into the activities performed by the customer. Do they match the customer expectations (and value-for-money perceptions)? Are they facilitated by the organisation in any way, or the right way? When there is a positive emotion, analysis is also useful to see if further improvement is possible, to learn how this positive emotion might be realised in other steps and activities, and to learn what causes this positive emotion to lessen (or further increase) in the next step(s) and how that experience can be transferred to other steps. The latter is, of course, also very important when trying to increase conversion rates (i.e. increase the number of potential customers who become actual customers).

Customer journey mapping finishes by identifying suggestions for improvement of each step, with the aim of increasing customer satisfaction (and thus sales).

Customer journey mapping benefits from being visualised. In this visualisation, the key steps in the interaction (from the customers' perspective) should be leading. When drawing up a customer journey map for business improvement, it might involve the following elements (see also Figure 39.1):

- Key journey steps – all the steps customers go through in chronological order.
- Actions and activities from the organisation in each step.
- Actions and activities to be performed by the customer in each step. Often the interactions between the customer and the company are specifically highlighted and referred to as touchpoints. These touchpoints are where activities by the organisation meet and overlap with activities by the

customer: this is when interaction occurs. However, touchpoints do not have to appear in every step.

- The emotional experience of customers (their thoughts and feelings) at each step, with a graphical representation of customers' emotional state and their satisfaction levels at each step of the process (often called a 'customer experience chart' or 'heartbeat chart').
- The barriers (as perceived by the customer) to moving forward to the next step – structural, process, cost, implementation or other barriers.
- Improvements and suggestions that would increase customer satisfaction in each step, and/or improvements and suggestions that would ease customer transition to the next step.
- Assessment of potential savings by optimising inefficient, combining (partially) overlapping and/or leaving out unnecessary activities in steps or even complete steps.

The final analysis

One of the strengths of customer journey mapping is that it helps to improve customer experiences in both offline and online interactions with the company. And it allows assessment of processes involving both tangible products and intangible service delivery. Another strong point is that it aims at both optimising the customer's experience (more sales) and the efficiency of the company's activities (less costs, more margin).

The model is scalable: it can be used both within a sales team meeting and at board level with extensive customer surveys. In both cases, it is likely that improvements will be found.

The visualisation of the 'customer journey' and the customer experiences is one of the reasons the model has seen increased popularity (especially in e-commerce). The visualisation is not necessarily linear, but could also take the shape of a 'wheel' with sequential steps in customer interaction. This shape also allows continued and replacement purchases to be linked up (as the 'after-sales step' and 'pre-purchase orientation step' connect in the wheel). Such a round, wheel-like shape is also called as a customer activity cycle, with Lego's customer experience wheel being a well-known example.

References

Liedtka, J., Ogilvie, T. and Brazonske, R. (2013) *The Designing for Growth Field Book: A Step-By-Step Project Guide.* New York: Columbia Business School Publishing.

Richardson, A. (2010) 'Using customer journey maps to improve customer experience'. *HBR Blog Network* (posted 15 November 2010). http://blogs.hbr.org/2010/11/using-customer-journey-maps-to/.

Shostack, G.L. (1984) 'Design services that deliver'. *Harvard Business Review* (84115), 133–139.

40

MABA analysis

The big picture

A MABA analysis compares the relative *market attractiveness* (MA) of a business activity or product–market combination with *business attractiveness* (BA), as determined by the ability to operate in a specific product–market combination. The MABA matrix is a useful tool to assess strategic options and help determine which option is the preferred one for the organisation (Figure 40.1).

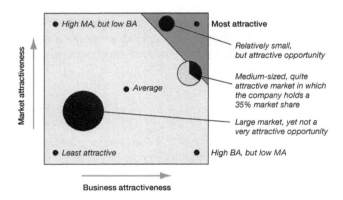

Figure 40.1 MABA analysis

When to use it

MABA analysis is used, in particular, to analyse and indicate new business opportunities. Market attractiveness is determined by external indicators such as profit margins; the size of the market; market growth (expectations); concentration; stability; and competitiveness. Porter's five forces analysis (see Chapter 8) and the BCG matrix (see Chapter 2) are appropriate models for assessing these indicators. Business attractiveness is determined largely by company-related indicators, such as the extent to which the product–market combination, market segment or business activity is a logical match with the company's current products, services, activities or competencies. The position of a company in the value chain or network of suppliers and customers is also of importance. Is the company able to benefit from economies of scale or other synergetic effects by taking on a particular alternative product–market combination?

How to use it

The first step in a MABA analysis is to decide which indicators are deemed important in determining the two dimensions of attractiveness, and how important they are relative to each other (weighting). It is obvious that an independently derived set of indicators and weights will lead to results that are more objective. The second step is to define the product–market combinations, the opportunities, and the segments or activities that will be subject to the MABA analysis. Although these need not be mutually exclusive, one important factor to take into account is the extent to which one opportunity affects the attractiveness of another.

Managers and consultants find it very useful to put the most attractive business opportunities in either the top-left or the top-right corner of the matrix. Some analysts create a matrix with quadrants or even more blocks within the matrix. Another way of emphasising the most attractive opportunities or weeding out better opportunities from worse opportunities is the application of curved or diagonal lines that serve as separators or thresholds. Sometimes points in the MABA matrix are replaced with 'bubbles', indicating the market size in units or money, and a pie segment to indicate a company's actual market share.

The final analysis

The MABA analysis is a very powerful model for helping companies to prioritise new opportunities. In particular, in situations where funds or management time are scarce, the model is a great help with decision-making. Make sure that the model does not lose its main quality: simplifying a complex situation.

The MABA analysis is much less powerful when discussing existing businesses. The managers and consultants involved will usually challenge assumptions and indicator ratings in such detail that the model loses its most profound quality, which is to simplify a complex situation.

The weakness of any MABA analysis lies in choosing and weighting indicators. Different indicators and weights can lead to very different results. There is a risk that a false sense of objectivity arises with the choice of some quantitative indicators, i.e. quantification only improves accuracy on a subjectively chosen scale.

The MABA analysis is limited to two (or three) artificially combined dimensions. Many, and more extensive, MABA analyses have to be performed using different indicators to compensate for this weakness.

Reference

Kotler, P. and Armstrong, G. (2011) *Marketing Management*, 14th edn. Prentice Hall.

Social network analysis

41

The big picture

'It is not what you know, it's who you know' – for a long time, this was a snobbish put-down for those without knowledge, but in today's network economy this argument is gaining relevance. The essence of a network analysis is to see whether the company has a competitive advantage through its partners in offline and online networks. A (social) network analysis assesses the contacts between individual employees of an organisation and individual stakeholders in the business environment of the organisation (e.g. contact with a supplier company's employees). These contacts are then depicted as a network, consisting of nodes or points (representing individual actors within the network) and ties or lines (representing relationships between individuals) – see Figure 41.1.

When to use it

A network analysis revolves around the mapping of the contacts of individuals. This is obviously a snapshot and often a complex and time-consuming task. It is a valuable exercise in analysing the position and reach of an organisation, e.g. when introducing a new product or when starting a new commercial campaign. It can also be very helpful to identify where the strength of the company's network lies and can potentially be exploited. It can be helpful to know, for instance, who to mobilise for a campaign or who can be consulted on specific topics, e.g. via crowdsourcing

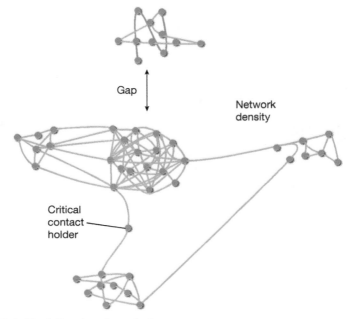

Gap

Network
density

Critical
contact
holder

Figure 41.1 (Social) network analysis

(see Chapter 38): most people find it an honour to be consulted or even considered an expert.

How to use it

A network analysis follows a number of steps:

- Map out the key players of your organisation on the organisation chart.
- Map out the most important contacts of these individual key players in the network of your organisation (e.g. with suppliers, customers, competitors, unions, trade agencies, etc.). You can find these by asking your employees and/or by analysing their online social network contacts.
- Cluster the contacts who are most relevant to the company: concentrate them around themes such as 'information' (e.g. knowledge or customer networks), 'resources' (e.g. financial or funding networks) and 'status' (e.g. persons or institutions with which the organisation would like to be associated).
- Assess the density of the network map. A dense network with many nodes (the dark spots in Figure 41.1) gives a good indication of how strongly your organisation is embedded in that network. A dense network with many lines is also an indication that information will be shared rapidly

and that mutual trust might be very strong within that group as there are so many relationships. A dense network will – almost automatically – strengthen the ties between its nodes. By ensuring the organisation has more than one representative in that network, it is more likely it will benefit from the network. But be careful, as the density says nothing about the quality of the network.

- Assess the gaps in the network. Where is there no connection? The lack of gaps is a proven indicator of a powerful network, which in turn benefits the strength, the entrepreneurship and the flexibility of a company.

- Identify the critical contact holders in your organisation. Who are the contact holders that link the organisation to critical partners? Make sure your organisation looks for a backup for these critical contact holders, as you don't want to jeopardise your network and strengths from the network when an individual employee leaves the organisation.

- Organise the network. Assign the management of networks to people who are explicitly responsible for that task. Go and fetch, but more particularly bring in. Don't transmit, but discuss and share it. Nurture the critical contact holders – try to bind them to the company and build bridges across the gaps.

The final analysis

This exercise is highly recommended, because most companies do not have a map of the organisation's network or of the strength this network offers the organisation; because networks play a crucial role in the value creation and business models of modern-day companies; and because on the internet the social networks of individuals (employees, customers, suppliers, key business partners) are becoming increasingly transparent.

References

Burt, R.S. (2009) *Social Capital: Reaching Out, Reaching In*. Cheltenham: Elgar Publishing.

Van den Berg, G. and Pietersma, P. (2014) *The 8 Steps for Strategic Success: Unleashing the Power of Engagement*. London: Kogan Page.

42 Stakeholder management

The big picture

Every company interacts with its environment and therefore has to deal with individuals, groups, companies and other organisations: the stakeholders. Some of these relationships are intentional and desirable, while others are not. All have in common the fact that they are involved with the organisation in a certain way and thus have an interest in the activities and objectives of the organisation. Stakeholder management helps to identify the interests of groups and individuals that are important to the company and then to act upon them. It consists of a set of tools to assess stakeholders and to analyse their interests and their relationship with the organisation. The most important factor in this is the assessment of the power of the stakeholder (Figure 42.1).

When to use it

With stakeholder management, a company can get a good idea of:

- the most important (dominant) stakeholders for the company;
- how the stakeholders relate to each other;
- what the various stakeholders contribute in their relationship with the company;

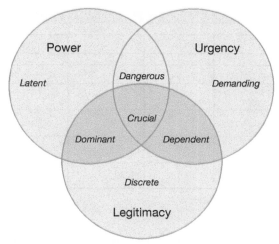

Figure 42.1 Stakeholder management

Source: after Mitchell, Agle and Wood (1997)

- what influencing power the stakeholders (should) have on the company;
- how the company could (and/or should) act upon the stakeholders' interest.

How to use it

Stakeholder management begins with an inventory of the organisation's stakeholders. The different stakeholders are then grouped, e.g. into 'the environmental movement', 'the staff' or 'the government'. Not all stakeholders are equally important to an organisation. Based on a classification, the organisation can prioritise relations with certain stakeholders. The classification is based on three characteristics of the relationship:

- the power of the parties to influence the organisation;
- the legitimacy of the relationship and actions of the stakeholders with the organisation in terms of desirability, accuracy or appropriateness;
- the urgency of the demands on the organisation made by the interested party, and the extent to which the sensitivity requirement is crucial for that person.

Stakeholders that only score high on one of the three characteristics are called *latent stakeholders* (see also Figure 42.1). Stakeholders that score high on all three are *crucial partners* for the organisation. Their interests and concerns should always be considered by the organisation. To complete the assessment of the power of stakeholders, you should also look into the relative position of the stakeholder amongst all stakeholders. This can be done by mapping out (Figure 42.2):

	Relation	Coalition	Interest	Power	Priority
Employees					
Customers					
Suppliers					
Competitors					
Regulars					
Trade unions					
Labour unions					
...					

Figure 42.2 Stakeholder analysis

- the current relationship of the stakeholder with the organisation;
- the possible coalitions of the stakeholder with any of the other stakeholders;
- the position of the stakeholder in the environment/market in which the organisation is active;
- the power of the stakeholder;
- the priorities of the stakeholder.

After the inventory and any prioritisation, the interest of each stakeholder or interested group should be determined, as well as the concerns they might have about the organisation's new strategy. Based on these concerns, an estimate can be made regarding which stakeholders will support the organisation's objectives and which still have doubts. The supporters are called *movers*. They will probably contribute actively and will seek others to do so as well. Opponents are called *blockers*, and those who are not in favour but who do not oppose are called *floaters*. Depending on the importance given to the relationship with an interested party, targeted action should be chosen as soon as that person's attitude seems to be moving in the same direction as the organisation. *Movers* should be informed about the organisation's objectives and (planned) activities, so that they can contribute. *Floaters* can usually be won over by the organisation. With regard to their doubts, the organisation can explain to them how their interests will be served by its plans. The *blockers* will have to be consulted too. Find out what they perceive to be a threat and what the organisation can do to remove that perception. Often, too much attention is given to blockers and too little to floaters.

For all actions and communication with the different stakeholder groups, key performance indicators (KPIs) are chosen to monitor whether the action actually contributes to the mobilisation or the creation of a win–win situation with that stakeholder. A stakeholder action card is a suitable tool to keep track of these (see Figure 42.3). It is a practical tool that gives a good overview of the interests, positions and roles of stakeholders, and the approach followed towards the stakeholder, as well as keeping track of progress and developments. It also allows further fine-tuning of actions and communication with the stakeholder when necessary.

Stakeholder (name)	Classification (latent-crucial)	Interest	Issue(s)	Coalition with	Attitude ('mover', 'floater', 'blocker')	Resistance/ response	Approach	KPI for approach	Monitoring method	Communication means

Figure 42.3 Stakeholder action card

The final analysis

Stakeholder management is an evergreen model that should always be used by any organisation. It can be particularly useful in any situation where there is resistance to (proposed) decisions, where there are changes among stakeholders and/or where a change in the actions, behaviour or attitude of one or more stakeholders of the organisation is required or would be beneficial. Stakeholder management provides practical guidance on how to convince any (internal or external) opponents and thus create support.

It is astonishing, however, how often in business a structured approach to the organisation's stakeholders is passed over. In a dynamic environment, a stakeholder analysis should be performed more frequently. Relevant groups change relatively rapidly, as do their power relations, interests and priorities. Not taking your stakeholders into consideration places the company's image and reputation in the public's mind at considerable risk and, with the advent of social media, this can bring your business to an immediate standstill.

References

Freeman, R.E. and Harrison, J.S. (2010) *Stakeholder Theory: The State of the Art*. Cambridge: Cambridge University Press.

Freeman, R.E. (2010) *Strategic Management: A Stakeholder Approach*. Cambridge: Cambridge University Press

Mitchell, R. K., Agle, B.R. and Wood, D. J. (1997) 'Toward a theory of stakeholder identification and salience: defining the principle of who and what really counts'. *Academy of Management Review* 22(4), 853–886.

[PART FIVE]

Operations, supply chain management and procurement

These models help to analyse and design operations and supply chain management.

Business process redesign

43

The big picture

Hammer and Champy (1993) define business process redesign (BPR) as the fundamental reconsideration and radical redesign of organisational processes, in order to achieve drastic improvement of current performance in cost, quality, service and speed. Value creation for the customer is the leading factor for process redesign, in which information technology often plays an important role (Figure 43.1).

1 Determine scope and goal	2 Redesign process structure	3 Install management	4 Implement and integrate
Indicator for need: • Conflicts • Meetings • Non-structured communication • Strategic dialogue	**Key elements:** • Focus on output requirements • Critical success factors • Efficiency	**Key elements:** • Define management tools • Performance measurement • Learning • Compensation	**Key elements:** • Install management • Manage change management

Figure 43.1 Business process redesign

Source: after Van Assen, Notermans and Wigman (2007)

When to use it

BPR is useful in cases where there are:

- numerous conflicts in (parts of) the organisation;
- high frequency of meetings;
- excessive amounts of non-structured communication (such as memos, e-mails and announcements).

How to use it

There are four important rules to bear in mind with any BPR project:

1 Determine strategy before redesigning.
2 Redesign each primary process first (i.e. a set of transformations of input elements into products with specific properties) and subsequently optimise the secondary processes (i.e. processes that support the proper working of the primary processes).
3 Optimise the use of information technology.
4 Organisational structure and governance models must be compatible with the primary process.

Furthermore, there is a general condition for success with BPR, namely that management and employees must both participate. Often, the decision to re-design entails a 'back to square one' approach. In an effort to allow discussion of any new views on how to design the organisation, the existing organisational structure and processes are considered as being 'non-existent' or irrelevant in the redesign.

Once the need for the redesign is established, the second step in the BPR process is redesigning (part of) the organisation in accordance with strategic requirements. The following questions have to be asked:

- What is the focus of our efforts (think of products, services and target customers)?
- What are the critical success factors?
- How can we achieve maximum efficiency based on the required output levels?

The third step is determining the required management of the newly designed organisation. Typical questions here are:

- How can we ensure that processes will function as intended?
- How can we measure performance?
- How can we adjust for improvements if necessary?
- How can we compensate or reward?

The final step comprises the implementation of the new organisational structure, the installation of management and procedures, and the integration of the organisation's work methods into its environment.

The final analysis

Business process redesign is a difficult concept to put into practice. Lack of adequate project management, limited management support and 'the delegation' of BPR projects to the IT department are generally fatal, and they are the top three reasons for BPR failure in practice. A further problem with BPR is that, although it makes sense on the 'hard' functional side, the 'soft' people side can be harder than initially foreseen (e.g. getting people to work in a new structure and with new rules). Many BPR projects stall during the design phase.

Neither redesigning organisational structures and processes nor implementing new technologies as part of a BPR project will automatically remedy all the flaws in an organisation, let alone provide a permanent, sustainable solution. That is the very reason why employees, management and an organisation's culture are called the 'key enablers' of BPR.

References

Hammer, M. and Champy, J. (1993) *Reengineering the Corporation: A Manifesto for Business Revolution*. New York: Harper Business.

Van Assen, M.F., Notermans, R. and Wigman, J. (2007) *Operational Excellence New Style*. The Hague: Academic Service (in Dutch: *Operational Excellence nieuwe stijl*).

44

House of purchasing and supply

The big picture

The house of purchasing and supply is a framework developed by A.T. Kearney. It can be used to plan, evaluate and monitor the leadership practices in procurement by following the example of successful firms. The framework is the outcome of the study 'Leadership practices in procurement' conducted by A.T. Kearney in 1996. Seventy-seven high-performing firms from various industries in North America and Europe participated. The framework consists of three basic levels – direction-setting processes, core procurement processes and supporting/enabling processes – and eight dimensions, so-called 'rooms' that comprise more than 100 detailed items that differentiate leaders from laggards (Figure 44.1).

Direction-setting processes

1. Procurement strategy. Capitalise on supply market opportunities as an integral part of the business strategy to drive value creation through innovation, cost leadership, and marketing and revenue realisation.
2. Organisational alignment. Embed procurement skills and knowledge in the organisation's key business processes.

Core procurement processes

3 Sourcing. Apply advanced techniques to leverage the full value potential across the entire expenditure base, thus helping the firm to understand its own core competencies.

4 Supplier relationship management. Effectively manage the tension between the value creation potential and the risks of each relationship.

5 Operating process management. Automate operating processes by the aggressive and innovative use of e-business technologies.

Supporting processes

6 Performance management. Link procurement figures to corporate results and strategic objectives by making transparent the contribution made by procurement towards results.

7 Knowledge and information management. Continuously capture and share knowledge across processes, geographies, business units and external relationships.

8 Human resource management. Create ambassadors of procurement excellence through training, incentives and the aggressive rotation of high-potential professionals throughout the organisation.

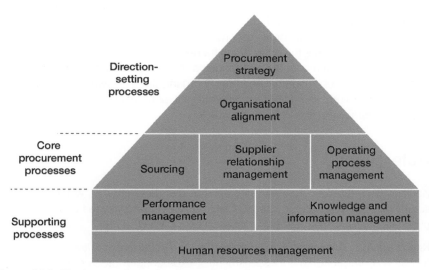

Figure 44.1 The house of purchasing and supply

Source: after Kearney (2002)

When to use it

The house of purchasing and supply is an appropriate framework for analysing and modifying any organisational procurement function to make it more effective. The framework helps to identify opportunities for improvement, with benchmark data regarding the procurement function, and consequently stimulates professionalism.

How to use it

The 'Assessment of Excellence in Procurement' study questionnaire is freely available online. Respondents receive a tailored feedback report containing their results as compared with those of other organisations, and even world-class leaders. Consequently, this assessment can accelerate professionalism by quickly identifying strengths and opportunities, and charting the course of action to prepare for the future. As such, many organisations use the assessment periodically to monitor their progress.

The final analysis

The house of purchasing and supply is one of many frameworks used to describe the scope of the procurement function and to determine its level of professionalism. Due to the available benchmark data, the framework can be used repeatedly, especially by large international organisations.

The study that forms the basis of the framework began with 50 respondents and grew into a study with over 600 respondents. As such, the framework has become a means of communication between many organisations. However, the benchmark is time-consuming, and the limited number of publications or other information about the framework is a serious drawback.

References

Kearney, A.T. (2002). 'The new procurement mandate: growing within tomorrow's supply webs'. White paper, downloadable at www.atkearneypas.com/knowledge/publications/2000/mandate.pdf (accessed on 17 March 2014).

Kearney, A.T. *Assessment of Excellence in Procurement Study.* http://www.atkearney.com/procurement/assessment-of-excellence-in-procurement-study

Kaizen/Gemba

The big picture

Kaizen literally means change (*kai*) to become good (*zen*). Key elements of kaizen are quality, effort, willingness to change and communication. The Gemba house, as the basis of kaizen, has five fundamental elements:

- teamwork
- personal discipline
- improved morale
- quality circles
- suggestions for improvement.

Based on this foundation, kaizen focuses on the elimination of *muda* (waste and inefficiencies (Figure 45.1).

When to use it

Kaizen can be used to solve several types of problems: process inefficiencies, quality problems, large inventories, and delivery and lead-time problems. Employees are encouraged to come up with suggestions during weekly meetings (kaizen events) for small and large improvements. Kaizen suggests eliminating *muda* (waste and inefficiencies) first. The types of waste are:

Figure 45.1 The Kaizen/Gemba model

Source: based on Imai (1997)

- **Defective products.** Defects in quality prevent customers from accepting the manufactured product. The effort to create these defects is wasted. New waste management processes must be added in an effort to reclaim some value from an otherwise scrap product.

- **Over-production.** Over-production is the production or acquisition of items before they are actually required. It is the company's most dangerous waste, because it hides production problems. Over-production has to be stored, managed and protected.

- **Transportation.** Each time a product is moved, it runs the risk of being damaged, lost, delayed, etc., as well as being a cost with no added value. Transportation does contribute to the transformation of the product that the consumer is disposed to pay for.

- **Waiting.** Refers to the time spent by the workers waiting for resources to arrive, the queue for their products to empty, as well as the capital sunk into goods and services that have not yet been delivered to the customer. It is often the case that there are processes to manage this waiting.

- **Excess inventory.** Whether in the form of raw materials, work in progress (WIP) or finished goods, excess inventory represents a capital outlay that has not yet produced an income for either the producer or the consumer. If any of these three items are not being processed actively to add value, it is waste.

- **Motion.** In contrast to transportation, motion refers to the worker or equipment, and is represented by damage, wear and safety. It also includes the fixed assets and expenses incurred in the production process.

- **Extra processing.** Using a more expensive or otherwise valuable resource than is required for the task, or adding features that are included in the design but are not needed by the customer. There is a particular problem with this factor. People may need to perform tasks for which they are overqualified to maintain their competency. This training cost can be used to offset the waste associated with over-processing.

After the reduction of waste, good housekeeping is put forward, which comprises the 5-Ss:

1 *Seiri* – tidiness. Separate what is necessary for the work from what is not. This should help to simplify the work.

2 *Seiton* – orderliness. You can increase efficiency by making deliberate decisions regarding the allocation of materials, equipment, files, etc.

3 *Seiso* – cleanliness. Everyone should help to keep things clean, organised, and looking neat and attractive.

4 *Seiketsu* – standardised clean-up. The regularity and institutionalisation of keeping things clean and organised as part of 'visual management' is an effective means of continuous improvement.

5 *Shitsuke* – discipline. Personal responsibility for living up to the other 4-Ss can make or break the success of housekeeping.

The last building block of the Gemba house is standardisation. Standardisation of practices and institutionalisation of the 5-Ss will make it easier for everyone in the organisation to improve continuously, including newcomers. Top management plays an important role in guarding and acting for the widespread implementation and coordination of kaizen, the 5-S method, and the standardisation of work.

A correct implementation of the kaizen concept will lead to:
- **Improved productivity**
- **Improved quality**
- **Better safety**
- **Faster delivery**
- **Lower costs**
- **Greater customer satisfaction**
- **Improved employee morale and job satisfaction.**

How to use it

The following steps should be taken in kaizen events:

- Define the problem and the goal of the event.
- Analyse the facts.
- Generate possible solutions.

- Plan the solution.
- Implement the solution.
- Check and secure the solution.

It is important that the solution is checked and secured. In the final phase of a kaizen event, people start to seek opportunities for new kaizen events, which may hamper the process of embedding each improvement into operational practice.

The final analysis

The kaizen philosophy resonates well with the speed of change at operational levels in the organisation. The sustainability of the improvements proposed and implemented by people on the work floor is perhaps the strongest argument in favour of kaizen. Its sheer simplicity makes implementation easy, although some cultures may not be as receptive to the high level of self-discipline that the Japanese are able to maintain.

Kaizen has more potential in incremental change situations than in abrupt turnarounds. A culture focused on short-term success and big 'hits' is not the right environment for kaizen. Cooperation and widespread discipline at all levels of the organisation are the absolute keys to its success.

Reference

Imai, M. (1997) *Gemba Kaizen: A Commonsense, Low-cost Approach to Management.* London: McGraw-Hill.

Lean thinking/ just-in-time

46

The big picture

Lean thinking is also known as lean manufacturing, or the Toyota philosophy. Lean focuses on the removal of *muda* (waste), which is defined as anything that is not necessary to produce the product or service. In lean thinking, inventories are considered to be the root of all evil. High inventories cover up all the real problems of an organisation and prevent it from becoming more flexible and efficient. If the inventories are reduced on a structural base, the real problems will become apparent, and they can then be solved accordingly.

Lean thinking, and in particular its operations strategy just-in-time (JIT), is a Japanese management philosophy developed by Taiichi Ohno for the Toyota manufacturing plants. Lean thinking forces any firm to continuously identify and remove sources of waste according to the *seven zeros*:

1 Zero defects
2 Zero (excess) lot sizes
3 Zero setups
4 Zero breakdowns
5 Zero (excess) handling
6 Zero lead-time
7 Zero surging

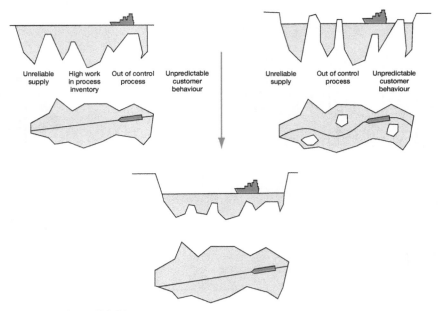

Figure 46.1 Lean thinking

Source: after Van Assen, Notermans and Wigman (2007)

According to the seven zeros, lean thinking advocates flow production, with the emphasis on JIT delivery (Figure 46.1).

When to use it

While lean thinking has shown itself to be very effective in high-volume repetitive operations, it can be applied to any organisation as long as management adheres to the assumptions underlying it:

- People value the visual effect of flow.
- Waste is the main restriction to profitability.
- Many small improvements in rapid succession are more beneficial than any analytical study.
- Process interaction effects will be resolved through value stream refinement.

How to use it

There are five essential steps in lean thinking:

1 Identify the drivers to create value (identify value and explore customer requirements). The evaluation of value drivers must be made from the

perspective of internal and external customers. Value is expressed in terms of how well a product or service meets the customer's needs, at a specific price, at a specific time.

2 Identify the value stream (the sequence of activities that add value to a product or service). Activities that contribute to value are identified with the aid of value stream mapping, in which all activities are evaluated according to whether they add value to the product or service. Finally, non-value-added activities are eliminated as much as possible.

3 Make the activities flow (ensure flow-type production: make products and services flow through the processes). Additional improvement efforts are directed towards making the activities in the value stream flow. Flow is the uninterrupted movement of a product or service through the system to the customer. Major inhibitors of flow are work in queue, batch processing and transportation. These buffers slow down the time from product or service initiation to delivery. Buffers also tie up money that can be used more effectively elsewhere in the organisation, and cover up the effects of system failures and other types of waste.

4 Let the customer pull products or services through the process (pull production control). Synchronise production with actual customer demand. Products must be pulled out of the system based on actual customer demand. The value stream must be made responsive to providing the product or service only when the customer needs it – not before and not after.

5 Optimise the system continuously. Search for perfection by continuously improving processes with the help of kaizen events (Chapter 45), the elimination of waste, and good housekeeping.

The final analysis

Implementing lean seems so easy! However, in order to implement lean successfully, various issues and elements must be considered (in the following order):

1 What results do we really want from JIT? Is it worthwhile in view of the costs and obstacles of implementation? Conduct a quick scan of costs and benefits, including a possible project plan.

2 The sequence of JIT implementation is of critical importance. Lowering inventories before creating flexibility in production can lead to poor delivery performance. In general, implementation has been at its most successful when it starts at the very end of the production process, and by then gradually working upstream. However, the 'best' order of implementation depends on the individual situation. Increasing inventory levels temporarily should be considered in order to ensure delivery performance during the implementation.

3 Definitely do not start by forcing suppliers to adopt JIT until implementation is well under way or completed.

4 Does the product design qualify for JIT production or delivery? Are alterations necessary?

5 Next, redesign the production process to enable JIT. More often than not, significant improvements and efficiencies can be created during this stage.

6 Adjust information systems to meet the demands of the primary process.

7 Seek improvements with suppliers and customers. This should yield the final, significant results of JIT.

The principal objective of lean is to reduce waste (especially excess inventories). Nevertheless, inventories cannot be eliminated altogether, as all supply systems require a work-in-process inventory to realise any output at all. The more variability (e.g. different types of order, different types of technologies) in the system, the more buffers are required to hedge for variability. Hence, for a lean production system to operate successfully, it is important not only to have a pull-controlled production system, small batch sizes and reduced setup times, but also to have stable and reliable demand, and a corresponding operation. In dynamic business environments, other approaches, such as the theory of constraints (Goldratt, 1984) or quick response manufacturing (Suri, 1998), are more appropriate.

Don'ts

- Do not expect to be able to just scrap waste.
- Do not believe that control is about output and process indicators.
- Do not underestimate the power of the Gemba house (Chapter 45).
- Do not underestimate the cultural and managerial aspects of lean thinking. These aspects are just as important as, or possibly even more important than, the techniques and tools of lean production. There are many examples of lean projects that failed due to a misunderstanding of the impact of lean on the organisation.

References

Goldratt E.M. and J. Cox, (1984). *The Goal: A Process of Ongoing Improvement.* Great Barrington: North River Press.

Ohno, T. (1988) *Toyota Production System: Beyond Large-Scale Production.* New York: Productivity Press.

Suri, R. (1998) *Quick Response Manufacturing.* New York: Productivity Press.

Van Assen, M.F., Notermans, R. and Wigman, J. (2007) *Operational Excellence New Style.* The Hague: Academic Service (in Dutch: *Operational Excellence nieuwe stijl*).

Purchasing model (Kraljic)

47

The big picture

Kraljic's (1983) purchasing model is used to determine an adequate purchasing strategy per product (or service) that optimises the trade-off between costs and risks. Appropriate guidelines can be derived from it to manage the relationships with various suppliers, by categorising supply items in a two-by-two matrix. Kraljic developed this model as an internal tool for BASF. However, the model became well known after it was published in the *Harvard Business Review* in 1983. The general idea of Kraljic's purchasing model is to 'minimise supply vulnerability and make the most of potential buying power'.

The model categorises products on the basis of two dimensions: *financial impact* and *supply risk*. This results in four quadrants, each of which requires a distinct purchasing strategy (Figure 47.1):

- Strategic items – these have a high supply risk and a high financial impact. In general, these items are scarce, high-value materials, such as rare metals and high-value components. Depending on the relative power position of the parties involved, the purchasing strategy for strategic items is aimed at partnership or collaboration.

- Leverage items – these are items with low supply risk, but high financial impact. An abundant supply is available; however, the items are very important to the organisation. Electric motors, heating oil and electronic data processing hardware are examples of leverage items. Leverage items require a purchasing strategy based on competitive bidding or tendering.

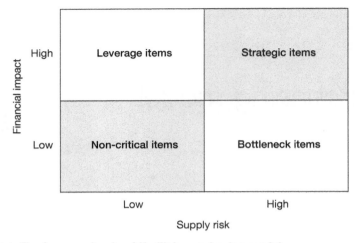

Figure 47.1 The four quadrants of Kraljic's purchasing model

- Bottleneck items – these have a low impact on the profit of the organisation, but they have a high supply risk. Mostly, this supply risk is due to production-based scarcity, and global, predominantly new, suppliers with new technologies. Examples of bottleneck items are electronic parts and outside services. The purchasing policy for bottleneck items aims at securing continuity of supply. Furthermore, alternative products and suppliers must be developed in order to reduce dependence on suppliers.

- Non-critical items – these are items that have low supply risk and low financial impact. An abundant supply is available, and the items are needed simply for functional efficiency. Examples of non-critical items are all types of commodities, such as steel rods, coal and office supplies. As the handling of non-critical items often takes more money than the value of the product itself, these products require a purchasing strategy aimed at reducing administrative and logistical complexity.

When to use it

Kraljic's model is used to determine distinct purchasing strategies per product (or service) that enable an organisation to develop different strategies for each of the suppliers, so that each supplier will receive the appropriate amount of attention. The model is an effective tool for supporting the discussion, visualisation and illustration of the possibilities of differentiated purchasing and supplier strategies. By offering a structured and systematic approach, the model enables an organisation to make its purchasing function more effective and efficient .

How to use it

In order to fill in the two-by-two matrix and subsequently determine the adequate strategy, all products (and services) must first be segmented. A good rule of thumb for grouping products logically is to evaluate whether they can be reasonably purchased from one or more supplier(s).

Secondly, the financial impact and the supply risk are determined for each of the product segments:

- The financial impact – this concerns the impact on the profit of a given supply item, measured against criteria such as purchasing volume, the percentage of the total purchase cost, product quality and business growth. The higher the volume or amount of money involved, the higher the financial impact.

- The supply risk – this relates to the complexity of supply, assessed according to criteria such as availability, number of suppliers, competitive demand, make-or-buy opportunities, storage risks and substitution possibilities. Sourcing a product from just one supplier without an alternative source of supply generally indicates a high supply risk.

Finally, the lines that divide the quadrants must be determined, because what exactly distinguishes high from low, for both supply risk and financial impact, is more or less arbitrary. This will result in a mapping of the segments in the matrix and a recommendation of the purchasing strategy to follow.

Note, however, that the appropriate purchasing strategy is not merely determined rationally by classifying the products, but also by the strategic choices of the organisation. Emotional and relational aspects are also important when choosing or maintaining suppliers.

The final analysis

Kraljic's model provided the first comprehensive portfolio management approach for purchasing and supply management. Kraljic's basic ideas and concepts have become the dominant approach in the profession. The Kraljic matrix has become the standard in the field of purchasing portfolio models. Its terminology has generally been accepted and it has become the standard for both scientists and practitioners.

References

Kraljic, P. (1983) 'Purchasing must become supply management'. *Harvard Business Review* 61(5), 109–117.

Van Weele, A.J. (2002) *Purchasing and Supply Chain Management: Analysis, Planning and Practice*. London: Thomson Learning.

48

Root cause analysis/ Pareto analysis

The big picture

Root cause analysis (RCA) is a class of problem-solving methods aimed at identifying the root causes of problems or events. It is based on the Ishikawa diagram (also fishbone diagram, or cause and effect diagram) named after its founder Kaoru Ishikawa (Figure 48.1a). The Ishikawa diagram shows the causes of a certain event. It was first used in the 1960s and is considered one of the seven basic tools of quality management, along with the histogram, Pareto chart, check sheet, control chart, flowchart and scatter diagram (Figure 48.1b). This principle is used in a root cause analysis and tries to explain the variations in a particular process. The analysis is generally used in both financial analysis and the analysis of operations, such as in business process redesign (BPR) projects (see Chapter 43).

When to use it

The RCA is used to explain the variation in any process (or outcome of a process). A certain amount of variability is normal and does not necessarily cause significant disturbance. However, unwanted variation can cause serious losses or damage, delays and reduced productivity, especially if it occurs in critical processes. The first essential step is to find the causes of variation and to quantify the effect. The main causes, which are generally easy to solve, should be taken care of first. The technique is particularly valuable for the analysis of critical processes that show undesirable variance.

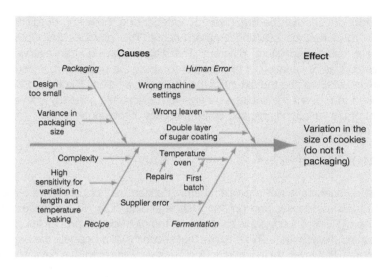

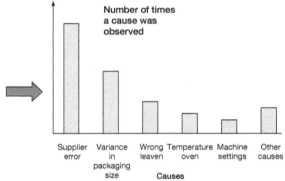

Figure 48.1 (a) Ishikawa diagram, or cause and effect diagram. (b) Pareto diagram

How to use it

Root cause analysis usually starts with the formation of a project team, including managers, suppliers, customers and employees. Next, the team defines the problem and decides which variation causes the most critical disturbance in the system under study. Then the team maps out the process and identifies the issues that can cause variance in the data/evidence-gathering phase. Following this, issues that contributed to the problem are identified and their root causes found. However, the root causes might not be immediately evident, in which case brainstorming techniques are required. Subsequently, the root causes identified (usually large in number) are illustrated on a whiteboard in order to discuss and sharpen the findings. Recommendations for solutions now have to be developed and actually implemented.

The root causes can be organised by categorising them and by distinguishing between main root causes and smaller effects. This provides the input needed to draw a 'cause and effect' diagram. The diagram provides an overview of the possible causes of variation. It is essential to study the possible root cause in the diagram in detail, to see the extent of the cause of variation. The Pareto diagram is often used to present the findings. Analysing root causes generally shows that 80 per cent of the variation is caused by 20 per cent of the causes.

The final analysis

Root cause analysis is not a single, sharply defined methodology; there are many different tools, processes and philosophies regarding RCA. To maximise the effect of the use of RCA, it is advisable to start with the most critical processes and/or the most disturbing variances. This ensures that success will propagate the broader use of the model. However, try to avoid finding causes of variation that have only a small effect on the lead time, productivity or costs.

Reference

Blanchard, K.H., Schewe, C., Nelson, R. and Hiam, A. (1996) *Exploring the World of Business,* New York: WH Freeman.

Six sigma

The big picture

The name six sigma originates from statistical terminology. Sigma is the mathematical symbol for standard deviation. Six sigma is a measure of the maximum number of defects that are allowed in a system. At the six sigma level, 99.999998 per cent of all products must be good, i.e. they fall within the tolerance limits. This implies that no more than 3.4 defects are produced in one million opportunities. This level can be achieved by reducing the variation of the process and controlling it. To reach this quality level, the processes must be improved. However, process and quality improvements are not the ultimate goal – financial improvement is the goal.

Six sigma first became rooted at Motorola. To confront heavy Japanese competition, in 1987 Motorola started to focus on quality improvement. The engineers at Motorola decided that the norm they were using, of defects per 1000 units, was no longer appropriate. They therefore decided to measure the defects per million. Allied Signal and General Electric have perfected the method. These firms have realised huge benefits by saving billions of dollars whilst improving customer satisfaction. Nowadays, six sigma projects are implemented not only in manufacturing firms, but also in the service industry.

Six sigma claims that focusing on reduction of variation will solve process and business problems. By using a set of statistical tools to understand the fluctuation of a process, management can begin to predict the expected outcome of that process. If the outcome is not satisfactory, other statistical tools can be used to further understand the elements that influence the process.

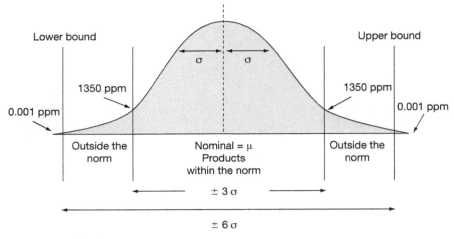

Lower bound

Upper bound

σ σ

1350 ppm

1350 ppm

0.001 ppm

0.001 ppm

Outside the
norm

Nominal = μ
Products
within the norm

Outside the
norm

± 3 σ

± 6 σ

Figure 49.1 Six sigma

Source: after Van Assen, Notermans and Wigman (2007)

When to use it

Six sigma is used to improve the operational performance of an organisation by identifying and dealing with its deficiencies. Six sigma projects help to achieve better financial results by improving quality and process reliability. Every six sigma project has to focus on financial improvements and cost savings. The six sigma philosophy suggests that top management should not authorise a project that does not have a savings target of at least $175 000.

Six sigma is a top-down method where management has to communicate the goal of each project and audit it. The organisation's employees carry out the projects in a very structured way. The employees have one of the following roles:

- *Executive management champions* – the CEO or other key management team members that have a clear overview of the six sigma projects.
- *Master black belts* – external consultants who train the black belts and support six sigma projects.
- *Black belts* – the project leaders, who execute overall project management.
- *Green belts* – the project leaders of a part of a project, who implement six sigma projects.
- *Project teams* – each green belt has a project team. These employees are trained in the six sigma techniques.

The infrastructure of a six sigma project is unique for every organisation. Nevertheless, general requirements for successful implementation can be determined:

- A good understanding of statistical tools and techniques.

- Spending adequate resources on the definition phase.
- Spending adequate resources on the implementation phase.
- Effective management leadership and commitment.
- Undergoing a cultural change before implementation.
- Having an effective communication plan.
- Providing adequate training for the improvement teams.
- Having black belts with the ability to facilitate.

How to use it

Six sigma includes five steps: define, measure, analyse, improve and control (commonly known as DMAIC):

1. Define. First of all, a selection of the processes that must be improved has to take place, and the goals for improvement should be defined (SMART – specific, measurable, acceptable, realistic and time-specific).
2. Measure. After the definition phase, data are collected to evaluate the performance of the current process for future comparison.
3. Analyse. The difference between the current state and the desired state is determined in this phase.
4. Improve. Subsequently the process is optimised based on the analysis.
5. Control. The new improved processes should be controlled and formalised.

The final analysis

Six sigma comprises hard and soft techniques. The harder ones include a structured problem-solving approach, statistical process control tools (applied using DMAIC methodology) and project management techniques. The softer ones include people management, creativity and improvement motivation.

Benchmarking (see Chapter 18) is used in six sigma projects. The important characteristics of the product, the client, the internal process and the manufacturing system are compared with the products and processes of competitors. This is useful for financially orientated management, because the comparison at process level makes it possible to use six sigma techniques.

In six sigma projects, it is important to have vision and enthusiasm, but a requirement for successful projects is a well-defined infrastructure for training, support and project coordination.

References

Breyfogle III, F.W. (2003) *Implementing Six Sigma: Smarter Solutions using Statistical Methods*. Hoboken, New Jersey: John Wiley & Sons.

Van Assen, M.F., Notermans, R. and Wigman, J. (2007) *Operational Excellence New Style*. The Hague: Academic Service (in Dutch: *Operational Excellence nieuwe stijl*).

The EFQM model

50

The big picture

The EFQM model developed by the European Foundation for Quality Management is a model that helps to translate strategy into five organisational areas ('leadership', 'policy and strategy', 'people', 'partnerships and resources' and 'processes') and four different result areas. The underlying philosophy is that, if the strategy is

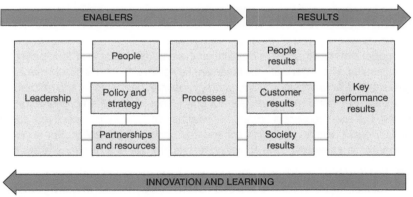

Figure 50.1 The EFQM excellence model

Source: after EFQM (1992)

properly translated and implemented, the five organisational areas are aligned and contribute to all four result areas, of which the outcomes will be satisfied customers and suppliers, satisfied employees, a satisfied society and satisfactory organisational performance and goal realisation (see Figure 50.1).

When to use it

Originally, the EFQM model was introduced as a tool to evaluate and improve the overall quality of the company, based on total quality management principles, by improving the alignment between the organisational areas and/or increasing their contribution to the results of the organisation. At its core, the EFQM model is a general model for assessing and designing a company's architecture in terms of best practices. It is based on different cultural and structural elements, with a view to developing an excellent organisation. It can be used by the management of any type of organisation that wants to implement strategy or to design and develop organisational structures and processes.

The EFQM model is also very useful in obtaining a clear overview of the interrelationships between the organisational areas of a company and how they contribute to the results of the organisation. The model explains performance gaps and identifies improvement directions. It is a non-prescriptive framework, underpinned by so-called 'fundamental elements':

- leadership and consistency of purpose;
- management by processes and facts;
- employee development and involvement;
- continuous learning, innovation and improvement;
- partnership development;
- public responsibility.

How to use it

The model distinguishes five organisational areas (enablers) and four performance areas (results). The organisational areas are key elements for effectively managing an organisation: *leadership*, *policy and strategy*, *people*, *partnerships and resources* and *processes*. Key performance results not only reflect how well an organisation is performing, but also measure a company's health from different perspectives: *customer results*, *people results*, *social results* and *key performance results*. For an excellent organisation and excellence in achieving results, the five organisational areas require:

- Leadership – requires managers who have a mission statement, vision and values; who are role models of a culture of excellence; who are personally involved in the development and improvement of the organisation; who care about customers, suppliers, partners and representatives of society; and who can motivate and support people in the organisation.

- Policy and strategy – require incorporation of current and future needs of all stakeholders; information for performance measurement, research and learning; continuous development and improvement; and communication

- People – employees play a key role. They should be carefully planned, managed and developed; their knowledge and competencies should be identified, developed and sustained; they must be involved and empowered; employees should interact at all levels in the organisation; and they should be rewarded and cared for.

- Partnerships and resources – require excellent management of external relationships, finances, buildings, equipment and materials, technology, and information and knowledge.

- Processes – require systematic design and management; should innovatively meet customer demands and increase value; should produce and deliver well-designed and well-developed products that meet customer needs and expectations; and should be well organised to contribute and enhance customer relations.

Using the model starts with (checking) the translation of the strategy in these five organisational areas. Next the desired results are mapped in the result areas. In the EFQM model, the organisational areas all contribute to four result areas. These represent the different types of results an organisation is hoping to achieve with its strategy. The result areas (i.e. 'employees', 'customers and suppliers', 'society' and 'financial return') present the activities delivered by the company.

An assessment is then made between the results that are sought by the company and those that are actually realised. In the EFQM model, the actual results are measured per result area using key performance indicators. For the 'customers', 'employees' and 'society' areas, perception indicators are also used to measure results.

Any gaps in performance, i.e. a lower performance than desired, are then identified. Suggestions for improvement (i.e. in certain organisational areas) can subsequently be determined. Ideally, these improvements are realised structurally. In the EFQM model, there is a feedback loop between the result areas and the organisational areas that represents a coordinated learning effect: it is the essential link between 'what we do' and 'what's in it'. Performance improvement efforts preferably utilise this learning loop.

The final analysis

The EFQM model is a recognised tool that provides companies with a structured approach to translate their strategy into functional areas in their organisation and to improve the overall quality in the organisation. The model provides core elements for the effective analysis, assessment, structuring, improvement and management of an organisation. The model also works well in conjunction with the balanced scorecard (see Chapter 17).

The EFQM model is frequently portrayed as a model to assist strategic decision-making. However, it is not a prescriptive model designed to assist with management analyses.

A valuable source of additional information on the EFQM model and on its use is the EFQM website (www.efqm.org), where benchmarks and tools for self-evaluation are also provided.

References

EFQM (1992) *Total Quality Management: The European Model for Self-appraisal.* Brussels: European Foundation for Quality Management.

Hakes, C. (2007) *The EFQM Excellence Model: For Assessing Organizational Performance: A Management Guide.* Van Haren Publishing

Oakland, J. (2000) *Total Quality Management: Text with Cases*, 2nd edn. Oxford: Butterworth Heinemann.

Value stream mapping

51

The big picture

Lean thinking (Chapter 46) focuses on adding value for customers and eliminating non-value-adding steps (waste). Value stream mapping is used in lean environments to map and analyse both the value-adding and non-value-adding activities and steps in information flows and processes. It visualises which activities add value for a customer, and which do not. Because of its fixed structure, it is often possible to find substantial improvement potential and corresponding improvement actions.

When to use it

Value stream mapping is used in lean environments to identify opportunities for improvement in lead time, as it identifies slack, waste and other non-value-adding activities. Mapping the processes involves making a diagram in which the processes, the material flows, the information flows and all other important data (e.g. inventory levels, processing times and batch sizes) are visualised with the help of standardised frameworks and symbols (see Rother & Shook, 2003). This map is the starting point for designing a desired future value stream that is lean.

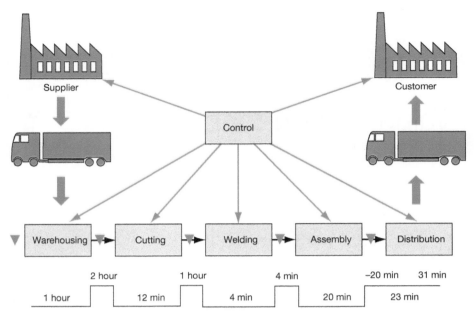

Supplier

Customer

Control

Warehousing → Cutting → Welding → Assembly → Distribution

| 2 hour | 1 hour | 4 min | −20 min | 31 min |
| 1 hour | 12 min | 4 min | 20 min | 23 min |

Figure 51.1 Example value stream map

Source: based on Rother and Shook (2003)

How to use it

The first stage in value stream mapping is the preparation of the *current state map*. Analysing the material flow in its current state provides information about value-adding and non-value-adding activities (e.g. machine time, unnecessary space, amount of rework, distance travelled and inefficiencies).

In the second stage, information from the current state map is used to prepare a desired *future state map*, where waste is eliminated, and the number of non-value-adding activities is minimised. Questions that must be answered during this step are, for instance:

- What is the 'takt time' (the desired time between units of production output, synchronised to customer demand)?
- Is it possible to introduce continuous flow?
- Can production be controlled with a pull system?

An important aspect to bear in mind during this stage is the need to adjust the production system to meet customer demand, while keeping the processes flexible.

The third and most important stage is to take action to change the manufacturing process from its current state to resemble the desired state as closely as possible. Thereafter, the process can start at the beginning again.

A stepwise plan could look as follows:

1 Identify which product (group) or service (group) needs to be analysed. Compose a team of process owners and employees who are involved in the different steps of the process.
2 Analyse the current state and translate this into a general process scheme.
3 Collect supporting data for the process scheme (e.g. throughput, throughput times, employees).
4 Formulate the ideal process based on the demands of the customers. (In this step, use parameters such as minimal work in progress, short setup times and a list of improvements needed to arrive at the ideal future state.)
5 Determine an action plan for realising the improvements needed to arrive at the future state. This action plan should contain priorities for the different improvements: actions that are coupled to persons, a clear time path and the involvement of sponsors.
6 Monitor progress and start again at step 1.

The final analysis

Value stream mapping involves more than just the elimination of waste. It is about the reduction of variability and levelling equipment utilisation. The core aim of value stream mapping is to process exactly what the customer wants. Therefore, the customer's demands and wishes have to be reviewed and assessed first. The data required for analysing the value stream may not always be present or available, perhaps because data are not systematically collected or because it is the first time the administrative process is being analysed in this way. The consequence is that the analysis is more time-consuming due to extra data collection activities.

Another important condition is that everybody respects the agreed method of working, so that the design of the ideal process yields the desired results. This sounds simple, but practical problems often arise because people are used to a certain level of freedom in performing their activities. This option is now substantially restricted. Initiative will now have to be channelled differently. Instead of improvising, using the existing working method, one should now think of how the existing working method may be continuously improved.

Determining the desired future state is an important starting point for improvements. The action plan is an enabler that starts the implementation of the improvements. However, the new situation often requires new rules, and sometimes it requires new behaviour. If these two elements are not carefully taken into account in the action plan (and implementation), there is a risk of regressing to the old situation. Developing the current and future state maps is a waste of time unless the necessary follow-up action is taken.

Reference

Rother, M. and Shook, J. (2003) *Learning to See: Value Stream Mapping to Add Value and Eliminate Muda*. Cambridge MA: Lean Enterprise Institute.

[PART SIX]

Innovation, technology management and e-business

These models help to guide and manage innovation, technology and e-business activities.

Diffusion model

52

The big picture

In 1969, Frank Bass introduced his diffusion model, or innovation adaptation model. The model forecasts how the market will adopt the introduction of a new product, innovation or technology. Competition is seen as either competing innovators or imitators: they will either compete with their own innovations or imitate (copy) the innovation (Figure 52.1).

When to use it

When introducing new products, technologies and/or innovations, the Bass diffusion model is very helpful in forecasting their adoption by the market. The model is especially useful for sales and technology forecasting of new products.

Despite a wide range of managerial decision variables, such as pricing, advertising, phasing of introductions, geographical differentiation and others, the Bass diffusion model fits nearly all introductions. Management decisions can shift the curve in the model (the adoption rate) in time, but its shape is always similar.

By differentiating competition in imitators and innovators (and adopters), the Bass diffusion model explains how competitive responses help to accelerate the adoption of the product, innovation or technology. As there is more supply, demand will pick up. This matches the concept of innovation diffusion by Everett Rogers, which explains how customers in the market adopt new products, innovations and

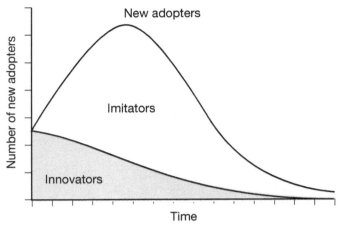

Figure 52.1 The Bass diffusion model

Source: after Bass (1969)

technologies. Beginning with the fastest adopters, Rogers identifies *innovators*, *early adopters*, *early majority*, *late majority* and *laggards*.

How to use it

The diffusion model is, at its heart, a mathematical model, stating there is a pool of X potential adopters (competitors that can take on or copy the product, innovation or technology that is to be introduced). Some of these potential adopters will adopt the new product on their own (innovators) with probability p. Others are imitators and their adoption probability depends on the imitation rate, q, multiplied by how many people already use their current product, Y. The number of new adopters N can then be calculated using the formula:

$$N = (p + qY)(X - Y)$$

where

N = new adopters

P = proportion who will adopt on their own

qY = proportion who will imitate

$X - Y$ = cumulative adopters

The final analysis

This model has been widely influential in marketing and management science. Although the concept of innovation diffusion by Rogers is commonly understood to be just that, a concept, the Bass diffusion model has proven over the decades not only to be an interesting concept but also to be mathematically valid.

Although the model appears to be very mathematical, its applicability is still strong. With the increasing attention being paid to communities, networks and user groups, the Bass diffusion model has gained in popularity as a means of estimating the size and growth rate of these (online) social networks.

References

Bass, F.M. (1969) 'A new product growth model for consumer durables'. *Management Science* 15(5), 215–227.

Rogers, E.M. (2003) *Diffusion of Innovations*, 5th edn. New York: The Free Press

53

Disruptive innovation

The big picture

Introduced by Joseph Bowyer and Clayton Christenson in their 1995 article, a disruptive innovation is an innovation that leads to a product or service designed for a new set of customers. By contrast, sustaining innovations are typically innovations

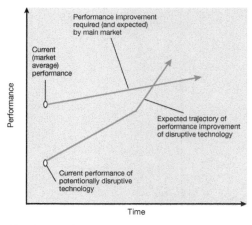

Figure 53.1 Disruptive innovation

Source: based on Bowyer and Christensen (1995)

in a new technology or application, whereas disruptive innovations change entire markets (Figure 53.1).

When to use it

The use of disruptive innovation helps to answer the question: what can firms do to avoid displacement brought on by radical, technological innovations? Contrary to the popular belief that established companies are unaware of (disruptive) innovations, most companies are hindered by their business environment (or value network) from pursuing them when they first arise. All too often, emerging, potentially disruptive innovations are – like most innovations – not profitable enough at first, and their development can take scarce resources away from other innovations (which are also needed to compete against the current competition). Start-up firms seem not to be hindered in this way and are often disruptive to established firms. Generally there are two types of disruptive innovation:

- **Low-end disruption** targets segments of the market that are not willing to pay a premium for extra performance. Often these are the least profitable customers. For a disruptive innovation, this is a good segment to start off with, as it is 'below the radar' of established firms and allows one to gain a (niche) position in a market. From this position, the disrupting party will seek to improve its profit margin and market position. This requires further innovation to be able to move upmarket and enter the segments where the customer is willing to pay more for greater performance. Once most segments are served, the disruptive party has driven most established companies out of the market and has set the new standard with the once disruptive technology. In some markets, e.g. data storage or computing hardware, developments and innovations speedily follow one another, showing a pattern of this type of disruption.
- **New market disruption** targets customers who have needs that were previously unserved by existing incumbents, for instance a new or emerging market segment.

How to use it

Disruptive innovation is a method that helps identify and manage potentially disruptive innovations. This is different from just research and development (R&D) management or technology development. The difference is mainly in the scope. Where few technologies are intrinsically disruptive or sustaining in character, a disruptive innovation is identified by the business model that the technology enables. In their article, Bowyer and Christensen suggest the following guidelines on how to foster disruptive innovations within any company:

- Determine whether the innovation is disruptive or sustaining.
- Define the strategic significance of the disruptive innovation.

- Locate the market for the disruptive innovation.
- Place responsibility for building business with the disruptive innovation in an independent organisation.
- Keep the disruptive innovation independent: do not integrate it into mainstream business activities as this tends to lower the disruptive power of the innovation.

The final analysis

Although the concept of disruptive innovation was first received almost as a radical innovation itself, it helps to explain developments in markets and industries. Similar to Moore's law (i.e. the observation of Gordon Moore, former CEO of Intel, that the number of transistors on integrated circuits doubles approximately every 2 years), disruptive innovation is best used descriptively, although it was presented as a method for spotting and cultivating disruptive technologies.

Disruptive innovation is built on a lot of assumptions, starting with the assumption that one can know which technology has the potential to be disruptive before it is readily available on the market and/or has a performance that is equal to that of the market average of currently available technologies. Next there is the assumption that the performance improvement that is required and expected by the market – based on currently available technologies – is known. The most important assumption is that the market will adopt a technology that outperforms not only the current market average but also the customers' expectations. It assumes that customers will be in awe and that the market will shift (or a new market will be created) in response to the performance of this technology.

With regard to this latter assumption, disruptive innovation does not take into account any aspects other than the technology's performance as being decisive for the adoption of the new technology by customers. Assessing the expected trajectory of performance improvement of the potential disruptive technology might better be done in conjunction with the Bass diffusion model (see Chapter 52), incorporating other market (entry) related factors.

References

Bowyer, J.L and Christensen, C.M. (1995) 'Disruptive technologies: catching the wave'. *Harvard Business Review* 73(1), 43–53.

Christensen, C.M. (1997) *The Innovators Dilemma: When New Technologies Cause Great Firms to Fail*. Boston, MA: Harvard Business School Press.

Leifer, R., McDermott, C.M., O'Connor, C.G., Peters, L. S., Rice, M.P. and Veryzer, R.W. (2000) *Radical Innovation: How Mature Companies Can Outsmart Upstarts*. Boston, MA: Harvard Business School Press.

Hype cycle

54

The big picture

Introduced in 1995 by Gartner Inc., a USA-based IT research and advisory firm, a 'hype cycle' provides a graphic representation of the maturity, adoption and social application of technologies and applications. It visualises the path that a new technology generally takes, from its initial introduction into the market and accompanying over-enthusiasm, through a period of disillusionment, to an eventual understanding of the technology's relevance and role in a market or domain and its maturation into useful components of broader solutions. A hype cycle characterises the typical progression of an emerging technology and is relevant to all kinds of technologies, not just IT-related ones.

When to use it

Hype cycles are used to assess the maturity level of a new technology. Based on this assessment, a company can derive what (type of) investments a new technology needs and what type of return can be expected from it.

Another application of hype cycles is in comparing different new technologies. Once a technology has been located on the hype cycle, it can be compared against others on the cycle, including those that are not directly related – for instance, when setting priorities for investments in different R&D and business development projects.

How to use it

Each hype cycle presents five key phases in the life of a piece of technology (Figure 54.1):

- **Technology trigger.** A potential technology breakthrough is identified. Often no usable products exist and commercial viability is unproven, but (public) interest is triggered.

- **Peak of inflated expectations.** Early publicity produces a number of success stories, often accompanied by scores of failures. Some companies take action; many do not. The hype is now at its highest point in terms of public and media interest: everyone is talking about the technology. The challenge here is to not simply 'join in because it's "in"', but to stay involved because the technology could actually be useful in a specific application or product of the company.

- **Trough of disillusionment.** Interest wanes as experiments and implementations fail to deliver. Producers of the technology start to fall away or fail. Investments continue only if the products are improved to the satisfaction of early adopters.

- **Slope of enlightenment.** More instances of how the technology can be beneficial start to crystallise and become more widely understood. Second- and third-generation applications (products) appear. More enterprises fund pilots; conservative companies remain cautious. The challenge now is to not 'miss out because it's "out"', but to keep exploring the possible application of the new technology in (new) products and services.

- **Plateau of productivity.** Mainstream adoption starts to take off. The technology's broad applicability and relevance are now clearly starting to pay off. As a high-profile technology matures, an 'ecosystem' often evolves around it. This ecosystem supports multiple providers of products and services, and also a market for related products and services that are based on, or extend, the technology. Criteria for assessing providers are also becoming clearly defined.

As a technology achieves full maturity and supports thousands of enterprises and millions of users, its hype typically disappears. Often there may be innovations around this technology that will follow their own hype cycles.

The hype cycle can be used in conjunction with the market adoption curve or the Bass diffusion model (see Chapter 52) to gauge the evolution and adoption of a technology. It can also be used in conjunction with the product life cycle (S-curve) to describe the maturity of the application of the technology beyond the hype cycle's 'plateau of productivity'. The hype cycle adds another dimension to these models. In addition to charting technology maturity, hype cycles also reflect human attitudes to technology. Most technologies conform to the hype cycle because the invariant in the equation is people, not the technology.

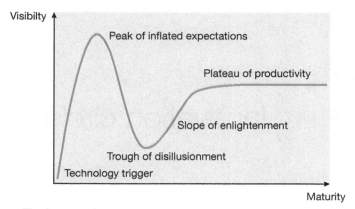

Figure 54.1 The hype cycle

The final analysis

Hype cycles are very well known not only in technology management but also in marketing. All companies want to be 'hyped' at some point through association with a (promising) innovation and to be at the centre of positive attention. There are, however, numerous criticisms of the model, the most basic of these being that the model isn't a cycle at all. Critics also point out that there is no scientifically validated method to assess the maturity of a technology. Nevertheless, in practice, almost any hype cycle that is published (not only by Gartner) is seen as accurate and representing the common view.

References

Fenn, J. and Raskino, M. (2008) *Mastering the Hype Cycle: How to Choose the Right Innovation at the Right Time*. Cambridge MA: Harvard Business School Press.

Gartner, Inc.: www.gartner.com/technology/research/methodologies/hype-cycle.jsp

55

Innovation circle

The big picture

The innovation circle is a model for efficiently analysing and successively managing the life cycle of a new innovation. Innovation – that is, the creation of new products, processes and services – is an essential process for creating a (long-term) competitive advantage. However, innovation processes are often complex and not easy to manage. This model identifies which phases in the life cycle of an innovation are the most important and in greatest need of management focus and attention.

The creation of new products, processes and services is a key challenge for management. The innovation circle identifies three main phases that are necessary to manage the life cycle of an innovation successfully – *creation*, *implementation* and *capitalisation* (Figure 55.1):

1 The creation phase. The 'seeds' of new products, processes and services are discovered and organised in the creation phase. This phase comprises three steps:

   (i) Receive incentives – in this step, the external incentives that initiate the innovation process are distinguished and interpreted. Examples of external incentives are diminishing growth, weakening of the brand, the decline of customer satisfaction and the development of new technologies (or other areas of knowledge).

   (ii) Generate ideas – in this step, the generation of new ideas is the key. The external stimuli (the incentives received) provide the initiative to create new (product) ideas. Idea creation can be stimulated by a creative climate in which variety and exploration stand central, and where chaos and energy are the main drivers. For example, brainstorming sessions in which out-of-the-box thinking is stimulated can result in the creation of (many) new ideas. The best new ideas will be selected and go through to the next phase. During this process, the focus should be on the needs of customers. Creation of (new) value for customers is the ultimate goal. The customer value can be recognised by identifying the rewards (return on investment), risks (technological and market) and resources (investment).

(iii) Function creation process (FCP) – in this step, the ideas are transformed into manageable functions. In addition, the risks are identified and can therefore be controlled. If the functions are clear, it is time to move on to the next phase.

2 The implementation phase. In this phase, the new product, process or service is further developed. The market introduction is prepared and executed. This phase is divided into two steps:

(i) Product creation process (PCP) – during the PCP, the new product and/or service is developed from the specifications created during the FCP phase. In this step, the product is tested, e.g. by developing a prototype and running demos.

(ii) Market introduction – in this step, all aspects of the market introduction are managed. This also implies the preparation of the following phase (see ORP below).

3 The capitalisation phase. In this final phase, the commercialisation of the new product, process and/or service is managed. This phase addresses the issue of how to create value (money) for the firm from the innovation(s). It is divided into three steps, in which operational excellence is key:

(i) Order realisation process (ORP) – in this step, the management of the continuous, repeating stream of product deliveries is executed. This is concerned with the management of the logistics and production of the new product. Integration with the existing logistics and the production of current products is crucial to generate synergy and scale advantages.

(ii) Service realisation process (SRP) – in this step, the management of providing (additional) services is undertaken. New services have to be integrated into the current service process.

(iii) Utilisation – the final step of the innovation circle concerns the management of the new product's revenues. This implies the continued preservation of the product's margin. Reductions in production costs and small adjustments to the product are ways in which the margin of a product can be preserved. This phase ends when the life cycle of the product has ended.

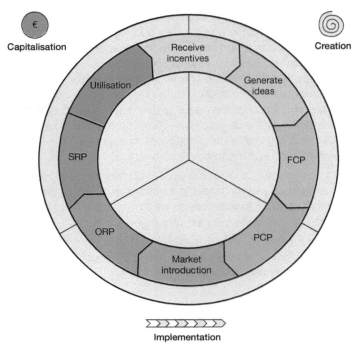

Figure 55.1 The innovation circle

Source: after Krebbekx and De Wolf (2008)

When to use it

The innovation circle can be used to manage the life cycles of a variety of innovations without overlooking relevant aspects of the innovation process. As the innovation process is divided into successive phases, management attention can be more easily directed to the correct subject during the life cycle of the innovation.

How to use it

The three phases of the innovation circle – creation, implementation and capitalisation – should be managed differently. In the creation phase, the search for new ideas is dominant. In this phase, management is directed towards managing creativity, but not in the same way as programme and project management, as search processes are not directed at a clear goal (clear goals are prerequisites in programme and project management). Rather, this phase can be managed by starting parallel research to explore different solutions. This iterative process ends when, with a degree of certainty, the most appropriate solution to the problem is found.

The implementation phase can be managed more tightly. The goal of this phase is clear from the outset and includes the different functions of the product, process

and/or service. The necessary resources (mainly time and money) are therefore reasonably well known and manageable. This phase can be managed well by project
management.

In the capitalisation phase, the new product, process and/or service is integrated into the ongoing operation, for which operational excellence programmes
are appropriate.

The final analysis

The innovation circle is an analytical tool for managing an innovation process that
provides a structure for overseeing its inherent complexity. Various analytical tools
for new product management have been developed during the past few decades.
The best-known tool is probably the Stage-Gate model (see Chapter 57). The
Stage-Gate model and the innovation circle are comparable, in that they both
provide an approach to managing the different stages of an innovation process.
However, the innovation circle differs from the Stage-Gate model in two ways. First,
the innovation circle directs more attention to the capitalisation phase. As such,
management is not only focused on creating new products, but also on the creation of new products that are commercially interesting, and which can be integrated
into the present operational infrastructure. Secondly, the innovation circle differs
because of its shape. It represents a continuous process, implying that innovation
should not stop at the end of a product's life cycle. The end of a product can be a
powerful incentive for new product ideas.

References

Camps, T.W., De Wolf, W. and Van den Berg, G. (2011) *Success!! Ten Lessons in
Innovation*. Utrecht: Berenschot (in Dutch: *Geslaagd! 10 Lessen in Innovatie*).

Krebbekx, J. and de Wolf, W. (2008) *Innovation in Dutch Industry: Towards
Excellence in Product Development*. Utrecht: Berenschot (in Dutch: *Innovatie in de
Nederlandse Industrie*).

56 Information Technology Infrastructure Library (ITIL®)

The big picture

The Information Technology Infrastructure Library (ITIL®) is a framework for designing the governance and service processes within an IT organisation. It is a set of best practices on how to align IT with business and how to organise IT service management.

Developed in the 1980s by Central Computer and Telecommunications Agency (CCTA) of the the British government, ITIL had been adopted by many organisations, both public and private. Version 3 (introduced in 2007 and amended in 2011) is currently available via Axelos Ltd., a UK government joint venture that licenses organisations to use ITIL. Today it is the biggest and most important framework for IT-service management worldwide.

When to use it

ITIL enables organisations to balance the opportunities of (information) technologies with the challenges of managing the required systems and data. Most IT solutions provide tremendous business opportunities, such as 'the internet of things' and 'big data', but at the same time present further challenges regarding the confidentiality, integrity and availability of services and data. Additionally, IT organisations need to be able to meet or exceed service expectations while working as efficiently as possible. Consistent, repeatable processes are the key to efficiency, effectiveness and the ability to improve services. These consistent, repeatable processes are outlined in ITIL.

The result of using ITIL is comparable to ISO 9000 accreditation in a non-ICT (information and communications technology) environment: all elements of the relevant processes and systems are described in a logical hierarchy of responsibilities and mandates.

A major benefit of using ITIL is the ability to share experiences with others. ITIL can also be adapted and used in conjunction with other good practices, such as:

- COBIT (a framework for IT governance and controls)
- Six sigma (a quality methodology; see Chapter 49)
- TOGAF (a framework for IT architecture; see Chapter 59)
- ISO 27000 (a standard for IT security)
- ISO/IEC 20000 (a standard for IT service management).

How to use it

ITIL is organised around a service life cycle with five phases – these are described in the five volumes that were released in 2011 as part of the latest edition of ITIL.

- Service strategy – understanding how IT service management brings value to the organisation. This means knowing who the (IT) customers are and what their needs are, what service offerings are required to meet the customers' needs, what IT capabilities and resources are required to develop these offerings, and what it takes to deliver the required and expected value to the customer.
- Service design – ensuring that new and changed services are designed effectively to meet customer expectations. This includes design of the technology, the architecture, the processes to manage the services, and the systems and tools to adequately monitor and amend the services to deliver the value expected.
- Service transition – building the design, testing it and adopting new or changed services and systems to enable the customer to achieve the desired value. This phase includes ensuring that end-users, support personnel and the production environment are ready for the release of the new service(s) and system(s).
- Service operation – once transitioned, this phase is about delivering the service on an ongoing basis and overseeing its daily overall health. This includes managing disruptions to service, handling daily routine end-user requests and managing service access.

- Continual service improvement (CSI) envelopes the service life cycle – this offers a mechanism for the IT organisation to maintain and improve the service levels, by improving the technology used and the efficiency and effectiveness of all service management activities.

Each of the phases consists of multiple steps, totalling 26 steps in ITIL, with numerous sources contributing to each step, for example:

- Standards alignment
- Case studies
- Templates
- Scalability
- Quick wins
- Qualifications
- Study aids
- Executive introduction
- Speciality topics
- Knowledge and skills
- Governance methods.

Implementing ITIL as the way of working for an organisation's IT service management is often based on a change management approach for implementing new processes.

The final analysis

ITIL is one of the best-known IT management models in the world. Its benefits are clearly stated: reducing costs, improving service levels, increasing customer satisfaction, and increasing effectiveness and productiveness – all thanks to the sharing of best practices in IT service management and to the standards upheld by the ITIL users community itself. Not every organisation sees these benefits, however: often the implementation of ITIL is seen as a superior solution that does not pay enough attention to company culture and to attaining the support of management and employees. In other cases, the implementation fails or only brings limited benefits, because the IT department and/or the rest of the organisation rigidly hold on to existing practice and procedures.

A strong point of ITIL is its continual service improvement, as this can exceed the improvement of the IT service management within an organisation. Aggregating and applying continuous improvement within ITIL itself, ITIL can rightfully be called a best practice!

References

Axelos Ltd: http://www.axelos.com/IT-Service-Management-ITIL/

ITIL®: www.itil-officialsite.com

57

Stage-Gate model

The big picture

The Stage-Gate model, also referred to as the Phase-Gate model, takes the often complex and chaotic process of taking an idea (e.g. for a new technology, a new product or a process improvement) from inception to launch and divides it into stages or phases (where project activities are conducted), separated by gates (where business evaluations and 'go/kill' decisions are made). At each gate, the continuation of the process is decided on. Originating in the chemical industry, the use of funnel tools in decision-making when dealing with new technology and product development was further developed by institutions like NASA. In the mid-1990s, Robert Cooper and Scott Edgett, two Canadian scholars, developed the Stage-Gate model as it is known today (Figure 57.1).

When to use it

The Stage-Gate model is based on the belief that product innovation begins with ideas and ends once a product is successfully launched into the market. In its entirety, Stage-Gate incorporates pre-development activities (business justification and preliminary feasibilities), development activities (technical, marketing and operations development) and commercialisation activities (market launch and post-launch learning) into one complete, robust process. Most firms suffer from having far too many projects in their product and technology development pipelines for the limited

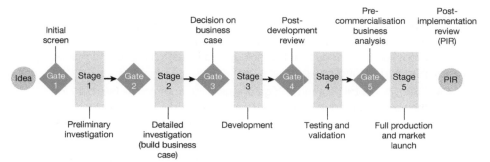

Figure 57.1 The Stage-Gate model

Source: after Cooper, Edgett and Kleinschmidt (2002)

resources available. A structured approach with clearly stated stages and gates at which a project can be stopped helps to prune the development portfolio of weak projects and deal with a gridlocked pipeline. In particular, the gates serve as quality control checkpoints in the process. They contribute to three goals: ensuring quality of execution, evaluating business rationale and allocating resources. In this way, the Stage-Gate model tries to ensure the right projects are done correctly.

How to use it

A generic Stage-Gate model has five phases and five gates. Ahead of the first phase is a preliminary or ideation phase called discovery. The result of this phase is an idea for a new technology or new product to be developed. This idea is then presented at the first gate: the initial screen. When it meets the requirements set at this gate, such as relevance to the company's aspired market position and/or complementarity within the product portfolio, the idea is taken on and a project is formulated. This project then – generically – moves through five phases:

- Scoping – stating the project definition, project justification and the proposed plan for development. Also, stating the initial thoughts on application(s) of, target customers for and benefits from the idea.

- Build business case – once past the second gate, the business rationale of the project is to be proven. By investigating the potential market(s) and potential application(s), the potential benefits offered by the idea (e.g. for a new technology or product) to potential customers are outlined. The comparative advantage over the competition and substitutes should also be stated. The feasibility of the new product and technology is also to be proven.

- Development – after passing the third gate, where management has reviewed the business rationale of the project, the actual detailed design and development of the new product or new technology take place. This often includes the design of the operations or production process required for eventual full-scale production.

- Testing and validation – after passing the fourth gate, where the technical feasibility (proof-of-concept and/or prototypes) is reviewed, tests or trials in the marketplace, laboratory and plant take place to verify and validate the proposed new product or technology and its associated brand/marketing plan and production/operations plan.
- Launch – once past the fifth gate, where the commercial feasibility (of the validated product) is reviewed, the new product or technology is commercialised and operations or production, marketing and selling start at full scale.

Often after the fifth phase there is an evaluation of the development process and of the launch. This evaluation is also known as the post-launch or post-implementation review.

The final analysis

The Stage-Gate model has a number of advantages that typically result from its ability to identify problems and assess progress before the project's conclusion. Poor projects can be quickly rejected by disciplined use of the model.

The Stage-Gate model can easily be used in conjunction with financial (project) valuation methods such as net present value (see Chapter 27) and technology assessment methods such as technology readiness levels to base decision-making on quantitative analysis of the feasibility and attractiveness of developing potential product ideas. Another advantage of the model is that, at each gate, there is an opportunity to interact with the project's executive sponsors and other stakeholders with regard to the progress and importance of a project.

An inherent disadvantage of the Stage-Gate model is that it structures the process of new product or technology development, which might interfere with creativity and innovation. The model regards these processes as linear, although in reality many creative and research-driven projects are largely iterative processes.

References

Cooper, R.G., Edgett, S.J. and Kleinschmidt, E.J. (2002) *Portfolio Management for New Products*. Reading: Perseus Books

Cooper, R.G. (2011) *Winning at New Products: Creating Value through Innovation*, 3rd edn. Basic Books.

European Industrial Research Management Association (EIRMA) (2002) No. 59: *Project Portfolio Management*. Paris: EIRMA.

Stage-Gate International: www.stage-gate.com

Strategic IT-alignment model

58

The big picture

Henderson and Venkatraman's strategic alignment model maps the relationships between the firm's strategy and IT, and between operations and the IT infrastructure. It helps to assess the alignment of the IT strategy with the business strategy. The model distinguishes two dimensions:

- The strategic fit – the degree to which the internal organisational infrastructure and processes are in harmony with the external strategy.
- The functional integration – the degree to which the IT-related technological planning and business planning are aligned.

The model uses the term 'strategic fit' for the degree of technological fit between the four strategic quadrants based on the two dimensions (as shown in the Figure 58.1) and it clarifies two things:

1. An effective support of the business strategy by IT.
2. An IT infrastructure that suits the operational processes resulting from the strategic choices.

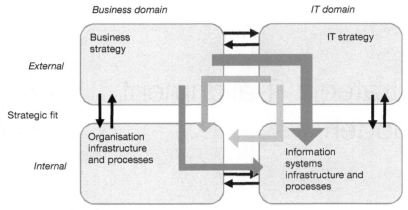

Figure 58.1 Strategic IT-alignment model

Source: after Henderson and Venkatraman (1991)

When to use it

The model underlines the fact that the IT strategy can never be considered, or modified, without being aligned to the business strategy. This is something that cannot be emphasised too strongly. The model functions as a tool to complete this necessary alignment.

The model should be used as a framework to map the relationships between business strategy and IT strategy, and between operations and IT infrastructure, in situations where IT is very important for realising the chosen business strategy. The model provides insight in three ways:

1 It identifies the link between the business strategy and the IT strategy.
2 It recognises the (strategic) value of the IT strategy and the automation system as providing support for, and possibly steering, the business strategy.
3 It optimises the potential for the use of IT within the company.

How to use it

Henderson and Venkatraman's vision entails four dominant strategic perspectives that are aligned as illustrated by the various arrows in Figure 58.1.

Strategic development (the anti-clockwise arrow from top left)

In this traditional view of strategic management, there is a hierarchical relationship between a company's business strategy and information systems infrastructure and processes. The (board of) management defines the strategy, which is subsequently translated into an IT infrastructure. Business strategy is considered to be the driver of both organisational infrastructure (structure follows strategy) and the logic of the IT infrastructure.

Technological potential (the clockwise arrow from top left)

The business strategy is the starting point for the IT strategy and infrastructure. The management view of technology, as defined within the business strategy, will drive the choices in IT strategy. The IT strategy is then translated into an appropriate IT infrastructure. The technological potential differs from the strategic perspective because it demands that the IT strategy is formulated in line with the business strategy. The IT strategy should also support the specification of the (internal) IT infrastructure and processes. The infrastructure, when implemented, must be consistent with the (external) IT strategy.

Competitive potential (the anti-clockwise arrow from top right)

The competitive potential differs in perspective from the previous strategic perspectives, because it assumes that the business strategy is changeable in line with IT capabilities. Exploiting the IT capabilities could influence the development of new products or services, new ways of steering and managing relationships, and new elements of the business strategy. The (board of) management only supports the business strategy in this perspective, in the sense that it envisages how emerging IT capabilities and new ways of governing will influence the business strategy. The IT manager should translate the developments and trends in the IT environment into opportunities and threats for the (board of) management.

Service level (the clockwise arrow from top right)

From the service level perspective, the business strategy is indirect and only barely visible. The organisational infrastructure is based on the IT infrastructure, which is the sole result of the IT strategy. There is a danger that an organisation built in this way will require huge investment in IT processes, acquisitions and licences. Management should therefore be involved in resource allocation.

The final analysis

The model assumes that both business strategy and IT strategy are the responsibility of top management. In reality, IT projects go wrong because top management considers them solely from the perspective of the IT strategy. In effect, they have 'delegated' the IT strategy to 'experts'. The model does identify the need for alignment, but it does not offer solutions for this frequent conflict.

References

Henderson, J.C. and Venkatraman, N. (1991) 'Understanding strategic alignment'. *Business Quarterly* 55(3), 72.

Henderson, J.C. and Venkatraman, N. (1993) 'Strategic alignment: leveraging information technology for transforming organisations'. *IBM Systems Journal* 32(1), 4–16.

The Open Group Architecture Framework (TOGAF®)

59

The big picture

The Open Group Architecture Framework (TOGAF®) is a framework for designing, planning, implementing and governing an enterprise information architecture. It is an open standard and basically a set of techniques, methods and best practices. TOGAF represents an industry consensus framework and method for enterprise architecture.

First published in 1995, TOGAF is based on the US Department of Defense Technical Architecture Framework for Information Management (TAFIM). It is developed and maintained by The Open Group, a collaboration of multiple companies and organisations to further technology development and adoption through setting industry standards, certifying and sharing best practices. Ever since, successive versions of TOGAF have been published at regular intervals on The Open Group's public website. They are currently at version 9.1 (as of December 2011).

When to use it

TOGAF can be used to design and govern an enterprise (information) architecture, as a conceptual blueprint of how to organise the organisation's business processes and IT infrastructure in a logical and structured way that reflects the firm's operating model. The intention of an enterprise architecture is to determine how an organisation can most effectively achieve its current and future objectives. TOGAF tries to give a well-tested overall starting model to information architects, which can then be built upon. It provides a high-level and holistic approach to design, which is typically modelled at four levels:

- Business architecture – the (key) processes of an organisation.
- Data architecture – the organisation's data assets and associated data management resources.
- Applications architecture – the organisation's application systems, their interactions and their relation to the organisation's (key) business processes.
- Technical architecture – the hardware, software and network infrastructure.

The data architecture and applications architecture together are sometimes also called the information systems architecture of an organisation.

How to use it

To develop the architectures on all four levels, TOGAF builds on three complementary resources:

- ADM: the architecture development method
- Enterprise continuum
- Resource base.

Core to TOGAF is the Architecture Development Method (ADM). The ADM is a method for developing an enterprise architecture that will meet the business and information technology needs of an organisation. It is to be tailored to the organisation's needs and is then employed to manage the execution of architecture planning activities. The ADM describes multiple steps to develop and design the enterprise architecture on all four levels (Figure 59.1):

- Preliminary phase: Framework and principles
- A: Architecture vision
- B: Business architecture
- C: Information systems architecture
- D: Technology architecture
- E: Opportunities and solutions
- F: Migration planning
- G: Implementation governance
- H: Architecture change management.

Each step consists of smaller steps. In principle, the steps are cyclical, starting with A and moving on to H. When at step H there is a need to change the architecture and start again at A. This makes the method not only cyclical but also iterative.

Use of the ADM is supported by the resource base, which is a collection of resources, guidelines, templates and background information on the use of ADM.

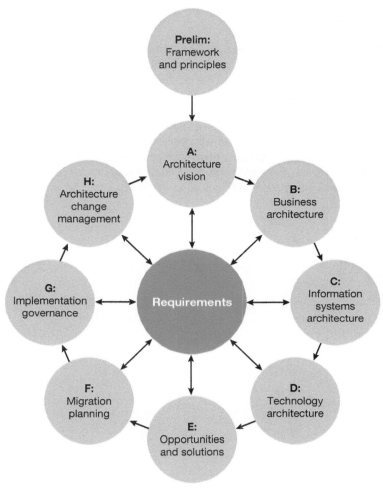

Figure 59.1 Architecture Development Method (ADM)

Source: after TOGAF.org.

The other important resource within TOGAF is the enterprise continuum. This is a (virtual) repository of all the architecture assets (models, patterns, descriptions) of an organisation. Each time the steps of the ADM are completed (the full cycle, but also some steps), this repository is filled. The enterprise continuum is a way of classifying solutions and architectures on a continuum that ranges from generic foundation architectures through to tailored organisation-specific architectures. With TOGAF there are tools available to organise this repository in such a manner that it can be exchanged with other organisations. These include, amongst others, the Technical Reference Model (TRM) for modelling technical systems; the Standards Information Base (SIB), listing all common industry standards used; and the Integrated Information Infrastructure Reference Model (IIIRM), for modelling application architectures.

The final analysis

TOGAF is a very well-known and popular framework in use by many organisations in both the public and private sectors. This is partly due to it being an open standard. Its appeal is also primarily related to the fact that TOGAF is one of the few enterprise information architecture frameworks that incorporates business processes.

At the same time, the downside of TOGAF is that it is clearly the result of a consensus: using the model still requires a lot of customisation by the organisation. More specific criticisms have to do with the steps in the ADM, as they can appear to be fairly trivial and (too) generic: does each step follow logically from the previous one, are all steps always needed and do all steps always influence the requirements of the enterprise information architecture?

Reference

The Open Group: www.opengroup.org/TOGAF and www.TOGAF.org

[PART SEVEN]

Human resources (HR) and change management

These models help to analyse and design human resources (HR) and change management.

Change quadrants

60

The big picture

The basic premise of the model is that the most appropriate change strategy depends on whether an organisation is *warm* or *cold*, and whether the motivation for change is *warm* or *cold*. A cold organisation is one where rules, regulations, systems, structures and procedures drive direction, control and coordination to get results; there is little or no intrinsic willingness to (out)perform. In a warm organisation, it is shared norms and values, and a common understanding of direction that make the organisation work.

A cold motivation for change is an objective response to a situation or emergency, such as a near bankruptcy, a drastic drop in market share, revenues, profits or an unavoidable (new) competitive threat. A warm motivation for change, on the other hand, is driven primarily by personal and professional ambitions. Based on the various warm/cold combinations of organisation and change, there are four possible change strategies: *intervention*, *implementation*, *transformation* and *innovation* (Figure 60.1).

When to use it

The change quadrants can be useful in determining the change agents; identifying active participants in the change process; and establishing the scope of change and the timing, in order to maximise the success of the change efforts. The model

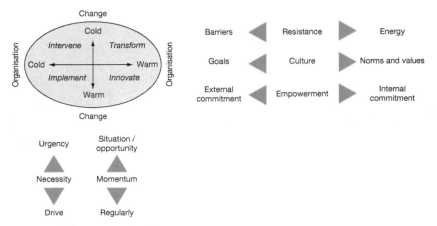

Figure 60.1 Change quadrants

Source: after Ten Have, Ten Have and Stoker (1999)

is used to determine the correct change strategy, given the type of change and the type of organisation in which the change is being proposed. The model of change quadrants is drawn up based on interviews with key figures within the organisation. This qualitative analysis is the key to determining the most suitable strategy for change.

How to use it

By analysing both the type of organisation and the type of change motives, an appropriate change strategy can be determined according to Figure 60.2.

For each change strategy, a matching approach for change communication can be chosen. In any change process, communication about the change (its purpose, its objectives, its progress, etc.) is of crucial importance. But the appropriate communication style, methods and instruments depend on what type of change should take place or is intended and the type of organisation in which the change is to take place (Figure 60.3):

- Intervention communication. As change is imposed on the organisation, a traditional top-down approach is also chosen in change communication: by line management and characterised as informing and telling. It requires a balance between mass communication and personal attention: clear and direct in group communication, attentive and specific in individual (one-on-one) communication. The messenger (the manager) is the 'face' of the message and is regarded as the personification of the change. This person's emotions and personal touch and communication style set the tone.
- Implementation communication. As change is driven more by ambition than by necessity, the communication style and method reflect this. It is

Warm organisation that is willing	Warm organisation that is obligated

RENEWING
Adopting the energy and ambition to create a long-term vision and realising it. Motivation to build something new together. Openness to bottom-up creativity. Final goal is open to change.

TRANSFORMING
Efficiently using available ideas according to the final goal. Participation is based on clear final goals. Large participation but because of time pressure it is not always possible to have a say.

Cold organisation that is willing	Cold organisation that is obligated

IMPLEMENTING
Mobilising the organisation to make the use for change clear. Top-down, driven by ambitions of management. Moving the employees through middle managers.

INTERVENING
Top-down design and implementation of change. Employees are being asked for a say only concerning operational consequences of the definite final goal.

Figure 60.2 Determining a change strategy

about convincing people of the benefits of the change and motivating them to help realise it. Communication is thus about sharing information (results, figures) and about keeping everyone focused on and motivated towards the same end result. It is often characterised as a public relations style of communication. Both project teams and management can be the communicator, although management is often more appropriate. You should be aware that the communicator is also expected to lead by example: not just to tell, but also to show.

● Transformation communication. As management is forced to take the initiative for change, communication is aimed at facilitating the quest for realising the necessary changes. Often management will set frameworks, and professionals in the organisation are invited to contribute and say what can be best done within that framework to realise the intended change. Communication is about closing the formal and informal information loops in the organisation, making sure that information is shared not only with the rest of the organisation by the people involved but also from a coordinated central point in the organisation. This requires balancing tight control with orchestration and facilitation of professionals.

● Innovation/renewal communication. As change is initiated as a result of ambitions from within the organisation, communication should also be organised from the bottom up with the joint goal of realising the change being the objective of communication. This approach to change communication is characterised by a strictly monitored communication process but with broad and extensive guidance and facilitation for communication by those leading change projects. Communication is thus

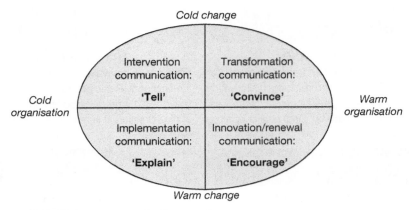

Figure 60.3 Change communication quadrants

Source: adapted from Van den Berg and Pietersma (2014)

decentralised and is often organised as a two-way interaction: informing about progress but also explicitly asking for suggestions and input.

The final analysis

A shortcoming of the change quadrants model is that in addition to the type of organisation and the type of change, the style and preferences of management should also be reflected upon when choosing the approach for change. Note that a cold change is easier to plan and communicate than a warm change and that many organisations consider themselves to be warmer than they actually are. Thus the sentiments and style of management should be aligned with the chosen approach for change in order to avoid hindering the change process. Therefore, the change quadrants model is often used in combination with models such as Kotter's eight phases of change (see Chapter 62).

The change quadrants allow for a matching communication strategy to support the change process. In practice, however, change communication is not always obviously linked to the situation or approach for change. All too often, change communication takes place on autopilot.

References

Kotter, J.P. (1990) *A Force for Change: How Leadership Differs from Management.* New York: Free Press.

Ten Have, S., Ten Have, W.D. and Stoker, J.I. (1999), The Idea Change, Amsterdam: Nieuwezijds (in Dutch: Het idee verandering).

Van den Berg, G. and Pietersma, P. (2014) *The 8 Steps for Strategic Success: Unleashing the Power of Engagement.* London: Kogan Page.

Compensation model

61

The big picture

The compensation model is a conceptual framework for the design, implementation and assessment of a remuneration strategy in organisations. It was originally designed by Milkovich and Newman (2013) in order to examine strategic choices in managing all aspects of compensation. The model describes three dimensions (Figure 61.1):

1 Policies – that outline the foundation of the system
2 Techniques – that link the policies and the pay objectives
3 Objectives – of the pay system.

When to use it

The compensation model provides a framework for examining current pay systems. It also plays a central role in creating and implementing an organisation's remuneration strategy.

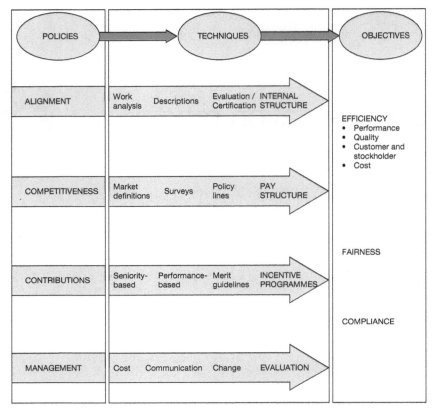

Figure 61.1 The compensation model

Source: after *Compensation*, 9th ed., McGraw-Hill (Milkovich, G.T. and Newman, J.M. 2008) Copyright ©
McGraw-Hill Education 2008

How to use it

1 Objectives – these are the central force of the system. Compensation
  systems are designed to achieve certain goals. The right-hand side of
  the model shows the basic objectives of pay systems: efficiency, fairness
  and compliance. *Efficiency* can be described as controlling labour costs
  while improving performance and quality, in order to satisfy customers and
  stakeholders. *Fairness* refers to treating employees fairly by recognising their
  contributions and needs. *Compliance* is about conforming to compensation
  laws and regulations.

2 Policies – these serve as guidelines for managing compensation in ways
  that accomplish the system's objectives. Employers must pay attention to
  all of the policy decisions shown in the column on the left of the model.
  The concept of *internal alignment* refers to pay relationships within the
  organisation and the logic behind these relationships. The extent to which

the organisation is willing to compensate in comparison with its market (*external competitiveness*) is of great importance. *Employee contribution* is concerned with individual differences in pay, based on output, competencies, length of service or seniority. The last important policy in the model concerns *managing* the pay system. Even the best pay system in the world would be useless without explicit agreements about who is responsible for application, maintenance and decision-making.

3 Techniques – these make up the pay system. Pay techniques vary from job analysis to surveys and merit guidelines, and reflect the method of tying the system's objectives to compensation policies. For example, benchmarking is a method used for mapping external competitiveness. Internal alignment can be determined by job evaluation and job matching. When using the pay model, it should be clear throughout the process whether the model contributes towards achieving organisational goals. In addition, as there is rarely a single approach to using the model, a constant re-evaluation of the current approach to the model is needed.

The final analysis

When designing, examining or implementing pay systems, it is essential to consider the organisational culture and organisational phase. This is foremost in determining which instruments to apply, as well as how sophisticated the application should be.

Reference

Milkovich, G.T. and Newman, J.M. (2013) *Compensation*. 11th edn, New York: McGraw-Hill.

62 Eight phases of change (Kotter)

The big picture

Kotters's eight phases of change is a systematic approach to achieving successful, sustainable change by breaking down the change process into eight phases. It is based on a study of more than 100 companies that have been through a change process. Kotter (1990, 1995) found that the most common mistakes made during change processes are allowing too much complacency; failing to create a substantial coalition; under-estimating the need for a clear vision; failing to communicate the vision clearly; permitting road blocks; failing to create short-term wins; declaring victory too soon; and not anchoring changes in the corporate culture. Kotter claims that these errors can be avoided by understanding why organisations change, and the numerous steps required to realise the change.

When to use it

In today's dynamic business world, the ability to *lead* change has become an important requirement for creating and maintaining success in all organisations. Kotter makes a clear distinction between leading change and managing it. He states that management consists of a set of processes that keep a complex system of people and technology running smoothly. Leadership, on the other hand, defines the future, aligns people with that vision and inspires them to pursue it. The eight phases of change approach provides a systematic tool for leading that process, enabling

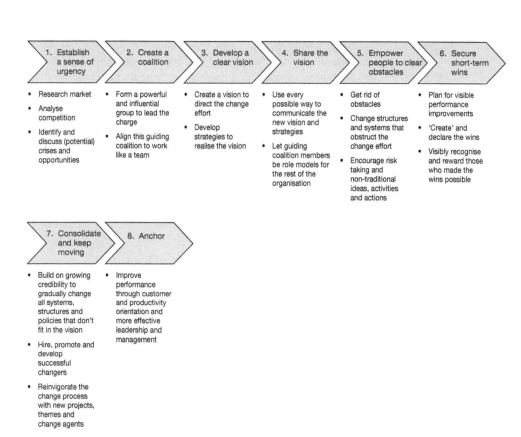

Figure 62.1 Kotter's eight phases of change

Source: after *A Force for Change: How Leadership Differs from Management*, The Free Press (Kotter, J.P. 1990) Copyright © 1990 by John P. Kotter, Inc.; all rights reserved. Reproduced with the permission of Simon & Schuster Publishing Group, a Division of Simon and Schuster, Inc. and the author.

people to bring about lasting changes within their organisations, and avoiding (possibly) fatal mistakes.

How to use it

Kotter stresses the importance of going through all eight phases as described in detail in the following list. However, if running multiple change projects, it is likely that an organisation will find itself in more than one phase of the model at any given time. The phases are as follows:

1 Establish a sense of urgency. In dealing with complacency, it is important to eliminate false signs of security. Management has to ensure that the relevant people feel a sense of urgency due to a crisis or a potential crisis, and that they are convinced that doing business as usual is no longer an acceptable option.

2 Create a coalition. A strong guiding coalition is needed in order to create change in an organisation. The members of this group need to recognise the value of the envisaged change, and must share trust and commitment. Furthermore, they should possess the credibility, skills, connections, reputations, and formal authority to provide change leadership.

3 Develop a clear vision. Vision is a central component in leading change. It is the bridge between current and future states, providing a sense of direction and aligning efforts. The best visions are sensible, clear, simple, elevating and situation-specific.

4 Share the vision. Communicating the vision to everyone involved is crucial if everyone is to understand and commit to the change. Communicating the vision inadequately and with inconsistent messages are both major pitfalls that hinder successful change.

5 Empower people to clear obstacles. The guiding coalition should remove any barriers to action that may be entrenched in the organisational processes and structures, or exist in the perception of employees. This allows everyone to participate in the change effort.

6 Secure short-term wins. Change may take time and significant effort. Therefore, people should be encouraged and endorsed by creating short-term wins. These wins should be unambiguous, visible to many, and closely related to the change effort.

7 Consolidate and keep moving. Build momentum by consolidating the accomplished gains, using them as stepping stones to greater wins and enabling people to generate new activities related to the vision driving the effort.

8 Anchor new approaches in culture. Having made effective changes, leaders must now make the changes permanent and prevent things from going back to the way they were. Kotter states that the real key to lasting change is in changing the corporate culture itself, through consistency of successful action over a sufficient period.

The final analysis

Kotter does not shy away from the complexity of organisational change by offering a simplistic approach. He recognises that there are many ways of making mistakes in change efforts. In fact, even successful change efforts are messy and full of surprises. However, anyone attempting to make a change effort in an organisational setting should consider Kotter's model precisely in order to prevent making the 'common mistakes' and be able to face challenges specific to the particular change effort in hand.

References

Kotter, J.P. (1990) *A Force for Change: How Leadership Differs from Management*. New York: Free Press.

Kotter, J.P. (1996) *Leading Change*. Cambridge MA: Harvard Business School Press.

Kotter, J.P. (2002) *The Heart of Change: Real-life stories of How People Change their Organisations*. Cambridge MA: Harvard Business School Press.

63 HR business roles

The big picture

In many organisations, the activities related to HR are organised in an HR department. This department supports the organisation with advice, procedures, administrative processing and other activities related to a managing human resources of the organisation. However, the HR department can take on different roles. The HR business roles model by David Ulrich introduces four roles for HR:

- Strategic partner
- Administrative expert
- Employee champion
- Change agent.

The best HR departments know how to act in each of these four roles, at the right time.

When to use it

Traditionally HR has to keep a balance in supporting the organisation as a whole and management in particular. This is where the HR business partner model is useful. By differentiating between the focus of the department (short-term or long-term) and the activities (process-oriented or people-oriented), David Ulrich introduced a framework that indicates four roles for HR:

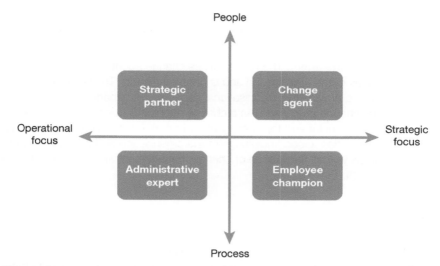

Figure 63.1 Ulrich's HR business partner model: four roles for HR

Source: after *Human Resource Champions*, Harvard Business School Press (Ulrich, D. 1996) Copyright © 1996 by the Harvard Business School Publishing Corporation; all rights reserved. Reproduced by permission of Harvard Business School Press

- **HR as strategic partner.** The role of HR as strategic (business) partner is aimed at the long-term focus of the organisation and is process-oriented. The key objective for HR is to enable the organisation to achieve its strategic goals. Organisational goals are translated into sub-goals for the HR department and, similar to performance indicators for the organisation, can be 'broken down' into performance indicators for the HR department in the balanced scorecard model (see Chapter 17). As a strategic partner, HR positions itself as a counterpart to senior and top management. Understanding the business is thus a key prerequisite for HR staff.

- **HR as administrative expert.** The role of HR as administrative expert is aimed at the short-term focus of the organisation and is process-oriented. The key objective for HR is to help the organisation with optimal processes for inflow, flow and outflow of people and optimal procedures for provision of HR services to both management and employees. HR administration is the backbone of any HR department and it needs to be organised efficiently. As an administrative expert, HR positions itself as a specialist, offering supportive and highly efficient processes and procedures. Being (more than) up to date with HR regulations and legislation is thus a key prerequisite for HR staff.

- **HR as employee champion.** The role of HR as employee champion is aimed at the short-term focus of the organisation and is people-oriented. The key objective for HR is to provide an effective employee-and-organisation relationship: to bind and capture (the right) employees for the organisation, for instance with active competence development programmes. As an employee champion, HR positions itself as a counsel to employees and less directly as a counterpart to management. The key prerequisites for HR staff are relational skills to be able to bind and advise employees.

- HR as change agent. The role of HR as change agent is aimed at the long-term focus of the organisation and is people-oriented. The key objective for HR is to provide the organisational capability to manage change and facilitate change processes. As a change agent, HR positions itself as a facilitator to senior and top management to realise the intended changes in the organisation. Good knowledge of the organisation and its strategy and culture, as well as knowledge of change management are thus prerequisites for HR staff.

How to use it

The HR business partner model is intended to allow HR professionals to show the added value of their activities. The model allows HR departments to become better connected to and embedded in the organisational processes and thus to contribute effectively to the organisation. It also gives HR and the organisation an insight into the roles HR can adopt that match the organisation's expectations of what the HR contribution should be.

Very often the model is also used by HR departments to set the agenda for their own development: to be able to take on any of the roles, HR needs certain capabilities and capacities, and to be able to take on more or all of the roles, HR needs to organise itself and its capabilities.

The final analysis

One of the most common challenges for HR is to maintain a balance between supporting employees and supporting management. In its relationship with employees, in particular, HR can have a dual agenda that sometimes conflicts: HR can have a policing role (carrying out management decisions) but also be a trusted counsel (answering employees' questions). Although the HR business roles model makes clear what roles HR can take on in an organisation, it does not provide an answer to this potential conflict.

One pitfall associated with the HR business roles model is that one of the roles becomes valued more than the others. Often the strategic partner role is considered the *nec plus ultra* level that an HR department can reach: being positioned as the counterpart of top management and being invited to think about the organisation's long-term strategy. The other roles are equally important, depending on the needs of the organisation (and not the ambitions of HR). Where the real challenge lies for an HR department is to master all roles and thus be able to take on the one role that is required (and expected by the organisation) in a specific situation.

References

Ulrich, D. (1996) *Human Resource Champions*. Cambridge MA: Harvard Business School Press.

Ulrich, D., Allen, J., Brockbank, W., Younger, J. and Nyman, M. (2009) *HR Transformation: Building HR Resources from the Outside In*. New York: McGraw-Hill.

64

Motivational insights

The big picture

Motivations are an important factor in understanding behaviour, both in under-standing ourselves and in understanding the people around us. Why is it that some people are difficult to work with, while working with others is so pleasant?

The American psychologist Dr Clarence W. Graves found in his research a number of motivations that explain people's behaviour under different circumstances. Building on the work of Carl Jung regarding personality types, he categorised this behaviour and attributed it to different personality types (Figure 64.1). Don Beck and Chris Cowan developed Graves' theories further in their book *Spiral Dynamics* (1996), in which they distinguish seven different motivations, each represented by its own colour. Everyone has developed a combination of these seven motives, and that combination is unique to each person. There is no right or wrong combination, no *good* or *bad* combination.

When to use it

Insights into your own motivations and into the motivations of your colleagues can help to put the right person on the job at hand. Insights into motivations can also explain how a person will react to changes in his or her environment. People by nature tend to react to circumstances as adequately as possible in order to survive or to keep developing. The behaviour involved in this reaction is key to how that

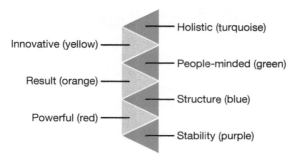

Figure 64.1 Personality types

Source: after Graves (1970)

person functions and will determine how he or she deals with the circumstances at hand.

A person's underlying motives can thus indicate how he or she is likely to respond to a change in circumstances (e.g. changes in the organisation).

The seven personality types with their characteristics and type-specific underlying motivations, that Beck and Cowan distinguish, are shown in the following table.

Colour	Motivation	Characterisation	Strength	Pitfall
Purple	Stability	● Subject yourself to the wishes of those above you ● Respect tradition and protect old values ● Honour recurrent rituals and customs ● Avoid unsafe situations ● Focus on avoiding danger ● The needs of the many always outweigh the needs of the individual	Able to bring people together and establish enduring bonds; has a deeper understanding of social relationships and a feel for traditions and historical values.	Difficulty in adapting to rapidly changing working environment; is often more loyal to group and supervisor than they are to him/her; makes personal sacrifices.

Colour	Motivation	Characterisation	Strength	Pitfall
Red	Power	• The world demands quick, fearless action • Respond quickly and impulsively • Live in the here and now • One must earn respect • Has little trust in other leaders • Friends are for life	Is good at making choices; takes quick and resolute action; responds instinctively; protects those close to him/her.	Distrust, overreaction; tends to divide the world into friends and foes.
Blue	Structure	• Living by the law ensures stability, and ultimately reward • Rules, agreements and discipline build character • Impulsiveness is restrained by shame • Everyone has their place • Eternal, absolute principles become a code of conduct • There is only one right way • Implementation only works when there is a structured approach and every step is carefully followed.	Is consistent, reliable, predictable and persistent; sets a good example; is loyal.	Has difficulty with multitasking; feels that older agreements are more important than new objectives; is sometimes blindly loyal.

Colour	Motivation	Characterisation	Strength	Pitfall
Orange	Result orientation	• Strategy, technology and competition lead to progress • Change is inherent to the way things are done • We achieve progress by seeking the best solutions in the most effective manner possible • Resources are used to make our lives more enjoyable • Optimistic, independent risk-takers deserve to be successful • Successful people should also be able to attain recognition.	Is driven and goal-oriented; seeks every opportunity to achieve results; continuously thinks about his/her own position; does not lose sight of opponents.	Sees competition where collaboration is possible; has difficulty sharing success; is inclined to break rules to achieve objectives; opportunist.
Green	People-minded	• Feelings, sensitivity and harmony are more powerful than cold rationality • We make decisions together through consensus • Everything revolves around creating harmony and ensuring personal development • Collective care for, and involvement with, the other is important • Everything must be fairly divided among everyone	Is very capable of creating group feeling and harmony; involves others in activities; coordinates and prevents unnecessary competition.	Has tendency to allow harmony to prevail above objectives; sometimes accepts compromises too easily; has difficulty with authority and authoritative decisions; falls into endless 'soft' discussions.

Colour	Motivation	Characterisation	Strength	Pitfall
Yellow	Innovative	• Flexibility, spontaneity and functionality are most important • The freedom to do and think are the highest objectives • Knowledge and competence are valued more than hierarchy, status and power • Differences can be integrated into mutual understanding • Existence in and of itself is more important than possession	Can handle complex situations; can work quickly due to model-based approach; can work in situations with much uncertainty; can do many things simultaneously.	First wants to understand, then to take action; sometimes impractical due to tendency to theorise and place everything in a larger framework; others may see him/her as chaotic.
Turquoise	Holistic	• The world is a cohesive organism with a collective consciousness • Everything is interconnected • Energy and information stream freely throughout • Everything revolves around holistic, intuitive thought and action	Can quickly make contributions when working on complex assignments; does not exhibit egotism or ambition; does not commit to a single ideology.	Often incomprehensible to others; is able to accept all perspectives so easily that others may see this as nihilism; does not easily show source of his/her own drive.

How to use it

To gain an insight into the underlying motivations of yourself and/or your colleagues, several tests are available for self-assessment. A commonly known one is 'The My Motivation Insights Colour Test'. This test is based on a questionnaire that poses questions on how you would react to certain situations or in certain circumstances. Based on your answers, a profile is drafted. This profile shows the order in which you

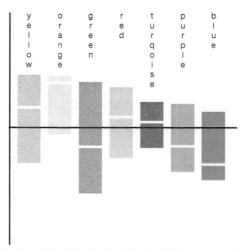

Figure 64.2 Insights from 'The My Motivation Insights Colour Test'

Source: after mymotivationinsights.com

normally tend to call upon the various motivators and to what degree. This order is a good predictor of behaviour in various situations and is usually very recognisable.

The profile also shows how susceptible you are to the negative aspects that play a role in each motivator. This susceptibility exhibits itself in the amount of negative energy that develops when you come into contact with the various motivators. This is a good indication of avoidance behaviour and stresses connected with experiencing these systems.

The net amount of energy remaining for each motivator is then presented visually (see Figure 64.2). You will see the sequence of motivators and a white horizontal line in each of the coloured stacks: above this line indicates a positive contribution of energy (positive aspects of the motivator), while below the line indicates a negative contribution (negative aspects of the motivator).

The final analysis

Motivational insights can be a useful tool for teams to get to know each other better and to prepare for team members' reactions to potentially challenging circumstances. It also can be useful for getting to know yourself and thus allow you to excel more often or to understand why you might not excel in certain situations.

Measuring your motivations is, however, much more difficult. Making use of self-assessments (such as online tests) will, by definition, colour the answers (self-bias). It is also difficult to observe yourself objectively. Making use of professional psychiatrists who observe you over a period of time (in your work) can overcome these shortcomings of self-assessment, but observations are insufficient to find out 'why you did what they saw you do'. They will therefore need to interview you about this, i.e. by asking you about your motivations.

References

Beck, D.E. and Cowan, C.C. (1996) *Spiral Dynamics: Mastering Values, Leadership, and Change.* Cambridge, MA: Blackwell.

Cowan, C.C. and Todorovic, N. (2005) *The Never Ending Quest: Dr. Clarence W. Graves Explores Human Nature.* Santa Barbara: ECLET Publishing.

Graves, C.W. (1970) 'Levels of existence: an open system theory of values'. *Journal of Humanistic Psychology* 10(2), 131–154.

Jung, C. (1921) *Psychologische Typen*, Zürich: Rascher Verlag

'The My Motivation Insights Colour Test': http://www.mymotivationinsights.com/Business/EN/ (accessed 24 March 2014).

Six thinking hats (De Bono)

65

The big picture

In his 1985 book, Edward de Bono introduced six thinking hats, each with its own colour, corresponding to the way participants think and the input they provide. Each participant gets a certain colour hat and therewith the assignment to think and talk from a specific perspective. De Bono (1985) states that human cognition and thought consist of different types, approaches and orientations. Most people develop thinking habits, which make them think in a limited way. De Bono believes that by defining the various approaches, people can become more productive and collaborative. By thinking from a different angle, represented by the coloured hat, the participants' initial responses will be changed. Someone who, for example, always talks about facts (white hat) is invited to look at possibilities instead (green hat). By deliberately trying on different 'hats' (perspectives), team collaboration can become more effective and efficient (Figure 65.1).

When to use it

The six thinking hats model forces us to shift from our normal way of thinking. As such, it helps us to understand the full complexity of a decision and see opportunities we would otherwise have missed; important decisions can be viewed from a number of different perspectives. The premise of the model is that people make better decisions if they are forced to move outside their habitual ways of thinking.

Hat	Focus	Typical questions
White	• Information / facts • Lacking information • Different kinds of information	• What information would we like? • What information do we need? • What information is available? • What information is lacking and how do we get it?
Red	• Feelings • Intuition	• What feelings do we have? • Are we committed to the subject? • What does our intuition say?
Black	• Downsides • Why it will not work • Pitfalls	• What are the risks? • What are the difficulties? • What are potential problems? • Does the idea suit the way we work?
Yellow	• Advantages • Optimism • Why it would work • Finding opportunities	• What are the advantages? • What are the good aspects? • How would it be feasible? • What are the potential opportunities?
Green	• Possibilities • Growth • New ideas • Creative thinking	• What other possibilities are there? • Can we challenge the existing situation?
Blue	• Management of communication • Summary and conclusions	• What are focal points? • Can we summarise? • What conclusions can we draw? • How do we proceed?

Figure 65.1 De Bono's six thinking hats

Source: after De Bono (1985)

This method also forces the participants to nuance their own perspective. Thus, more creative and lateral thinking is encouraged. Furthermore, the technique can be used to speed up decision-making.

It is a convenient method to use when a team has to be reminded what it means to act as a team and how to complement each other. Thinking hats can also be used in a team situation to obtain a picture of what is communicated, how it is communicated and where there may be gaps in team cooperation.

How to use it

The six thinking hats model can be used in a meeting, a workshop or a brainstorming session, but it can also be used by individuals. Each thinking hat refers to a different style of thinking. If applied in a group, each participant wears the same hat at the same time.

De Bono distinguishes the following thinking hats:

- White hat (factual). With this hat, one can focus on available data. Analyse the information and see what can be learned from it.
- Red hat (emotional). With this hat, one considers the problem with intuition and emotion. Try to imagine how other people would respond emotionally and try to understand these responses.
- Black hat (critical). With the black hat, one looks at all the bad points of the decision. Look in a cautious and defensive way: why would it work? Highlight the weak points in a plan.
- Yellow hat (positive). With the yellow hat, one has to think positively. Look from an optimistic point of view and try to see all the benefits of the decision.
- Green hat (creative). With the green hat, one thinks in a creative way. Create solutions to a problem in a free way of thinking.
- Blue hat (process control). A blue hat is worn by the chairman of the meeting or workshop. The session leader intervenes in the process and says when to change hats.

The final analysis

This model allows for various ways of thinking, i.e. it allows a problem to be considered from a variety of perspectives. De Bono claims that the key to successful use of this model is to choose a deliberate focus *during the discussion*. A particular approach has to be chosen that suits the needs of a particular stage in the discussion. Hence, a discussion may start with one hat to develop goals and objectives, while another hat may be used to collect reactions and opinions. By choosing a deliberate focus during each stage of the discussion, all people will simultaneously be focused on the same aspect of the 'problem', and hence be more collaborative in solving it and working towards a 'solution'. This can be beneficial in change projects.

Reference

De Bono, E. (1985) *6 Thinking Hats*. London: Little Brown.

66 Socially engineered change

The big picture

Changes in organisations do not always succeed. This may be because manage-ment has no shared vision, because there is no connection between the programme team and the organisation, or between the project teams themselves, or because of fragmented communication. The model for socially engineered change provides guidelines on how change can be made a sustainable success, whether it involves the introduction of a new method, a reorganisation or a (post-merger) integration of organisations (Figure 66.1).

When to use it

Socially engineered change is a useful concept and model to effectively manage change processes. It offers help with embedding a chosen strategy or new way of working (or whatever the topic is that involves a change in the organisation and its day-to-day activities) into the organisation and getting a rapid, but structured and sustainable, payoff. The socially engineered change model increases the likelihood of successful change. The basic principle is that change must be planned well in advance, with clarity about the end situation ('Begin with the end in mind,' as Covey describes one of the habits of effective people; see Chapter 76). The likelihood of success increases when the intended change is translated into fairly detailed guide-lines and principles for daily business.

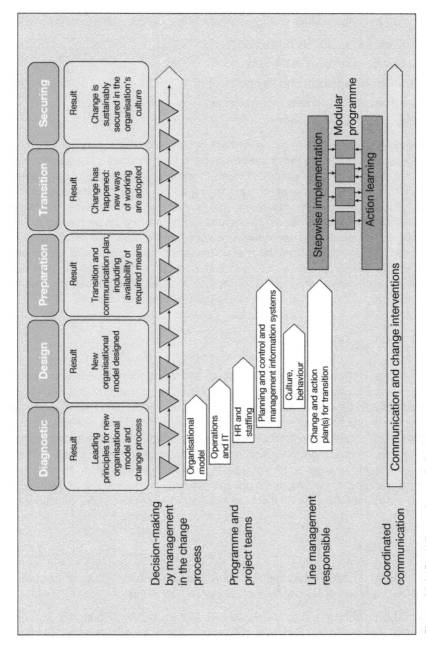

Figure 66.1 Socially engineered change

Source: adapted from Wobben, Kalshoven and De Groot (2009)

How to use it

The socially engineered change model uses five main principles, which provide guidance on the approach for change and which can be used as a benchmark:

- Use an integral approach for change.
- Reflect the final result in the approach.
- Position management and key people.
- See communication as a two-way street.
- Change through learning.

The change process itself involves a number of core activities. Once the intended change has been decided on, it needs to be operationalised into specific elements and aspects of the organisation and in the preparation of a change plan. Direction from the top management team during all the steps is at the core of the change process. In addition, managers and possibly employees are responsible for various change projects, possibly coordinated by a programme manager. The actual change is based on an experiential learning programme. The central pivot is at the heart of the organisation: the executives effectively manage and implement change in the workplace. This is achieved in a modular manner. Finally, throughout the process, communication and cultural interventions are directed at employees to inform them about the change and/or boost the willingness to change.

The final analysis

Socially engineered change is a useful concept and model for many types of organisational change. Hence the name itself is based on the conviction that change in organisations can be engineered as long as there is a good plan that is executed consistently. In practice, however, change programmes often are not as idealistic as hoped at the outset. In particular, in highly unpredictable situations and situations where evolution seems more appropriate than revolution, planned changes such as socially engineered change tend to fare badly. Where change is driven by strategy, can be planned and/or centrally directed, as in strategy processes with the strategic dialogue model (see Chapter 3), the model of socially engineered change fits well.

References

Van den Berg, G. and Pietersma, P. (2014) *The 8 Steps for Strategic Success: Unleashing the power Of Engagement*. London: Kogan Page

Wobben, J. J., Kalshoven, A. and De Groot, R. (2009) *Socially Engineered Change, a Targeted Approach for Successful Change*. The Hague: Academic Service. (In Dutch: *De Maakbare Verandering: een Doelgerichte Aanpak voor Succesvol Veranderen*.)

Team roles (Belbin)

67

The big picture

Belbin (1985) distinguishes nine complementary roles of successful business teams that can be classified as follows:

People-orientated roles	Cerebral roles	Action-orientated roles
1. Coordinator 2. Team worker 3. Resource investigator	4. 'Plant'/creator/ inventor 5. Monitor/evaluator 6. Specialist	7. Shaper 8. Implementer 9. Finisher

1 The coordinator is a mature and confident person. He or she probably brings experience as a chairperson or leader of some kind to the table. Coordinators clarify goals, encourage decision-making and delegate tasks, but can, however, be manipulative or bossy, especially when they let others do work that could and should be done by themselves.

2 The team worker is cooperative, mild, perceptive and diplomatic – in a nutshell, everybody's friend. Team workers listen, build, balance and avert friction. Their inherent indecisiveness surfaces in crunch situations. The doers in the team tend to think team workers talk too much.

3 The resource investigator is an enthusiastic, communicative extrovert

who explores opportunities and develops contacts that he or she thinks will benefit him/her now or later. Although opportunistic and optimistic, resource investigators tend to have a short span of attention and they quickly lose interest.

4 The 'plant' is Belbin's name for the creator or inventor. Plants are creative and imaginative, even brilliant at times. Their unorthodox thinking helps to solve difficult problems. Plants ignore incidentals and are too preoccupied to communicate effectively. The problem is that this self-aware genius has a tendency to get other team members' backs up.

5 The monitor evaluates actions and ponders the strategy. Monitors are sober yet discerning, and keep track of progress. They oversee all options and judge accurately, but lack drive and the ability to inspire others.

6 The specialist is a single-minded, dedicated self-starter. Specialists provide rare knowledge and skills, and therefore their contribution is limited to a narrow front. These people get a kick out of technicalities and need to be told to get to the point.

7 The shaper is challenging, dynamic and thrives on pressure. Shapers have the drive and courage to overcome obstacles, see no evil and hear no evil. They might rub people up the wrong way in their zealous efforts get things going.

8 The implementer is a disciplined, reliable, conservative and efficient person who turns ideas into practical actions. Once at work, the implementer will keep going and stick to the plan. They might, however, be a little rigid and unwilling to adopt alternative approaches or solutions along the way.

9 The finisher is meticulous, punctual, conscientious and anxious to make sure that everything turns out perfectly. Finishers deliver on time, but sometimes worry too much. They certainly hate to delegate work – nobody else seems to understand that it has to be perfect.

When to use it

Analysis of (the roles of) team members using the Belbin model is especially useful in situations where a team must be created that can undertake an assignment requiring a certain set of skills and combination of roles, or in order to optimise cooperation in an existing team.

To make use of the model, members of a prospective team should first determine which roles they can and want to fulfil. Each member should subsequently be assessed to see whether, and to what extent, he or she could play one or more of the nine roles.

Such an assessment is in itself beneficial, in that it encourages individuals to take a closer look at their own strengths and weaknesses, at those of the other team members, and at their cooperation. These can then be exploited or corrected as necessary, resulting ultimately in a more flexible, complementary and stronger team.

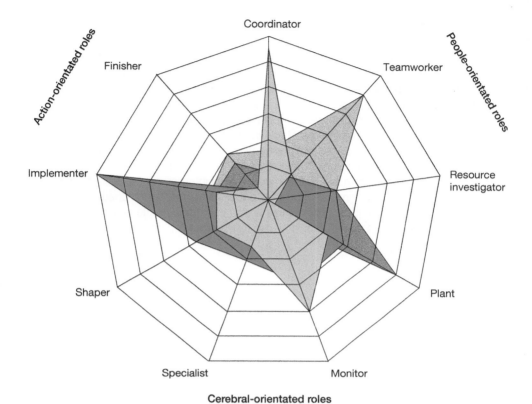

Figure 67.1 Belbin's complementary roles plotted

Source: based on Belbin (1985)

How to use it

The assessment can be done in various ways:

- self-assessment (apply scores, rank, rate or distribute weights), possibly supervised by a third party;
- team assessment (let the team work on a small assignment or game, and let the members grade each other);
- assessment by an unprejudiced individual such as a mentor, a former team member, or perhaps a co-worker or supervisor.

With a profile of each team member's ability to fulfil one or more roles, it is possible to detect the potential under- or over-representation of certain roles in the team. If necessary, management may decide to use this information to pay greater attention to certain roles during the execution of team tasks and to make arrangements regarding the way in which the team members work together.

The final analysis

The way Belbin observes teams and the roles of team members assumes that there is an objective basis for assessing team members, but this is open to debate. A team assessment based on Belbin's team roles is nonetheless a very useful exercise. People will recognise themselves and team dynamics in this model.

Whilst the different roles are complementary, it can be fatal to have too many representatives of the same type of role in one team: too many coordinators in the same team results in a clash, and having two monitors in the same team may hold up a team's progress because they keep waiting for others to take action.

The model does not address the importance of interpersonal relationships within a team. Many teams that look good on paper fail to function properly in practice because they do not 'click'. The reverse is also true: for example, a person who has no history of being a coordinator may rise to the occasion and fill a vacuum.

Reference

Belbin, R.M. (1985) *Management Teams: Why they Succeed or Fail*. London: Heinemann.

The Deming cycle: plan–do–check–act

68

The big picture

The Deming (or plan–do–check–act, PDCA) cycle is a method to structure improvement and change projects. It refers to a logical sequence of four repetitive steps for continuous improvement and learning: *plan*, *do*, *check* and *act*. Planning ('plan')

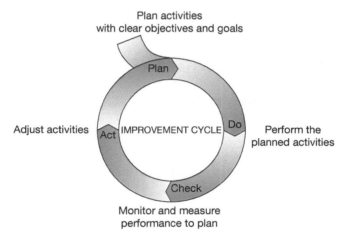

Figure 68.1 The Deming cycle: plan–do–check–act (PDCA). Four stages of a single cycle.

Source: based on Walton and Deming (1986)

the improvement of an activity should be followed by execution of the activity ('do') according to the plan. One should then measure and study ('check') the results and the improvement. Action should then be taken ('act') towards adapting the objectives and/or improvement. The consequent learning should be implemented in planning the new activities (Figure 68.1).

When to use it

The PDCA cycle allows an organisation to manage improvement initiatives in a disciplined way. When confronted with this model for the first time, many will realise that they are steering, but not really managing their organisation. It can be used to structure and discipline the process of continuous improvement. Pictorially, the process of improvement may look as if one were rolling the PDCA wheel uphill. Each problem-solving cycle corresponds to a PDCA cycle (Figure 68.2).

It is important to teach all the managers who have to work with this improvement method how to use the cycle. By making explicit use of the PDCA cycle, people will become aware of the improvements and benefits. This will encourage people to continue with the improvement projects. The cycle can be applied to different subjects, e.g. to achieving a mission, objectives, control points or in training.

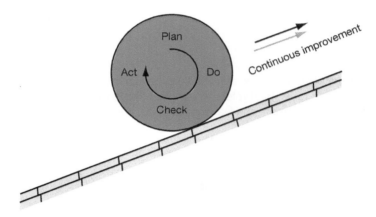

Figure 68.2 Continuous improvement with successive PDCA cycles

How to use it

Go through the four steps systematically when pursuing improvement in specified activities.

1. Plan

Plan ahead for change. Analyse the current situation and the potential impact of any adjustments before you do anything else. Predict the various results expected, with or without the theory. How can you measure the impact when the desired result has been achieved? Plan to include result measurement in the execution. Make an implementation plan with assigned responsibilities for participants.

Experience shows that it is useful to ask the following questions:

- What are we trying to achieve?
- How can this be linked to the higher purpose of our organisation?
- Who is going to be affected?
- Where will it happen?
- When will it happen?
- What is the step-by-step procedure?
- How can we measure the improvement, if at all?

2. Do

When executing the plan, you must take small steps in controlled circumstances in order to be able to attribute improvements (or failures) to the planned changes in the activity.

3. Check

Check the results of your experiment. Was the desired result achieved? Analyse why success is realised – and if not, find out why not.

4. Act

Take action when results are not as desired. Try to standardise procedures by including those actions that have already been proved to contribute to success and eliminating those that do not contribute. Or, in the event that the result proved to be other than what was desired, use the experience as input for new attempts at improvement.

The final analysis

Many organisations are unable to specify objectives, activities and desired results, let alone manage their own improvements systematically and consistently, with or without the PDCA cycle. In addition, it requires discipline to practise the whole PDCA cycle, to stop firefighting and to stop undertaking only plan–do–plan–do. There have been several adaptations of the PDCA cycle. For example, *plan* can be split into 'determine goals and targets' and 'determine methods of reaching goals'; and 'do' can be split into 'training and education' and 'implementation'. The PDCA cycle constitutes an important part of the kaizen thinking described in this book (see Chapter 45).

Reference

Walton, M. and Deming, W.E. (1986) *The Deming Management Method*. New York: Dodd.

[PART EIGHT]

Leadership and (inter)cultural management

These models help to guide managers in leadership styles and roles, and to analyse and act upon (inter)cultural aspects within organisations.

Bottom of the pyramid

69

The big picture

When the spread of purchasing power in the world is visualised as a pyramid (see Figure 69.1), a very small group of people have a lot to spend, and a larger group of people have something to spend. But, according to the United Nations, more than half of the world's population has a very low annual per capita income. This very large group of people is referred to as being 'at the bottom of the pyramid'. But there are fortunes to be made in this market, according to C.K. Prahalad: collectively, the world's poor have vast untapped buying power. They represent enormous potential for companies who learn how to serve this market by providing the poor with what they need, and who are willing to adopt specific strategies to enter these markets, which requires a combination of cost reduction and innovation.

When to use it

By far the largest group in the world of potential consumers cannot be reached via existing developed markets (Figure 69.2). These existing developed markets are becoming saturated, which will eventually lead to severe price competition. To continue to grow, new markets must therefore be sought. Bottom of the pyramid (BoP) markets offer valuable opportunities – as long as sufficiently affordable and appropriate products can be offered, and as long as the people at the bottom of the pyramid can be reached to spend what little money they have on the products of your company.

Annual per capita income*	Tiers	Population in millions
More than $20,000		75–100
$1,500 – $20,000		1,500–1,750
Less than $1,500		4,000

* Based on purchasing power parity in US$
Source: UN World development reports

Figure 69.1 The world economic pyramid

Source: reprinted with permission from 'The Fortune at the Bottom of the Pyramid' by C. K. Prahalad and Stuart L. Hart from the First Quarter 2002 issue of *Strategy+Business* magazine, published by PwC Strategy& Inc. © 2002. All rights reserved. PwC refers to the PwC network and/or one or more of its member firms, each of which is a separate legal entity. Please see www.pwc.com/structure for further details. www.strategy-business.com

The concept of the BoP model is about lifting people out of poverty either by helping them to reduce the expense and effort needed to meet their basic needs or by engaging them in new (entrepreneurial) activities related to creating products to meet their needs. A 'narrow' BoP strategy looks at poor people as potential consumers, while a 'broad' BoP strategy also includes them as potential producers.

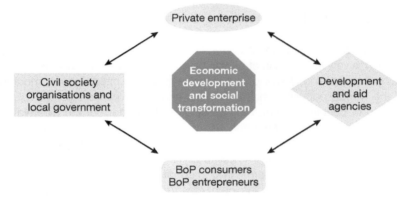

Figure 69.2 Bottom of the pyramid framework

How to use it

Companies targeting BoP consumers need to take a bottom-up approach: they need to get as close to the local BoP market as possible to understand the various influencing factors that will determine consumer behaviour. The rules of the game can be astonishingly different from those that companies are used to playing by in developed markets. They might need to sell different products with different strategies and with different business models and different earnings per customer.

To reach BoP markets, companies must not only adapt their products, but must also educate and inspire customers to buy the products and develop efficient channels for communication and distribution in BoP markets.

To be successful in BoP markets, companies must overcome:

- lack of and/or poor market data, with markets often fragmented;
- lack of information on consumer behaviour;
- latent needs of consumers;
- lack of infrastructure for both transportation and communication;
- lack of support structures such as legal frameworks or societal organisations;
- adversity to outsiders of local social networks;
- lack of affordable products readily available at the company;
- lack of spending power: a different price–performance relationship is required

The BoP model is even more effective when people at the bottom of the pyramid are addressed not only as consumers, but also as producers. When buying from a (large) base of local (small) producers, companies will alleviate poverty significantly. In turn, these local producers will have the money to spend on the companies' products. And they will see that it is beneficial to them and the companies alike to improve local infrastructure and distribution systems and other problems faced when targeting BoP consumers. In this way, BoP markets will gradually be transformed into more developed markets.

The final analysis

The BoP model was hailed enthusiastically when it was first introduced, receiving excited reviews even from people like Bill Gates, who finds it 'an intriguing blueprint for how to fight poverty with profitability'.

Striving for a win–win–win situation (poverty alleviation, profitable growth for companies and economic development of developing countries), the BoP model gets a lot of its appeal from the combination of doing good and doing business. It is respectful to people in less well-developed countries, as it treats them as simply the next customer group (and not as 'under-developed' or 'needy' people), while still aiming to improve their situation. It also offers a new – and often exciting – opportunity for companies from developed countries to continue growing profitably. And one major positive side-effect of the need to adapt and innovate products is that it sometimes leads to improved or new products for developed markets.

References

Prahalad, C.K. and Hart, S.L. (2002) 'The fortune at the bottom of the pyramid'. *Strategy+Business* 26.

Prahalad, C.K. (2005) *The Fortune at the Bottom of the Pyramid: Eradicating Poverty through Profits*. Upper Saddle River, NJ: Prentice Hall.

CAGE distance framework

The big picture

The CAGE distance framework, introduced by Pankaj Ghemawat, identifies differences between countries that organisations must address when doing business internationally. The framework disaggregates differences on four dimensions: cultural, administrative, geographic and economic (see Figure 70.1). Differences along these dimensions generally have a negative impact on international interactions: the bigger the distance, the more likely it is that international interactions will be (very) unsuccessful.

When to use it

The CAGE framework is very useful on the level of a single organisation with international business activities or with the intention to start them. The framework can be used to assess the industry in the target country. It makes differences visible on each of the dimensions. Next it can be used to assess the attractiveness of foreign markets (and even your home market), discounting the market attractiveness and market potential with any distance on each of the four dimensions.

The framework can also be used to assess the so-called 'liability of foreignness', pinpointing differences that might handicap the foreign company. This assessment using the CAGE framework can also be done on home markets, to identify (if there are any) barriers to foreign competitors. Subsequently, the framework can

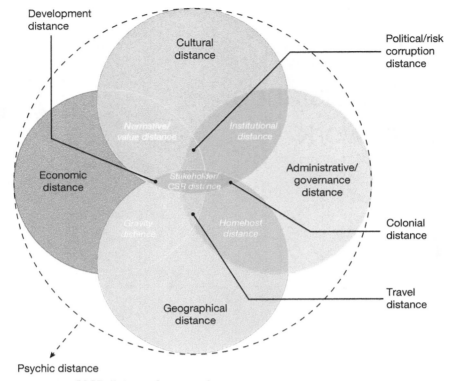

Development
distance

Cultural
distance

Political/risk
corruption
distance

Normative/
value distance

Institutional
distance

Economic
distance

Stakeholder/
CSR distance

Administrative/
governance
distance

Gravity
distance

Homehost
distance

Colonial
distance

Travel
distance

Geographical
distance

Psychic distance

Figure 70.1 CAGE distance framework

Source: after *Redefining Global Strategy: Crossing Borders in a World Where Differences Still Matter*, Harvard Business School Press (Ghemawat, P. 2007) Copyright © 2007 by the Harvard Business School Publishing Corporation; all rights reserved. Reproduced by permission of Harvard Business School Press.

also be used to assess the strength of foreign competitors in your home markets, their home markets or other foreign markets. The framework lets you discount any competitive advantage (either yours or your competitor's) with any distance on each of the four dimensions.

How to use it

The CAGE framework is used by measuring the distance on each of the four dimensions for which differences between countries can be assessed:

- Cultural distance. This encompasses differences in (the collection of) religious beliefs, race/ethnicity, language, values and social norms. Organisations can even differ in their attitudes toward market power and internationalisation (globalisation), with effects on how business operates both formally via regulation and informally.
- Administrative distance. This encompasses differences in (the collection of) legislature, corruption levels, colonial links, historical and political associations and (free) trade agreements.

- Geographic distance. This encompasses both the distance between the borders of countries, and other distances and differences between countries on geographic aspects (e.g. contiguity within countries to borders, topography, time zones and natural barriers such as lakes and rivers, etc.).
- Economic distance. This encompasses differences in (the collection of) consumer wealth, cost of labour, availability of resources and (economic) infrastructure.

Between these four dimensions, several differences can be found and even categorised into sub-dimensions (see Figure 70.1). Different types of distance matter differently to different industries. For instance, geographic distance affects costs for transportation, but that is only relevant for industries involving a lot of transport. Cultural distance shapes the consumer product preferences, but that is only relevant for consumer goods industries (and not a cement business).

To measure the distance on each of the dimensions, extensive databases are available from Pankaj Ghemawat on all relevant aspects of each dimension, which are validated to determine the likelihood of success of international trade with the target country. These databases can also be accessed via an online tool.

The final analysis

The CAGE framework is an important contribution in the field of international business. The four dimensions combine the insights from well-established theories (mostly on cross-cultural management) with intuitive and implicit business knowledge about doing business in foreign countries. The tools and databases available (especially the Cage Comparator) make this framework concrete and useful.

However, the model is indicative rather than decisive. Even with exact numbers from the databases, the framework does not tell you what country to target. All it can tell you is what differences there are between the country (countries) you are currently active in and the country (countries) you aspire to be active in. You still have to analyse which differences are relevant to your business and what distance is acceptable (and/or what similarity is required).

Another difficulty with this model is that it only indicates relative differences: a company's home base affects which countries are close and which ones are further away.

References

CAGE Comparator: www.Ghemawat.com

Ghemawat, P. (2007) *Redefining Global Strategy; Crossing Borders in a World Where Differences Still Matter*. Cambridge MA: Harvard Business School Press.

71

Competing values

The big picture

The competing values framework is a model for judging the effectiveness of organisations (Quinn & Rohrbaugh, 1983), but it can also be used to assess and define supervision and management development programmes. The study by Quinn and Rohrbaugh was an attempt to gain a better understanding of organisational effectiveness criteria, which resulted in a multi-dimensional scaling or spatial model with three dimensions (Figure 71.1):

- internal vs external focus of the organisation;
- flexibility vs stability of the organisation;
- process vs goals orientation (the means to achieving the end).

When to use it

In an organisational context, the framework can be used in four ways:

- to develop supervision and management development programmes;
- to understand various organisational functions and processes;
- to examine organisational gaps;
- to diagnose an organisation's culture.

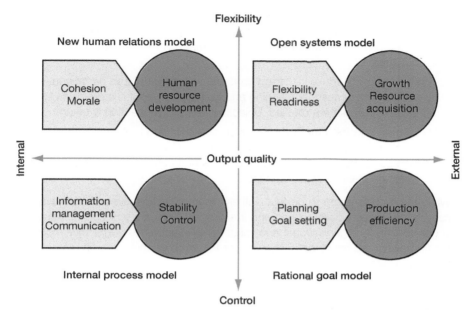

Flexibility

New human relations model

Cohesion
Morale

Human
resource
development

Open systems model

Flexibility
Readiness

Growth
Resource
acquisition

Internal ←———————— Output quality ————————→ External

Information
management
Communication

Stability
Control

Planning
Goal setting

Production
efficiency

Internal process model

Rational goal model

Control

Figure 71.1 Competing values

Source: based on Quinn and Rohrbaugh (1983)

How to use it

The dimensions of the model reflect well-known organisational dilemmas. The first dimension (internal vs external organisational focus) represents a basic organisational dilemma in which, at one end of the scale, the organisation is viewed as a socio-technical entity, and at the other as a logically designed tool for accomplishing business goals.

Flexibility vs stability is another basic organisational dilemma. Order and control do not mix well with innovation and change. Many social theorists have (successfully) argued for authority, structure and coordination, while others have found evidence for individual initiative and organisational adaptability.

Finally, a study of organisational effectiveness cannot be complete without observation of the tendency of means, methods, procedures and rules to become functionally autonomous, i.e. to become goals in themselves.

The integration of these dimensions results in four basic models of organisational effectiveness:

1 Internal process model – based on hierarchy, with an emphasis on measurement, documentation and information management. These processes bring stability and control. Hierarchies seem to function best when the task at hand is well understood and when time is not an important factor.

2 Open systems model – based on an organic system, with an emphasis on adaptability, readiness, growth, resource acquisition and external support. These processes bring innovation and creativity. People are not controlled but inspired.

3 Rational goal model – based on profit, with an emphasis on rational action. It assumes that planning and goal-setting results in productivity and efficiency. Tasks are clarified, objectives are set, and action is taken.

4 Human relations model – based on cohesion and morale, with an emphasis on human resources and training. People are seen not as isolated individuals, but as cooperating members of a common social system with a common stake in what happens.

While the models seem to be four entirely different perspectives or domains, they can be viewed as closely related and interwoven. They are four sub-domains of a larger construct: organisational and managerial effectiveness. The four models in the framework represent the unseen values for which people, programmes, policies and organisations live and die.

The final analysis

The debate surrounding the model that describes organisations and the issues they face is ongoing. In an effort to derive a framework for organisational analysis, Quinn and Rohrbaugh approached a large number of organisational researchers and experts to determine the key dimensions of organisational issues. The fact that the three dimensions of the model so closely describe three major areas of debate and research indicates that the authors have been quite successful in their effort to provide a framework for organisational effectiveness.

In anticipation of criticism, Quinn and Rohrbaugh agree that the spatial model is a type of oxymoron: a combination of seemingly contradictory and simple concepts. However, the theoretical paradoxes are not necessarily empirical opposites. They argue that an organisation might be cohesive and productive, or stable as well as flexible. Does its apparent simplicity limit the scope of the model? Quinn and Rohrbaugh would seem to argue the contrary, as they state that the process of creating the model is, in itself, productive. Quinn and Rohrbaugh present a number of alternative methods for comparing and describing their model; for instance, using Parson's functional prerequisites model, in which core values, coordination mechanisms and organisational structures are presented.

References

O'Neill, R.M and Quinn, R.E. (1993) 'Editor's Note: Applications of the competing values framework'. *Human Resource Management* 32(1), 1–7.

Quinn, R.E. and Rohrbaugh, J. (1983) 'A spatial model of effectiveness criteria: Towards a competing values approach to organisational analysis'. *Management Science* 29, 363–377.

Quinn, R.E. (1988) *Beyond Rational Management: Mastering the Paradoxes and Competing Demands of High Performance*. San Francisco: Jossey-Bass.

72

Core quadrants

The big picture

Every person has certain core qualities that truly describe the 'self'. A core quality pervades every aspect of an individual's life, such as words, feelings, deeds and values. Stripped of all the conscious and unconscious external protective and regulatory barriers of everyday life, your core quality describes 'the real you'. What is your core quality? The core quadrants model of Ofman (2001) can help you to determine, describe and diagnose your core quality (Figure 72.1).

When to use it

The core quadrants can be used to find out what your strengths and weaknesses are, as well as your pitfalls, challenges and allergies. Once you are aware of these, you can more easily recognise these characteristics in others as well. Furthermore, it gives you a better understanding of your reactions to others. When you have a better understanding of your own core competencies, you can gain a greater insight into the rational problems of others, as well as increased self-awareness.

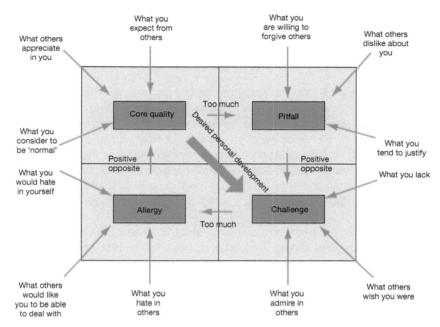

Figure 72.1 The core quadrants

Source: based on Ofman (2001)

How to use it

Although it is difficult to put your finger precisely on your core quality, it is easier when you look at it from different perspectives:

- What is your major *pitfall*? (Too much of your core quality.)
- What is your biggest *challenge*? (The opposite of your pitfall.)
- What is your *allergy* in terms of core qualities in others? (The opposite of your core quality – and too much of a challenge.)

The core quadrant shows the different, yet interdependent, perspectives of your core quality. An understanding of, and active consideration for, these core qualities, pitfalls, challenges and allergies strongly increases efficiency and effectiveness of human interaction.

The power of this model lies in the fact that it offers four perspectives on a 'core quality'. Nevertheless, there are subtle differences. The same core quality may have slightly different pitfalls, challenges and allergies. It is therefore important to specify the quadrants in more detail for each individual.

To this end, Ofman suggests that three additional perspectives be added to each of the four elements, which can then be combined to form a personalised 'super quadrant':

- something that *you* would say, feel, like, condone, wish, miss or hate *about yourself*;

- something that *you* would say, feel, like, condone, wish, miss or hate *about others*;
- something that *others* would say, feel, like, condone, wish, miss or hate *about you*.

The super quadrant is uncomfortably revealing: inconsistencies between the three 'super quadrant' perspectives are a relatively sure indicator that you are not who and/or how you want to be. You are, in fact, trying to hide your true feelings, avoid your pitfalls and curb your dislike of your allergy. In other words, you are 'acting'.

Incongruity in a core quadrant can also be an indicator that you might be describing the symptoms or effects of a pitfall. For example, the core quality 'enthusiasm' could lead to the pitfall fanaticism, leading to negative feedback, causing disappointment, fuelling retreat and, eventually, egotism. Yet, egotism itself is not the pitfall.

The core quadrants can be used to prepare for meetings where people with opposing core qualities interact. Instead of a confrontation, both parties can muster (more) respect and try to learn from each other.

The final analysis

Core quadrants have proved to be very helpful in increasing mutual understanding and respect amongst people with opposing core qualities. There is, however, an inherent danger in 'classifying' oneself or someone else incorrectly. It is important to involve others in the perspectives.

At the end of the day, the continual effort of remaining aware of one's core quality, though difficult, is perhaps the closest approximation of being true to oneself and succeeding in life.

Reference

Ofman, D.D. (2001) *Inspiration and Quality in Organizations*, 12th edn. Antwerp: Kosmos-Z&K.

Cultural dimensions (Hofstede)

73

The big picture

Hofstede's cultural dimensions can be used to develop an effective strategy to cooperate with people from various countries. By studying survey data on the values of employees at IBM in over 50 countries, Hofstede concluded that there were big differences in these cultural values. In many countries, the challenges and problems around these cultural values seemed the same, but the interpretations and subsequent solutions differed strongly by country. His model is an aid to becoming more effective when interacting with people from other countries. The types of (different) values identified in the study represent the four dimensions of culture:

1 Power distance
2 Individualism/collectivism
3 Masculinity/femininity
4 Uncertainty avoidance

However, based on the differences between western and eastern countries, a fifth dimension was added, namely:

5 Long-term orientation.

Knowing the differences between national cultures makes it possible to understand specific behaviour. Becoming aware of and recognising these differences is the first step to becoming more effective when interacting in multicultural environments (Figure 73.1).

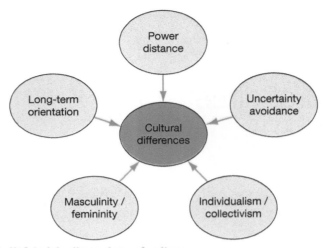

Figure 73.1 Hofstede's dimensions of culture

Source: after Hofstede and Hofstede (2005)

When to use it

The chances are that most of us have business dealings with people from different cultural backgrounds on a daily basis. Internationalisation leads to more international clients, partners and suppliers, and may also result in hiring employees from all around the world. This trend increases the risk of cultural misunderstandings and failures. Hofstede's cultural dimensions model and the scores of nationalities involved on these dimensions may help to prevent these frictions and to get off to a good start with potential clients or partners.

How to use it

Hofstede's cultural dimensions model is not a guideline for interaction between people; it merely helps to understand certain behaviour:

- Power distance index (PDI) is the extent to which the less powerful members of organisations and institutions accept and expect power to be distributed unequally amongst individuals. If an Austrian and a Malaysian marketing manager working on the same hierarchical level within an organisation are compared, the difference in PDI becomes visible. The Malaysian manager (high PDI) has hardly any responsibility or power compared with the Austrian (low PDI). In a Malaysian organisation, power is much more centralised.

- Individualism (IDV) (and collectivism, on the other side of the continuum) describes the relationship between the individual and the collective that prevails in a given nation. Individualism pertains to societies in which the ties between individuals are loose; everyone is expected to look after themselves and their immediate family. Collectivism pertains to those societies in which people are integrated into strong, cohesive in-groups. The in-groups continue to protect these people throughout their lifetime in exchange for unquestioning loyalty. In US companies, for instance, people are more self-interested and less interested in the well-being of the whole team than is the case in Asian companies.

- **Masculinity (MAS)** is the opposite of femininity. These constructs refer to the differences between the sexes. In masculine cultures, assertiveness is the predominant characteristic, as opposed to personal goals and nurturing. In Japan, ambition, competitiveness and accumulation of wealth and material possessions are valued, whereas in Sweden relationships and quality of life are much more important.

- **Uncertainty avoidance index (UAI)** indicates to what extent a culture programmes its members to feel threatened by ambiguous situations. Uncertainty-avoiding cultures try to minimise the possibility of such situations by strict laws and rules and safety and security measures. In addition, these cultures are characterised by long-term employment. Others have a low UAI and are therefore more likely and relatively willing to take risks.

- **Long-term orientation (LTO)** vs short-term orientation. Values associated with long-term orientation are thrift and perseverance; values associated with short-term orientation are respect for tradition, fulfilling social obligations and protecting one's 'face'. Asian countries, such as China, Vietnam and Japan, score relatively high on the LTO index, whilst western countries, such as Australia, Germany and Norway, score relatively low.

Do's
- **Realise that the actions and reactions of people from other countries may be completely different to what you are used to.**

Don'ts
- **Be aware that the possible differences are no guarantee for effective interaction, as no two individuals are alike.**

The final analysis

Hofstede's cultural dimensions model has been useful in creating awareness of the various cultural differences that become apparent when a firm starts to operate internationally. However, during the past few decades, distances have decreased, cultures have mingled and differences are often less visible. In addition, one could question the ratings of some countries, depending on whether all cultural groups within that country are represented or not. In either case, ratings on dimensions may vary amongst the inhabitants of that specific country. Finally, no two individuals are alike, and one must therefore realise that misunderstandings can still happen.

References

Hofstede, G. (1991). *Cultures and Organisations: Software of the Mind.* London: McGraw-Hill.

Hofstede, G. (2001) *Culture's Consequences: Comparing Values, Behaviours, Institutions, and Organisations across Nations* Thousand Oaks, CA: Sage Publications.

Hofstede G. and Hofstede G.J, (2005) *Cultures and Organizations: Software of the Mind*, revised and expanded 2nd ed. New York: McGraw-Hill

Culture dimensions (Trompenaars)

74

The big picture

In their 1997 book, Fons Trompenaars and Charles Hampden-Turner introduced seven dimensions of culture that help in understanding and managing cultural differences. They are commonly referred to as 'Trompenaars' culture dimensions', but are also known as 'Trompenaars' seven dimensions of national culture' (or 'Trompenaars' model of national culture differences').

Based on extensive research into the preferences and values of people in cultures around the world, Trompenaars and Hampden-Turner found that people from different cultures differ in very specific ways, and that these differences can be predicted, as each culture has its own values and beliefs, its own way of thinking and its own different preferences. In this way, it is possible to differentiate people from one culture and another along seven dimensions (Figure 74.1):

1. Universalism vs particularism (rules vs relationships).
2. Communitarianism vs individualism (the group vs the individual).
3. Neutral vs affective (the range of feelings and emotions expressed).
4. Diffuse vs specific (the range of involvement).
5. Achievement vs ascription (how status is accorded).
6. Sequential vs synchronic time (how we manage time).
7. Inner-directed vs outer-directed.

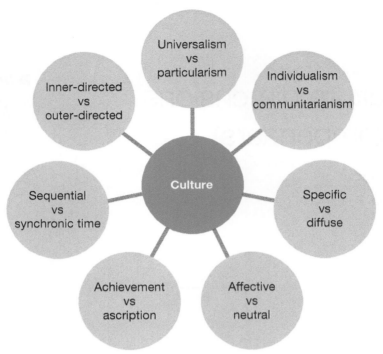

Figure 74.1 Trompenaars' culture dimensions

Source: after *Riding The Waves of Culture: Understanding Diversity in Global Business*, 2nd ed., McGraw-Hill (Trompenaars, A. and Hampden-Turner, C. 1998) Copyright © McGraw-Hill Education 1998

When to use it

Many people have colleagues, clients and/or business partners from different cultures and backgrounds. Very often these cultural differences do not interfere with doing business, but sometimes they do. Some people find it interesting to learn about the other person's perspective, while others simply cannot understand (or respect) the other person's position. Being aware that cultural differences exist is a first step, but knowing the dimensions along which these differences can occur is another – and knowing how to deal with them is yet another. To become truly effective when interacting in multicultural environments requires a good understanding of the differences between cultures, but also of how to overcome them. Or, in the words of Trompenaars and Hampden-Turner, how to reconcile the dilemmas that result from tensions (on one or more of the seven dimensions) between different cultures. This is the key to intercultural management: one culture is not necessarily better or worse than another; people from different cultural backgrounds simply make different choices.

How to use it

Trompenaars' culture dimensions model provides a classification of national cultures on seven dimensions. National cultures are assessed on each dimension and then positioned on the sliding scale of that dimension (although often a nation is referred to as a 'typical' exponent of one of either extremes on a dimension). To use the model, you should thus first identify which national culture your business partner (or colleague) is from and then look up the scores of that nation on the seven dimensions. When comparing these scores with the score of your own nation, you will discover the dimension(s) on which the preferences differ. With regard to these differences, you should then start a dialogue, trying to learn about each other's opinions, and see how differences can be respected or even overcome. On each of the seven dimensions, there are strategies for doing this:

1 Universalism vs particularism. This dimension concerns the standard by which relationships are measured. Universalist societies tend to feel that general rules and obligations are a strong source of moral reference. They are inclined to always follow the rules – even when friends are involved – and believe that their 'standards' are the best and that others should (thus) adjust to match their beliefs. Particularist societies tend to put relationships, family and friends over rules and regulations. They are inclined to act depending on the situation and who is involved.

2 Individualism vs communitarianism. This dimension is about the conflict between individual and group interests. An individualistic culture tells people to take care of themselves and sees group efforts as a means to achieve individual objectives. By contrast, a communitarian culture knows a strong sense of loyalty and embedding in local societies, tells people to take care of their fellow human being and sees individual advances as a step towards the group's prosperity.

3 Neutral vs affective. This dimension is about the extent to which people express their emotions and the interplay between reason and emotion in relationships. In neutral cultures, cool and self-possessed conduct is admired and one rarely shows feelings. In affective cultures, warm, expressive and enthusiastic behaviours are admired and people freely and spontaneously show emotions.

4 Specific vs diffuse. This dimension is about the degree to which people engage others in specific areas of their lives and at single levels of personality, or the degree to which they engage others diffusely, in multiple areas of their lives and at several levels of personality at the same time. People from specific cultures tend to keep private and business agendas separate, having a completely different relationship to authority in each social group. People from diffuse cultures tend to interweave relationships throughout the various aspects of their lives, referring to the authority level at work in the social arena as well (e.g. when meeting one's manager outside office hours).

5 Achievement vs ascription. This dimension is about how people attribute status. People from achievement-oriented countries respect their colleagues for their performance and actions. People from ascription-oriented cultures respect their colleagues for their attributes, such as position in life, age, gender, education, function, job title, etc.

6 Sequential vs synchronic. This dimension is about how people manage time. There are two aspects to this dimension: the relative importance given to past, present and future; and the approach to structuring time. People in past-oriented cultures tend to show respect for ancestors and older people and frequently put things in a traditional or historic context. People in present-oriented cultures enjoy the activities of the moment and current relationships. People from future-oriented cultures enjoy discussing prospects, potentials and future achievement. With regard to the second aspect, cultures that sequentially structure time view life as a series of events: they tend to do one thing at a time and follow plans and schedules (strictly). Cultures that synchronically structure time view the past, present and future as being interrelated: they do several things in parallel and view time commitments as desirable but not absolute.

7 Inner-directed vs outer-directed. This dimension is about how people relate to their natural environment and the extent to which they believe they can control nature. Inner-directed cultures have an internally controlled mechanistic view of nature: they can dominate nature and they themselves are the starting point for all action. Outer-directed cultures have an externally controlled organic view of nature: they believe humans are controlled by nature, that harmony is valuable, and that others, or external factors, are the starting point for (adaptive) action.

The final analysis

Trompenaars' culture dimensions have helped organisations and individuals around the world to better understand the 'other side', whether that be a colleague, business partner or client. Better understanding reduces the number of culture-driven misunderstandings and conflicts, thereby reducing the coordination costs of doing business internationally. A strong aspect of this model is that it takes into account the fact that national cultures develop and (inter)mingle: in their consulting practice, Fons Trompenaars and Charles Hampden-Turner actively keep the data underlying the model up-to-date, in a cross-cultural dataset with data from over 100 countries. Periodically they publish new (updated) scores of nations on the dimensions.

A criticism of the model – similar to Hofstede's cultural dimensions (see Chapter 73) – is that the model does not take into account the fact that cultures within nations can differ enormously, even though Trompenaars and Hampden-Turner, in their 1997 book, put forward South Africa as a nation with many cultures. Another criticism – also similar to other models on cultural differences – is that it does not take into account the fact that individuals might differ in their preferences from their average countrymen.

References

Trompenaars, A. and Hampden-Turner, C. (1993) *Riding The Waves of Culture: Understanding Diversity in Global Business*. New York: Random House.

Trompenaars Hampden-Turner Consulting: www.THTconsulting.com

Focus–energy matrix

75

The big picture

Managers who take effective action – those who seem to make the impossible happen – rely on a combination of two critical aspects: energy and focus. In their 2002 book, Heike Bruch and Sumantra Goshal found that the most effective managers are those who put their energy into their actions and concentrate their attention on those actions. They found that by plotting the two dimensions of energy and focus against each other, a framework emerges that helps to explain managerial behaviour and the reasons for managerial (in)effectiveness.

When to use it

By understanding what types of managerial behaviour lead to what levels of effectiveness, organisations and managers can better understand how to improve their actions and impact. In the focus–energy matrix, four types of managerial behaviours are identified:

- Procrastination. The procrastinators put little energy into their work and have little focus. They dutifully perform routine managerial tasks, such as attending meetings, holding appraisal interviews and so on, but fail to take the initiative and raise the level of performance. Procrastination describes the phenomenon whereby a person knows what he or she wants to do, is

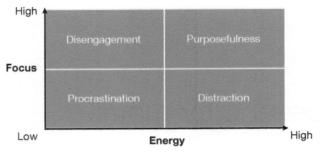

Figure 75.1 The focus–energy matrix

almost always also able to do it and, sometimes, is even trying to do it a little, but isn't really doing it. The reasons for this hesitant behaviour can be insecurity, fear of the negative consequences of taking the initiative, being overwhelmed by developments and/or not knowing one's own abilities.

- **Disengagement.** The disengaged have high levels of focus but lack the energy to bring their initiatives to a (positive) result. Often they have some (or even very strong) reservations about the task they are being asked to do and, as a result, they approach it half-heartedly. Alternatively, they might simply deny that the task is necessary or relevant at this moment in time, even when it is obvious to all that it is, in fact, needed. The reasons for this behaviour can be that the person is overwhelmed by negative developments (high burnout rate), has strong emotional reactions (anxiety, alienation, uncertainty) and/or has difficulty dealing with his or her own emotions.

- **Distraction.** The distracted have high levels of energy but lack the focus to complete a task once it is started. Often they have good intentions and are highly energetic, but have difficulty concentrating their actions. They find it difficult to reflect on their actions and adjust them as required to stay focused on the objectives. Typically, when situations become more difficult, these types of managers can become the proverbial 'bull in a china shop', as they often feel a desperate need to do something – anything. They shoot first and aim later. The reasons for this behaviour can be that they find it difficult to adjust their own actions to changing situations, they have an urge to be busy and to make something happen, and/or they lack discipline.

- **Purposefulness.** The purposeful have high levels of energy and good focus on what to achieve with their energy. They have strong willpower and tend to realise what they set out to realise. They also tend to be more self-aware than others: they are clear about their intentions, clear about their purpose and objectives, clear about their contribution and clear about the contributions they expect from others. One reason that purposeful managers are effective is that they manage their own energy, so they can use it when it is needed and it doesn't 'leak away' into ordinary daily tasks. Another reason is that they actively manage the circumstances in which they have to operate: when the context is right (enough), it takes less energy to realise your objectives. The reasons for this behaviour can be a strong commitment to the organisation and its objectives, high levels of self-discipline and/or being aware of one's capability to think and act strategically.

How to use it

In any organisation, you will find all types of managers. According to Bruch and Goshal, some 30 per cent of managers can be typecast as procrastinators, some 20 per cent as disengaged, some 40 per cent as distracted and a mere 10 per cent as purposeful. The focus–energy matrix can help managers to better understand their own behaviour. It can also help senior management and board members iden-tify which managers to ask to lead certain (strategic) projects in the organisation.

The matrix can also help management and senior management change the man-agement behaviours of individual managers. By considering the reasons why they behave in a certain way, it might be possible to make changes [e.g. by taking away the fear of negative consequences of taking the initiative (for the procrastinators) or by helping managers to focus on one objective instead of several (for the distracted)] and thus help those managers to become more effective. According to Bruch and Goshal, senior management can help to prevent managers from losing energy or focus, or both. By giving managers the right challenges and (delegated) choices, given their expressed generic management behaviour, they can be pointed in the right direction, increasing their levels of energy or focus, or both.

The final analysis

The focus–energy matrix strives to explain the idea that effective managers are not necessarily busy managers. On the one hand, it offers the insight that willpower, the accumulation of energy and focus, is the major source of (and force behind) success. By categorising managerial behaviour into four types along the axes of focus and energy, it also offers an insight into what to change in your behaviour to become more effective and increase your purposefulness. On the other hand, using the matrix requires a difficult (self-)assessment of managers' behaviour – in different circumstances and different situations, managerial behaviour can be quite different.

A criticism of the model is that it does not pay attention to actually changing behaviour. The matrix does not offer any suggestions regarding what effective (and/ or corrective) actions to take to change a manager's behaviour: how does a dis-engaged (low energy levels) manager get the energy to begin changing his or her personal behaviour?

References

Bruch, H. and Goshal, S. (2002) 'Beware the busy manager'. *Harvard Business Review*, February 2002.

Bruch, H. and Goshal, S. (2004) *A Bias for Action: How Effective Managers Harness Their Willpower, Achieve Results, and Stop Wasting Time*. Cambridge MA: Harvard Business School Press.

Seven habits of highly effective people (Covey)

76

The big picture

Wildly popular throughout the 1990s and into the twenty-first century, Stephen Covey (1989) has changed the face of many an ambitious manager's bedside table. Covey claims that highly effective people have *seven habits* that make them very successful in life and business:

1 Be proactive.
2 Begin with the end in mind.
3 Put first things first.
4 Think win–win.
5 First understand, and then be understood.
6 Synergise.
7 'Sharpen the saw'.

In addition, Covey argues that highly effective managers do exactly what they feel is both right and important, and they do it consciously.

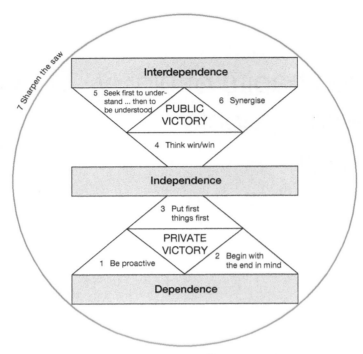

Figure 76.1 Covey's seven habits of highly effective people

Source: after Covey (1989)

When to use it

The seven habits model is a theory that tries to give an insight into why successful people are successful, in both business and in their personal lives. It is therefore highly applicable for leaders and managers. The model provides a self-help programme, based on an inside-out approach. According to Covey, our personal paradigms affect our interactions with others, which in turn affect how others interact with us. Improving interactions thus starts with a thorough understanding of our own paradigms and motives. To become successful, one should examine how effectively one acts and interacts.

How to use it

According to Covey, one first has to break loose from being dependent on others. People may become independent by adopting the first three habits:

- Be proactive. From now on, *you* take responsibility for your own behaviour. You don't blame circumstances, conditions, or – perhaps most importantly – your conditioning for your behaviour. You actively choose your response to any situation and any person. You must be prepared to respond in a way that makes you feel proud. If that requires extra hard work or makes you feel uncomfortable, so be it.

- **Begin with the end in mind.** Whatever you undertake, you must visualise the result or future that you want to achieve. You have a clear vision of where you want to go, or you will not go there at all. You know exactly what you want to accomplish, or you choose not to accomplish it at all. You live your life and make decisions according to your deeply held beliefs, principles or 'fundamental truths'.

- **Put first things first.** By taking full control and remaining disciplined, you can focus on the most important, but not necessarily the most urgent, activities. Covey's list of such important activities includes building relationships, writing a personal mission statement, making a long-range plan, doing your workout and preparing for that presentation next week. Do all those things now that otherwise would be squeezed in at the last minute, delayed or even dismissed. They will help you eliminate those urgent activities that recently topped your overweight to-do list, but really were not as important. Now that you have reached the point of being independent, and you are using your time to *pursue* your most important goals in life *effectively*, you must increase your effectiveness with others around you.

- **Think win–win.** You must believe in 'abundance' – there is plenty for everyone. One person's success does not necessarily require someone else's failure. You seek solutions to problems that allow all parties involved (including yourself) to benefit.

- **Understand first, before trying to be understood.** By this means you can make people around you feel like winners. You might actually learn something from them in the process, now that you have finally decided to shut up *and* listen. In fact, you must listen with the firm intention of understanding the other person fully and deeply on an intellectual, analytical and emotional level. Diagnose before you prescribe, says Covey.

- **Synergise.** Finally, you need to open your mind to fresh, creative ideas. You become an agent for innovation, a trailblazer and a pathfinder. You are convinced that the whole is greater than the sum of its parts. You value differences between people and try to build upon those differences (see references, and further reading on Belbin's team roles, Chapter 67). You think of creative ways to resolve conflict.

- **'Sharpen the saw'.** You have now reached a stage of interdependence. You are effective and admired by family, friends and co-workers. Nevertheless, you should never allow yourself to rest on your laurels. You must constantly trying to improve yourself, and retain a relentless eagerness to learn and explore.

The final analysis

The question is, what drives people to do the things they do, and how can they become happy doing them? Covey appeals to business managers and all other professionals who take themselves seriously, by bringing it all back to one commonly understood concept: effectiveness. What happened to that world trip you dreamed of 20 years ago? Effectiveness, and having the time to do all those important things that make us love life and make others love us, is the ultimate dream of the overworked manager.

References

Covey, S.R. (1989) *The Seven Habits of Highly Effective People*. New York: Simon & Schuster.

Covey, S.R. (2004) *The 8th Habit: From effectiveness to greatness*. New York: Free Press, New York.

Situational leadership

The big picture

In the 1970s and 1980s, Paul Hersey and Ken Blanchard developed their theory on leadership. They stated – and found in their research – that leadership is not a static principle or a fixed state. Effective leadership is task-relevant, and the most successful leadership is the one that adapts to the situation: the task at hand and the individual or group that is to be led.

In their Situational Leadership model, they differentiate between task-related aspects (task behaviour) and relation-related aspects (relation behaviour): on either aspect or both, the leader can put more or less emphasis vis-à-vis the situation.

When to use it

Effective leaders need to be flexible, and must adapt themselves according to the situation. They are able to switch between the different leadership styles of the Hersey-Blanchard Situational Leadership model.

When the group that is to be led, is very capable of doing the task at hand, leadership should place less emphasis on task related aspects: team members do not need strict guidance on how to accomplish the task. In the Hersey-Blanchard Situational Leadership model this is expressed as the maturity of the individual or group, with maturity referring to the capacity to set high but attainable goals, the willingness and ability to take responsibility for the task, and the relevant education and/or experience of an individual or a group for the task. The task behaviour of the leader should match the maturity of the team: less able teams need more guidance on how to do the task at hand, whereas able teams need less guidance.

When the group that is to be led is very willing of doing the task at hand, leadership should place less emphasis on relation aspects: team members do not need motivation (or monitoring or control) to do the task at hand. The relation behaviour of the leader should match the willingness and commitment of the team: less committed teams need more motivational leadership.

How to use it

Effective leadership adapts to the group that is to be led and to the task at hand. Based on these aspects, the Hersey-Blanchard Situational Leadership model has four leadership styles.

- Telling – Teams or organisations that are less able to do the task at hand but are committed to completing the task, require strong directive behaviour but little supportive behaviour by the manager or (team)leader. Leadership is characterised by one-way communication in which the leader defines the roles of the individual or group and provides the what, how, why, when and where to do the task. It places strong emphasis on task-related aspects and less on relation-related aspects. The more focus on the task at hand, the more *directive* the leadership style will be. With more focus on the (relation with) the group that is to be led, the more *guiding* the leadership style will be;

- Selling – Teams or organisations that are less able to do the task at hand or less committed to completing the task, require strong directive behaviour and strong supportive behaviour by the manager or (team)leader. Leadership needs to explain how the task can be completed and why it is in the interest of the team or organisation to complete the task. This is characterised by two-way communication and providing the socio-emotional support that will allow the individual or group being influenced to buy into the process. It has strong emphasis on both task-related and relation-related aspects The more focus on the task at hand, the more persuading the leadership style will be. With more focus on the (relation with) the group that is to be led, the more explaining the leadership style will be;

- Participating – Teams or organisation that are able to do the task at hand but are less committed to completing the task, require little directive behaviour but strong supportive behaviour by the manager or (team) leader. Leadership is characterised by motivating the team or organisation. There is often shared decision-making on aspects of how the task is to be accomplished. It has strong emphasis on relation-related behaviour and less on task-related behaviour. The more focus on the task at hand, the more *problem solving* the leadership style will be. With more focus on the (relation with) the group that is to be led, the more *encouraging* the leadership style will be;

- Delegating – Teams that are able to do the task at hand and are committed to completing the task, require little directive behaviour and little supportive behaviour by the manager or (team)leader. Leadership is characterised by leaving decision making mostly to the group (or team), with the manager or leader facilitating and monitoring progress (and ensuring it when needed). It has little emphasis on relation-related behaviour and little on task-related behaviour. The more focus on the task at hand, the more *monitoring* the leadership style will be. With more focus on the (relation with) the group that is to be led, the more *observing* the leadership style will be.

The final analysis

The Hersey–Blanchard Situational Leadership model turns out to be a solid model for explaining the type of leadership and the fact that leadership styles vary with the situation at hand. However, this is also the difficulty with this model: how to assess the situation correctly. How do you know whether your team requires guidance on the task at hand and/or on relation-related aspects? It is not easy to assess without prejudice or without stigmatising team members, if individual team members who are to be led are (un)willing (commitment) and (un)able (capability/maturity) to carry out the specific task at hand. Besides, in modern-day organisations, most teams have multiple tasks to perform for which their abilities and commitment vary. To make a clear assessment of which team member needs what style of leadership could thus be very confusing for both team member and manager. Nevertheless, on the level of the task and the level of the team as a whole, for most situations effective leadership can be situational: managers can apply different styles for different tasks to the same team.

Reference

Hersey, P. and Blanchard, K.H. (2012) *Management of Organizational Behavior – Utilizing Human Resources*, 10th edn. New Jersey: Prentice Hall.

Appendix: Model matrix and categorisation

	Corporate and business strategy	Organisation and governance	Finance	Marketing and sales	Operations, supply chain management and procurement	Innovation, technology management and e-business	HR and change management	Leadership and (inter)cultural management
4Ps of marketing (Kotler)				x				
7-S framework (McKinsey)		x						
Activity-based costing			x					
Ansoff's matrix and product market grid	x							
Balanced scorecard (Kaplan & Norton)		x						
BCG matrix (Henderson)	x							
Benchmarking		x						
BHAG (Collins & Porras)	x							
Blue ocean strategy (Kim & Mauborgne)	x							
Bottom of the pyramid (Prahalad)								x

	Corporate and business strategy	Organisation and governance	Finance	Marketing and sales	Operations, supply chain management and procurement	Innovation, technology management and e-business	HR and change management	Leadership and (inter)cultural management
Branding pentagram				x				
Business model canvas (Osterwalder)	x							
Business process redesign (Hammer & Champy)					x			
Business scope (Abell)	x							
CAGE distance framework (Ghemawat)								x
Capital asset pricing model (CAPM)			x					
Change quadrants (Kotter)							x	
Client pyramid (Curry)				x				
Compensation model (Milkovich)							x	
Competing values (Quinn & Rohrbaugh)								x
Competitive analysis: five forces model (Porter)	x							

	Corporate and business strategy	Organisation and governance	Finance	Marketing and sales	Operations, supply chain management and procurement	Innovation, technology management and e-business	HR and change management	Leadership and (inter)cultural management
Core competencies (Hamel & Prahalad)	x							
Core quadrants (Ofman)								x
Crowdsourcing				x				
Cultural dimensions (Hofstede)								x
Culture dimensions (Trompenaars)								x
Customer journey mapping				x				
Diffusion model (Bass)						x		
Discounted cash flow (DCF) and net present value (NPV)			x					
Disruptive innovation (Christensen)						x		
Dupont analysis			x					
Economic value added (EVA) and weighted average cost of capital (WACC)			x					

	Corporate and business strategy	Organisation and governance	Finance	Marketing and sales	Operations, supply chain management and procurement	Innovation, technology management and e-business	HR and change management	Leadership and (inter)cultural management
Eight phases of change (Kotter)							x	
Financial ratio analyses: liquidity, solvency and profitability ratios			x					
Focus–energy matrix (Bruch & Ghoshal)								x
House of purchasing and supply (Kearney)					x			
HR business roles (Ulrich)							x	
Hype cycle (Gartner)						x		
Information Technology Infrastructure Library (ITIL)						x		
Innovation circle						x		
Internationalisation strategy framework	x							
Investment stages			x					
Kaizen/Gemba					x			
Lean thinking/just-in-time (Ohno)					x			

	Corporate and business strategy	Organisation and governance	Finance	Marketing and sales	Operations, supply chain management and procurement	Innovation, technology management and e-business	HR and change management	Leadership and (inter)cultural management
MABA analysis				x				
Motivational insights (Jung)							x	
Offshoring and outsourcing		x						
Organisational configurations (Mintzberg)		x						
Organisational growth model (Greiner)		x						
Overhead value analysis		x						
Purchasing model (Kraljic)					x			
Real options theory			x					
Risk management		x						
Risk–reward analysis			x					
Road-mapping	x							
Root cause analysis/ Pareto analysis					x			
Scenario planning	x							

	Corporate and business strategy	Organisation and governance	Finance	Marketing and sales	Operations, supply chain management and procurement	Innovation, technology management and e-business	HR and change management	Leadership and (inter)cultural management
Seven habits of highly effective people (Covey)								x
Situational Leadership model (Hersey–Blanchard)								x
Six Sigma					x			
Six thinking hats (De Bono)							x	
Social network analysis				x				
Socially engineered change							x	
Stage-Gate model (Cooper and Edgett)						x		
Stakeholder management				x				
Strategic IT-alignment (Henderson & Venkatraman)						x		
Strategic dialogue	x							
Strategy maps (Kaplan & Norton)	x							
SWOT analysis	x							

	Corporate and business strategy	Organisation and governance	Finance	Marketing and sales	Operations, supply chain management and procurement	Innovation, technology management and e-business	HR and change management	Leadership and (inter)cultural management
Team roles (Belbin)							x	
The Deming cycle: plan–do–check–act							x	
The EFQM model					x			
The Open Group Architecture Framework (TOGAF)						x		
The value chain (Porter)		x						
Value stream mapping					x			
Value-based management			x					
Value disciplines (Treacy & Wiersema)	x							

Index

3M 39
4Ps of marketing 145–8
5-S method 183
7-S framework 71–4
80/20 rule/Pareto analysis 120, 154, 194

abandon/exit options 133
Abell, D.F. 28
achievement vs ascription 295, 297
activities, key 25–6
activity ratios 127
activity-based costing (ABC) 97, 98, 109–11
activity-based management (ABM) 111
adaptive organisational learning 52
administrative distance (CAGE framework) 282
affective vs neutral 295, 297
alliances 43, 87, 106
Allied Signal 195
Ansoff product/market grid 3–7, 251
anticipation in scenario planning 52
Apple 39
Architecture Development Method (ADM) 234, 235, 236
ascription vs achievement 295, 297
Asian companies 293
Australia 293
autonomy crisis 86
Axelos Ltd 222

backward integration 33
balanced scorecard (BSC) 55–6, 57, 75–8, 120
  EFQM model 201
banks 13, 101, 113, 129
Barney, J.B. 36
barriers
  as perceived by customer 161
  to entry 32–3
  to exit 34, 137
  to foreign competitors 281
BASEL III 101
BASF 189
Bass, F. 209
BCG (Boston Consulting Group) matrix 8–10, 163
Beck, D. 254, 255
Belbin's team roles 267–70, 305
benchmarking 79–83, 98, 118, 180
  remuneration 245
  six sigma 197
beta (β) 112, 114
BHG ('big hairy audacious goal') 18–20
big data 222
binomial (or trinomial) pricing model 134

Black–Scholes model 134
Blanchard, K.H. 307–9
blockers 170
blue ocean strategy 21–3
bonuses 141
bottleneck items 190
bottom of the pyramid (BoP) 277–80
Bowyer, J.L. 212, 213–14
brainstorming 48–9, 137, 193, 219, 263
branding 32, 34
  corporate vs product 67
  pentagram 149–52
break-even points 110
Brown, F. Donaldson 120
Bruch, H. 299, 301
budgeting 141
  capital 116, 123, 139
build/make-or-buy 67, 104
business attractiveness (BA)
  MABA analysis 162–4
business model canvas 24–7, 30
business process redesign (BPR) 175–7, 192
business scope (Abell) 28–30
business-to-business (B2B)
  services 67
business-to-customer (B2C)
  crowdsourcing 156
buyers: five forces model 33

CAGE distance framework 281–3
Canon 39
capital asset pricing model (CAPM) 112–14, 125
capital budgeting 116, 123, 139
capitalisation phase 219, 221
cash cows 9
cause and effect diagram 192–4
champions 49, 196
  HR as employee 251–2
Champy, J. 175
change management
  change quadrants 239–42
  Deming cycle: plan–do–check–act 271–4
  eight phases of change 246–9
  HR as change agent 252
  socially engineered change 264–6
China 91, 293
Christensen, C.M. 212, 213–14
client pyramid 153–5
collaboration
  phase of growth 87
  purchasing strategy 189
collectivism/individualism 291, 292–3

Collins, James 18, 19
communication
    change 240–2, 246, 248, 266
    road-mapping 49
    of strategy 16
communitarianism vs individualism 295, 297
compensation 141
    model 243–5
competence–research road maps 47
competencies, core 36–40, 89, 288
    BHG ('big hairy audacious goal') 19
competing values 284–7
competitive advantage 21
    Ansoff's matrix 5–6
    branding 151
    CAGE framework 282
    core competencies 36–7
    innovation 218
    value chain 103–6
competitive analysis
    Porter's five forces model 31–5, 36, 163
competitive bidding 189
competitive strategy 3
    Ansoff's matrix 6–7
concentric diversification 7
confidentiality 15
confrontation matrix 60
conglomerate diversification 7
conglomerate firm 6
constraints, theory of 188
consultants 66, 82, 106, 163
    road-mapping 49
    six sigma 196
context and strategy process 11, 15
control crisis 86
Cooper, R. 226
coordination phase of growth 86–7
core competencies 36–40, 89, 288
    BHG ('big hairy audacious goal') 19
core quadrants 288–90
corporate and business strategy 3–67
corporate road maps 46
cost of capital 122–3, 139
    weighted average (WACC) 117, 123–5
cost of equity 125
cost(s)
    activity-based costing 97, 98, 109–11
    advantages 32
    coordination 298
    differentiation 23
    fixed 34, 89
    leadership 23
    low 23
    opportunity 116
    overhead value analysis 96–9
    reduction 158, 161, 196, 224
    structure 26
    sunk 43
    switching 32, 33, 34
    transportation 182, 283

    value chain 104
cost–benefit analysis 90
Covey, S.R.
    seven habits of highly effective people 264,
        303–6
Cowan, C. 254, 255
creation phase 218–19, 220
creativity 19, 26, 228, 286
    Greiner's growth model 85
    six thinking hats 263
critical contact holders 167
cross-selling 153
crowdsourcing 156–7, 165
cultural dimensions
    Hofstede 291–4
    Trompenaars 295–8
cultural distance (CAGE framework) 282, 283
Curry, J. and A
    client pyramid 153–5
customer journey mapping 158–61
customer(s) 94
    activity cycle 161
    adoption of new products 209–10
    bottom of the pyramid (BoP) 277–80
    client pyramid 153–5
    disruptive innovation 212, 213, 214
    evaluation 97
    intimacy 64, 66, 67
    lean thinking/JIT 187, 188
    network analysis 166, 167
    perspective (BSC) 75, 77
    relationship 25, 66, 155
    satisfaction surveys 160, 161
    segments 25, 26, 153–5
    touchpoints 160–1
    value 219
    value stream mapping 204, 205
    what do they value 22
    who, what needs, how to serve 28–30

databases
    benchmark 82
    CAGE framework 283
De Bono, E.
    six thinking hats 261–3
decentralisation 43, 86, 87, 95, 97
    change communication 242
defer/waiting to invest options 133
delegation phase of growth 86
Delphi method 157
Deming cycle: plan–do–check–act 271–4
developing countries
    bottom of the pyramid (BoP) 277–80
differentiation 23, 34, 104
    cost 23
diffuse vs specific 295, 297
diffusion model 209–11, 214, 216
discount rate 116, 117, 123
discounted cash flow (DCF) 115–17, 123, 133,
    139

disengagement 300, 301
disruptive innovation 212–14
distraction 300–1
diversification 7
    portfolio of shares 114
    strategic flexibility 6
diversity 51
DMAIC 197
dogs 10
DuPont scheme 118–21

e-business technologies 179
e-commerce 158, 161
early adopters 210
earnings per share 139, 140
economic distance (CAGE framework) 283
economic value added (EVA) 76, 122–5, 139
economies of scale 5, 32, 43, 44, 163
Edgett, S. 226
effectiveness
    activity-based costing 110
    competing values model 284–7
    core quadrants 289
    focus–energy matrix 299–302
    seven habits of highly effective people 264,
        303–6
efficiency
    activity-based costing 110, 111
    core quadrants 289
    customer journey mapping 161
    kaizen 181–3
    labour costs 244
    operational and capital 118–19
    portfolio 114
EFQM model 199–202
egotism 290
eight phases of change 246–9
80/20 rule/Pareto analysis 120, 154, 194
emotions 138, 160, 161
    change communication 240
    neutral vs affective cultures 295, 297
    six thinking hats 263
    suppliers 191
employees 98, 120
    brands 151
    business process redesign 176, 177
    change projects 266
    crowdsourcing 156
    EFQM model 201
    HR as employee champion 251–2
    kaizen 181
    network analysis 165–7
    six sigma 196
    value stream mapping 205
empowerment 248
energy
    focus–energy matrix 299–302
enterprise information architecture
    TOGAF® (The Open Group Architecture
        Framework) 233–6

entry barriers 32–3
exit barriers 34, 137
exit/abandon options 133
expert panels 157
external vs internal focus of organisation 284, 285

'face' 293
fairness 244
family-owned companies 131
feedback loop 201
femininity/masculinity 291, 293
finance 109–42
financial impact: purchasing model 189–91
financial perspective (BSC) 75, 76
financial ratio analysis 126–8
    return on assets (ROA) 118, 120
    return on capital employed (ROCE) 118, 120
    return on equity (ROE) 118–19, 120, 140
    return on investment (ROI) 48, 76, 137, 139,
        219
    return on net assets (RONA) 125
financing, sources of
    investment stages 129–31
fishbone diagram 192–4
five forces model 31–5, 36, 163
5-S method 183
flexibility 19
    lean thinking 185, 187
    network analysis 167
    options 133
    organisation: stability vs 284, 285
    strategic 5, 6
floaters 170
focus strategy 23
focus–energy matrix 299–302
foreignness, liability of 281
formulation
    strategy 12–13, 15, 16
forward integration 34
4Ps of marketing 145–8
function creation process (FCP) 219
functional prerequisites 286
fuzzy pay-off method 134

Gartner Inc. 215
Gates, Bill 279
Gemba/kaizen 181–4
General Electric 195
geographic distance (CAGE framework) 283
Germany 293
Ghemawat, P. 281, 283
global model companies 43
globalisation see internationalisation
goals
    BHG ('big hairy audacious goal') 18–20
    vs process orientation 284, 285
Goldratt, E.M. 188
Goshal, S. 299, 301
governance and organisation 71–106
government 35, 169

Graves, C.W. 254
Greiner's growth model 84–8
growth/phasing options 133

Hamel, G. 36, 38, 39
Hammer, M. 175
Hampden-Turner, C. 295, 296, 298
heartbeat chart 161
Heijden, K. van der 51, 53, 54
Henderson, J.C. 229, 230
Hersey–Blanchard Situational Leadership model
 307–9
Hofstede, G.
 cultural dimensions 291–4
Holweg, M. 106
Honda 39
horizontal diversification 7
house of purchasing and supply 178–80
human relations model 286
human resources (HR) 106
 house of purchasing and supply 179
 HR business roles 250–3
hype cycle 215–17

IBM 291
imitators 209, 210
implementation
 blue ocean strategy 23
 phase 219, 220–1
 strategy 12, 13, 14, 15, 16
independence 304–5
India 91
individualism
 collectivism and 291, 292–3
 communitarianism vs 295, 297
industry road maps 46
information
 bargaining position 33
information technology
 Infrastructure Library (ITIL®) 222–5
 strategic IT-alignment model 229–32
 TCO 110
 TOGAF® 233, 234
infrastructure 106
inner-directed vs outer-directed 295, 298
innovation 228
 adaptation model 209–11, 214, 216
 circle 129, 218–21
 disruptive 212–14
 Stage-Gate model 133, 221, 226–8
inside-out approach 15, 35, 36–7, 48, 304
institutional investors 113
insurers 101
integration
 backward 33
 forward 34
 tapered 33
 vertical 7
intercultural management
 CAGE distance framework 281–3

cultural dimensions 291–4, 295–8
interdependence 305
 real options theory 134–5
internal growth crisis 87
internal process model 285
internal process perspective (BSC) 75, 77
internal vs external focus of organisation 284,
 285
internationalisation
 bottom of the pyramid (BoP) 277–80
 CAGE distance framework 281–3
 cultural dimensions 291–4, 295–8
 strategy framework 41–5
internet 156, 161, 167
 social media 158, 172
 of things 222
intranet 156, 157
inventory
 excess 182, 188
 just-in-time 185–8
investment analysis 116, 123, 139
investment fund 6
investment stages 129–31
investors 113, 114, 117, 125, 131
Ishikawa, K. 192
ITIL® (Information Technology Infrastructure
 Library) 222–5

Japan 293
job evaluation 245
Jung, C. 254
just-in-time 185–8

kaizen/Gemba 181–4
Kaplan, R. 55, 57, 75, 77
Kearney, A.T. 178
Kim, W.C. 21, 22, 23
knowledge and information management 179
Kotler, P.
 4Ps of marketing 145–8
Kotter, J.P.
 eight phases of change 246–9
Kraljic, P.
 purchasing model 189–91

laggards 210
leadership
 change 246–7
 cost 23
 crisis 85
 delegating 308
 EFQM model 200
 participating 308
 product 64, 66, 67
 selling 307–8
 situational 307–9
 telling 307
lean thinking 185–8
 value stream mapping 203
learning and growth perspective (BSC) 75, 77

learning loop 201
learning options 133–4
Lego 161
lemniscate 16
leverage items 189
life cycle
    costs 110
    ITIL®: service 223–4
    product 8, 47, 66, 110, 216
liquidity ratios 127
logistics 104
long-range plan 305
long-term orientation 291, 293

MABA analysis 162–4
make/build-or-buy 67, 104
manufacturing 91
    lean 185–8, 203
    quick response 188
    value stream mapping 187, 203–6
maps, strategy 55–7
market adoption see diffusion model
market attractiveness (MA)
    MABA analysis 162–4
market development 6
market growth
    BCG matrix 8–10, 163
market penetration 6
market research 137
market share
    BCG matrix 8–10, 163
market value added model 125
market/product grid
    Ansoff 3–7, 251
marketing and sales 104, 145–72
masculinity/femininity 291, 293
Mauborgne, R. 21, 22, 23
mergers 87
    and acquisitions (M&A) 106
Milkovich, G.T. 243
Mintzberg, H.
    organisational configurations 92–5
mission statement 16
    personal 305
mobilisation
    strategy 12, 13
monitoring 57, 62, 148
    risk 101, 102
    strategy and strategic goals 15
Monte Carlo simulation 134
Moore, G. 214
motivational insights 254–60
Motorola 195
movers 170
muda see waste
multi-domestic model companies 42–3
multicultural environments
    cultural dimensions 291–4, 295–8
multinational companies
    local business models 44

NASA 226
national cultures
    cultures within nations 298
    intercultural management see separate entry
net operating profit after taxes (NOPAT) 123, 124, 125
net present value (NPV) 115–17, 123, 133, 134, 228
network analysis, social 165–7
neutral vs affective 295, 297
new entrants 32–3
Newman, J.M. 243
Norton, D. 55, 57, 75, 77
Norway 293

offshoring/outsourcing 89–91, 104
Ofman, D.D. 288, 289
Ohno, T. 185
open systems model 286
operating company 6
operating model 64, 66, 233
operational excellence 64, 66, 67
opportunities 58–63
opportunity costs 116
order realisation process (ORP) 219
organisation and governance 71–106
organisational
    alignment 178
    configurations 92–5
    culture 177, 245, 248, 252
    effectiveness 284–7
    learning 52
    phase 245
    risk 23
Osterwalder, A. 24
outer-directed vs inner-directed 295, 298
outside-in approach 15, 36, 48
outsourcing 89–91, 104
overhead value analysis 96–9

Pareto analysis 120, 154, 194
Parsons, T. 286
particularism vs universalism 295, 297
partners 35
    crucial/key 26, 169
    EFQM model 201
    HR as strategic 251
    strategic items 189
pay see remuneration
pension funds 113
performance
    benchmarking 79–83, 98, 118, 180, 197, 245
    key indicators 75, 77–8, 120, 170, 201
    management 139, 141, 179
    targets 56, 57
Phase/Stage-Gate model 133, 221, 226–8
phasing/growth options 133
Pil, F.K. 106
pitfalls 138
    core quadrants 288–90

HR business roles model 252
strategy 13–14
place (distribution)
4Ps of marketing 145–8
planning 141
scenario 51–4
plan–do–check–act (PDCA) 271–4
policy and strategy
EFQM model 201
Porras, Jerry 18, 19
Porter, M.E. 23
five forces model 31–5, 36, 163
value chain model 97, 103–6
portfolio of shares 113, 114
portfolio strategy 3
Ansoff's matrix 3–6, 7
poverty
bottom of the pyramid (BoP) 277–80
power distance 291, 292
Prahalad, C.K. 36, 38, 39, 277
price 155
disruptive innovation 213
entry deterring 33
4Ps of marketing 145–8
sensitivity 33
wars 34, 61, 148
proactive 304–5
process vs goals orientation 284, 285
processes and EFQM model 201
procrastination 299–300, 301
procurement 105
Assessment of Excellence in 180
house of purchasing and supply 178–80
product characteristics
4Ps of marketing 145–8
product creation process (PCP) 219
product development 7
blue ocean strategy 21–3
product leadership 64, 66, 67
product life cycle 8, 47, 66, 216
costs 110
product preferences 283
product/market grid
Ansoff 3–7, 251
production
lean 185–8, 203
partial in-house 33
products, defective 182
product–technology road maps 47–9
profitability ratios 127
see also individual ratios
promotion
4Ps of marketing 145–8
purchasing management 118
purchasing model 189–91
purposefulness 301

quality 181, 182, 192, 200
circles 181
six sigma 195, 196

question marks 9
quick response manufacturing 188
Quinn, R.E. 284, 286

ratio analysis 126–8
return on assets (ROA) 118, 120
return on capital employed (ROCE) 118, 120
return on equity (ROE) 118–19, 120, 140
return on investment (ROI) 48, 76, 137, 139,
219
return on net assets (RONA) 125
rational goal model 286
real options theory 132–5
realisation
blue ocean strategy 23
strategy 12, 13, 15, 16
red oceans 21, 22
red tape crisis 87
regional model companies 43–4
relationships
building 305
rules vs 295, 297
remuneration 141
compensation model 243–5
research and development (R&D) 47, 48, 49, 106,
133
hype cycle 215
resource-based view 36
resources 49
activities consume 109, 111
EFQM model 201
innovation circle 219
key 25
network analysis 166
risk–reward analysis 137, 138
return on assets (ROA) 118, 120
return on capital employed (ROCE) 118, 120
return on equity (ROE) 118–19, 120, 140
return on investment (ROI) 48, 76, 137, 139, 219
return on net assets (RONA) 125
revenues 25
Ringland, G. 51, 53
risk(s)
aversion 14, 114, 137
financial 42
innovation circle 219
management 100–2
operational 42
premium 116, 117, 123
product development 22–3
profile 137
purchasing model: supply 189–91
risk-free rate 116, 134
road-mapping 48–9
systematic and unsystematic 112, 114
uncertainty avoidance index (UAI) 293
risk–reward analysis 136–8
road-mapping 46–50
Rogers, E. 209–10
Rohrbaugh, J. 284, 286

root cause analysis (RCA) 120, 192–4
Rother, M. 203
Royal Dutch Shell 52, 53
rules vs relationships 295, 297

sales and marketing 145–72
scenario planning 51–4, 61, 137
Schwartz, P. 53
self-awareness 288, 301
sensitivity analysis 137
sequential vs synchronic time 295, 298
service 104–5
service realisation process (SRP) 219
seven habits of highly effective people 264, 303–6
seven zeros 185–6
7-S framework 71–4
shareholders 13, 75, 94, 122, 123, 125, 141
Shook, J. 203
short-term orientation 293
situational leadership 307–9
six sigma 195–8
six thinking hats 261–3
skills (7-S framework) 71–4
SMART targets 151
social media 158, 172
social network analysis 165–7
social networks and diffusion model 211
socially engineered change 264–6
solvency ratios 127
Sony 39
South Africa 298
specific vs diffuse 295, 297
stability vs flexibility of organisation 284
staff (7-S framework) 71–4
Stage-Gate model 133, 221, 226–8
stakeholder(s)
    action card 170, 171
    crowdsourcing 156–7
    management 168–72
    network analysis 165–7
standardisation of work 183
stars 9
start-up firms 129, 213
Stern Stewart & Co 122
strategic architecture 38
strategic dialogue 11–17, 266
strategic flexibility 5, 6
strategic IT-alignment model 229–32
strategic partner, HR as 251, 252
strategy (7-S framework) 71–4
strategy, corporate and business 3–67
strategy maps 55–7
strengths 58–63
structure (7-S framework) 71–4
style (7-S framework) 71–4
substitutes 33, 34
super quadrants 289–90
supplier(s) 94
    five forces model 33–4
    just-in-time 188

network analysis 165, 166, 167
    purchasing model 189–91
    relationship management 179
supply chain 137
Suri, R. 188
sustainability 67
Sweden 293
switching
    costs 32, 33, 34
    options 133
SWOT analysis 58–63
synchronic vs sequential time 295, 298
synergies 5, 6, 41, 163, 219
    highly effective people 303, 305
    road-mapping 48
system thinking 54
systems (7-S framework) 71–4

tapered integration 33
taxation
    interest costs 124
teams 259, 262
    team roles 267–70, 305
technology
    development 106, 228
    product–technology road maps 47–9
    see also innovation
tendering 189
threats 58–63, 137
time
    context and limited lead 15
    sequential vs synchronic 295, 298
TOGAF® (The Open Group Architecture
        Framework) 233–6
total cost ownership (TCO) 110
touchpoints 160–1
Toyota 185
trade model companies 42
transnational model companies 43
transparency 51, 167
Treacy, M. 64
trinomial pricing model 134
Trompenaars, A.
    cultural dimensions 295–8

Ulrich, D. 250
uncertainty 51
    avoidance 291, 293
    offshoring 91
    real options theory 133, 134
    scenario planning 52–3
understand, then be understood 305
unique selling points (USPs) 48
universalism vs particularism 295, 297
up-selling 153
US companies 293

value
    chain 97, 103–6, 163
    curve 22

disciplines 64–7
drivers 186–7
grid 106
proposition 22, 25, 64, 155
value-based management (VBM) 123, 139–42
value stream 187
    mapping 187, 203–6
values, shared (7-S framework) 71–4
Van der Heijden, K. 51, 53, 54
Venkatraman, N. 229, 230
vertical integration 7
Vietnam 293
vision 16, 75, 305
    change 248
    road-mapping 49
Volvo 38

Wack, P. 54
wage erosion 91
waiting to invest/defer options 133
waste 185, 186, 187, 188
    and inefficiencies 181–3
    value stream mapping 203, 204
weaknesses 58–63
weighted average cost of capital (WACC) 117, 123–5
Wiersema, F. 64
Williams, J.B. 117
wins, short-term 248
win–win 305

Do you want your people to be the very best at what they do?

Talk to us about how we can help.

As the world's leading learning company, we know a lot about what your people need in order to be better at what they do.

Whatever subject or skills you've got in mind (from presenting or persuasion to coaching or communication skills), and at whatever level (from new-starters through to top executives) we can help you deliver tried-and-tested, essential learning straight to your workforce – whatever they need, whenever they need it and wherever they are.

Talk to us today about how we can:

- Complement and support your existing learning and development programmes
- Enhance and augment your people's learning experience
- Match your needs to the best of our content
- Customise, brand and change it to make a better fit
- Deliver cost-effective, great value learning content that's proven to work.

Contact us today:
corporate.enquiries@pearson.com